FOREIGN PLAYERS AND FOOTBALL SUPPORTERS

MANCHESTER 1824
Manchester University Press

Foreign players and football supporters

The Old Firm, Arsenal, Paris Saint-Germain

David Ranc

Manchester University Press
Manchester and New York

distributed in the United States exclusively by Palgrave Macmillan

Published by Manchester University Press
Oxford Road, Manchester M13 9NR, UK
and Room 400, 175 Fifth Avenue, New York, NY 10010, USA
www.manchesteruniversitypress.co.uk

Distributed in the United States exclusively by
Palgrave Macmillan, 175 Fifth Avenue, New York,
NY 10010, USA

Distributed in Canada exclusively by
UBC Press, University of British Columbia, 2029 West Mall,
Vancouver, BC, Canada V6T 1Z2

British Library Cataloguing-in-Publication Data
A catalogue record for this book is available from the British Library

Library of Congress Cataloging-in-Publication Data applied for

ISBN 978 0 7190 8612 0 hardback

First published 2012

Typeset
by Carnegie Book Production, Lancaster
Printed in Great Britain
by CPI Group (UK) Ltd, Croydon, CR0 4YY

To Trinity Hall,
for the continued support
I have received from its members.
Row Hall!

Football unites all those people who love the game, whether in agreement or disagreement, at the same time as it divides the supporters of the different clubs. The more you know about the game, the deeper the enjoyment; the more passionately you support your club, the deeper your involvement. The amount of intellectual energy generated by football is unimaginably massive; the effect of such passion is to dramatise the lives of people who might otherwise be snared in disadvantage, poverty and disability, with very little to look forward to if not their club's promotion. This cultural activity receives no support whatever from government because it needs none. (Germaine Greer, *The Guardian*, 24 March 2008)

Football is an art more central to our culture than anything the Arts Council dare to recognise. (Germaine Greer, *The Guardian*, 28 May 1996)

Contents

Preface

Having studied (political) history, then political sciences (note the plural) in France, I wanted to research an object which is clearly political but at the level of the people, rather than the level of political or administrative machinery. I was lucky enough to be introduced to the importance of sport in the study of international relations through coursework and research in a seminar led by Dr Paul Dietschy at Sciences Po, in Paris. I realised that sport could provide me with the object I was looking for, in the field that I was and still am most interested in: European studies. I was then fortunate enough to be able to undertake research on this topic in an M.Phil., which later became a Ph.D., at the Centre of International Studies and Trinity Hall, in the University of Cambridge, under the supervision of Dr Geoffrey Edwards. This study is an updated, revised and abridged version of the Ph.D. thesis I submitted in 2007.

Acknowledgements

I would like to thank first and foremost Trinity Hall for funding the years of research needed to write this book, as well as Mr and Mrs Johnson Ng Wai Yee and their children, whose financial assistance was invaluable in the last year of my Ph.D. At Trinity Hall, I am very thankful especially for the help and assistance provided in numerous circumstances by Dr Christopher Padfield, Julie Powley, Dr Nick Bampos, Dr James Montgomery and Dr Nigel Chancellor.

Thanks also to everyone who helped me at the Centre of International Studies. A most conspicuous thank you to my supervisor Dr Geoffrey Edwards who has offered guidance and advice on academic matters, and who convinced me to finish this work: Geoffrey's enthusiasm for a dissertation on football, a sport he confesses to know very little about (or in his own words 'not even like very much'), has proved priceless too. I have also learned a lot from the feedback I received on successive drafts of the chapters in the thesis which has given birth to this book.

Thanks also go to the Foundation Wiener-Anspach who allowed me to spend a very interesting year at the Université Libre de Bruxelles in a research group headed by Professor Jean-Michel De Waele, to whom I also express my warmest thanks.

Thanks also to my family and all the friends (too numerous to mention here), who have supported and helped me. A special thanks to LA to whom I originally planned to dedicate this book.

List of abbreviations

AFP	Agence France Presse
ASSE	Association Sportive de Saint-Étienne
EC	European Community
ECJ	European Court of Justice
EU	European Union
FC	football club
FCNA	Football Club de Nantes Atlantique
FFF	Fédération Française de Football
FIFA	Fédération Internationale de Football Association
KoB	Kop of Boulogne
OM	Olympique de Marseille
PSG	Paris Saint-Germain
UEFA	Union Européenne de Football Association
UK	United Kingdom
US	Union Sportive

Introduction

On 15 December 1995, the European Court of Justice (ECJ) ruled on the case of the disputed transfer of a Belgian football player, Jean-Marc Bosman,[1] and professional sport in the European Union (EU) entered a new era.[2] In *Bosman*, the ECJ established its full jurisdiction on the rules made for the organisation of football competitions by football's governing body at European level, the Union Européenne de Football Association (UEFA). The court also followed the principle established in two of its earlier rulings, *Walrave*[3] and *Donà*:[4] Community law (the law of the European Community, or European Union, EC/EU) applies to sport whenever sport is an economic activity. Consequently, and as forecast by Stephen Weatherill as early as 1990,[5] the Court concluded in *Bosman* that some rules imposed by UEFA were incompatible with the European Community Treaty, more precisely with article 48 on the freedom of movement of workers. The consequences were far reaching. Before *Bosman*, in many Member States of the European Union (but not, for example, in France or Spain), clubs were allowed to retain a player and demand a transfer fee, even when that player's contract was over. After *Bosman*, this aspect of the transfer system became illegal within the whole of the EU.

The application of UEFA's system of quotas to players hailing from Member States was also declared unlawful. Under UEFA's so-called '3+2' rule (which applied only to European competitions), football clubs had been forbidden to field more than three foreigners, plus two foreigners who had resided and played in an Association for three years or more ('assimilated players'). In football terms, an 'Association' is broadly synonymous with a 'country'. The main exception is the United Kingdom, which (for historical reasons) is divided between the four Associations of England, Scotland, Wales and Northern Ireland).

Misunderstandings on these two consequences of the *Bosman* ruling abound, even in academic publications.[6] As Stephen Weatherill has argued, both international transfers within the EU and transfers between clubs of the same Member State are affected by *Bosman*.[7] Similarly, the *Bosman* ruling did not prevent countries from establishing quotas on foreign players. *Bosman* simply forbade these countries to consider citizens from other countries of the European Union (Member States) as foreigners. Quotas could still be applied to players from countries outside the EC/EU. After *Bosman*, UEFA decided to lift all restrictions on nationality for their club competitions. However, most national associations or leagues (which are typically in charge of professional football within the association) still have quotas on non-EU players for the domestic competitions they organise.

It is tempting to argue that the new transfer rules brought about by *Bosman* are merely following on, and furthering long-term trends affecting football, i.e. its increased globalisation and commercialisation. *Bosman* has arguably led football's global governing body, the Fédération Internationale de Football Association (FIFA) to change the international transfer system entirely.[8] However, the new rules on quotas are distinctively a consequence of the construction of the EC/EU. *Bosman* created a single European market for professional sportspersons. It is part of a process of regionalisation or Europeanisation[9] and only rather indirectly constitutive of wider trends of globalisation. Logically, consequences have been most clearly felt in team sports, and above all in the wealthiest of them: football. As a result, the best footballers now play in the richest clubs throughout the EU, their salaries have risen considerably and their transfers have become more frequent.[10] Some European clubs currently have fielded a majority of foreign players or all-foreign teams.

The governing bodies of football, FIFA and UEFA, have been firmly opposed to the post-*Bosman* system. UEFA and FIFA claim there is a specificity of sport, which would justify its exemption from the general application of the treaty. Their claims have found an echo in the media and they have prompted debate in some political institutions. Various vague declarations of intention (for example in an annex to the 2000 Treaty of Nice)[11] were followed by reports (most famously the *White Paper on Sport* from the Commission)[12] until the Treaty of Lisbon (in its article 165) finally provided the EU with a soft competence on sport. This increasing involvement of the EU in sport has triggered a growing body of academic literature on the matter. The birth and development of an EU sport law has been extensively analysed from a legal perspective,[13] and political scientists have analysed which forces are shaping the EU's embryonic sport policy.[14] Richard Parrish for example[15] uses an advocacy coalition framework, and contends that there is a sports policy subsystem at work in the European Union, composed of two coalitions. The *Single Market* coalition wants to protect the legal foundations of the Single Market by refusing to grant sport an exemption, for fear other industries would follow. The *sociocultural* coalition, conversely, sees sport more as a social and cultural activity and, accordingly, wants the specificity of sports to be recognised by the European Union. Parrish argues that as long as the balance of power between the two coalitions remains as it is, European sports law and policy will remain fundamentally unaltered and changes will remain only minor.

Football's governing bodies have, indeed, used sociocultural arguments to support their cause.[16] They have argued that the compensation fee for out-of-contract players allowed for a transfer of wealth from rich to smaller, sometimes amateur, clubs ('solidarity'). They have also claimed that the limitation on the number of foreign players was important to protect the development of young 'home' players. It thereby ensured national teams kept a big enough pool from which to select the best players. Two other arguments have further emphasised the national character of football clubs, which are said to represent their countries when they play European games. Furthermore, football's governing bodies have claimed that:

> the identification of the spectators with the various teams is guaranteed only if those teams consist, at least as regards the majority of players, of nationals of the relevant member state.[17]

This last argument has proved remarkably resilient. Ten years after the *Bosman* ruling, Sepp Blatter, President of FIFA, still claimed publicly, but without providing supporting evidence, that 'we should maintain the national identity of a club',[18] and that 'the national identity of clubs is very important'.[19] Calling for limits on foreign signings, he added that the presence of home-grown players 'helps the public identify with the players in the team'.[20]

This alleged inability of football supporters to identify with foreign players (EU or not) raises fundamental questions about the persistence of national identities within the European Union, about the rejection of others and therefore xenophobic attitudes, and how they are sometimes expressed through sport. This is particularly interesting since the Adonnino report to the European Council proposed as early as 1985 that a European citizenship be promoted through sport.[21] Yet, the veracity of the claims from football's authorities has not been investigated in the existing academic literature. The subject at hand here is therefore the assessment of how the *Bosman* ruling from the

ECJ has affected a vast number of citizens throughout the Union in one of the leisure activities (supporting football) which form part of their daily life. Does the presence of a majority of foreign players in a football club prevent fans from supporting and identifying with this club? This could only be the case under three conditions. First, clubs are (at least, primarily) representative of a national identity. Second, football fans cannot identify with foreign players (or they have a lesser propensity to identify with them than with 'natives'). Third, the identification with players is the main (but not necessarily the only) reason why fans come to support a club. To erase any bias that might be introduced by the claims of the football authorities (or more widely, what Richard Parrish had termed the 'sociocultural coalition'), it is therefore important to study the existence of other means through which supporters identify with their club and the relative importance of each means in stimulating support. It is also important to question whether football clubs are actually representative of national identities (and to what extent), and to question how such identities are instrumental in gathering support for the club.

Because of the sheer number and the complexity of possible correlations and causal relationships between the presence of foreigners in a team and the support that this team receives, and because of the possible existence of other means that stimulate team support, the case study approach has appeared to be the most suited to this topic. Case study methods allow for the discovery of new variables, the emergence of new hypotheses and the research into multiple interactions.[22] In particular, case study methods are very useful to identify causes when a correlation has been perceived in a given context. The same general correlation (for example: supporters do or do not identify with their football teams through the players) can have different precise causes in different clubs. History, precise events in the history of a club are crucial when it comes to process-tracing: the establishment of one, or multiple, process of causality. In order to ensure that the results of this study can be generalised, the research has therefore selected three cases and followed a logic of replication defined by Robert Yin as 'if similar results are obtained from all three cases, replication is said to have taken place'.[23]

The research questions are relevant for all countries within the European Union, but their very nature demands that they are researched as close to the supporters as possible: i.e. at the level of the club. Material circumstances (languages spoken and resources available) have played a part in the choice of the three case studies in France and the United Kingdom. Also, in order to minimise the external variables that can impact the results, the clubs have been selected in the capital cities of England, Scotland and France. Nevertheless, the three cases provide different contexts in which to seek an answer to the questions. Glasgow's Rangers club was, for a long time, one of the clearest (and most famous) examples of a club whose identity was carried by the composition of the team, the very means of identification that *Bosman* has been accused of destroying. Rangers has self-defined as Protestant, when its arch rival, the Glaswegian club Celtic has been described as having a clear Irish and Catholic support and identity. Accordingly, Rangers long followed a policy of not recruiting Catholic players. In 1989, though, for the first time in living memory, Rangers signed a Catholic. In a context of exacerbated tension between the supporters of these two clubs, the Glaswegian case of Rangers' opposition to Celtic therefore provides an opportunity to study the consequences for club support of the introduction of 'strangers' (football players who are not necessarily foreign but whose identity is undoubtedly at odds with the team's established identity), and the subsequent ability (or inability) for fans to identify with such players.

Glasgow answers the main questions posed here based on differences that have a clear (but perhaps not exclusive) sectarian dimension. The cases of Paris Saint-Germain and the London club Arsenal broaden it to the national level. They bring to the fore the questions of whether, and how, clubs symbolise a national identity in contexts that could barely be more different. Arsenal can rely on a large number of faithful supporters, which is characteristic of the English passion for football. Throughout its long history, the club has also developed a strong English identity, which can be partly explained by the interdiction on English teams from hiring non-UK footballers between 1931 and 1978. Paradoxically, following *Bosman*, Arsenal undoubtedly became the European club most open to foreign influence. Since 2006, they have even been known to line up teams made up entirely of non-UK nationals. In contrast to these other clubs, the foundation of Paris Saint-Germain is comparatively recent and, especially given the general lack of fervour for football in France, the club has had to recruit an audience, actively. Playing in a French league that has always allowed foreign players, Paris Saint-Germain have also constantly lined up French as well as foreign footballers, and still do, in part specifically to win support.

According to Benedict Anderson,[24] the press plays a crucial role in the creation of 'imagined communities' as it shapes the values and memories that these communities share. The largest spectator sport in Europe, football entertains a particular relationship, of reciprocal dependence, with the media. Football's presence in the media certainly helps increase the sales and audiences of both print and audiovisual media but is also responsible for football's current success.[25] In football, the press may therefore be instrumental in defining national identities and xenophobia (or in Glasgow sectarianism), which may directly impact on the ability for supporters to identify with their club through players (native or foreign), or through other means. Research on the press, through a selection of representative newspapers in each case study, has therefore been central to this work. Assessing the supporters' reaction to what they read in the printed media has been an important aspect of the press study: it allows to understand whether the press has a real influence on the fans' perception of their club and in the definition of their identity as supporters. The press is the main source in process-tracing throughout this study of identification and identity.

Identity is clearly understood here as a social concept. Following Henri Tajfel: a (social) identity can be understood as 'that part of an individual's self-concept which derives from his knowledge of his membership in a social group (or groups) together with the value and emotional significance attached to that membership'.[26] Identification is therefore seen as the movement by which an individual joins a group or stays in a group, because attributes of the group are congruent with the individual's self-concept, are valued and have emotional significance. Following, partisanship is here defined as the support given by someone or by a group to a football club. Partisan identification is defined as the identification of supporters with a group (club, supporters, other collectives).

Before moving on to the case studies themselves, a review of the existing literature on sport (and the sport press) will inform, frame and define the study of football partisanship. The literature review will help identify the theoretical approach to be adopted and other possible variables in the identification with a club, in order to define a framework of typological theories used for this research.[27]

Notes

1 Arrêt de la Cour de Justice des Communautés Européennes du 15 décembre 1995, *Union Royale Belge des Sociétés de Football Association e.a.* v. *Bosman e.a.* (at: http://eur-lex.europa.eu/smartapi/cgi/sga_doc?smartapi!celexplus!prod!CELEXnumdoc&lg=en&numdoc=61993J0415; last accessed 8 April 2007 (hereafter *Bosman*)).

2 David McArdle. 'They're playing R. song. Football and the European Union after *Bosman*', *Football Studies*, 3(2) (2000), 42–66.
3 Arrêt de la Cour de Justice des Communautés Européennes du 12 décembre 1974, *B.N.O. Walrave, L.J.N. Koch contre Association Union cycliste internationale, Koninklijke Nederlandsche Wielren Unie et Federación Española Ciclismo* (at: http://eur-lex.europa.eu/LexUriServ/LexUriServ.do?uri=CELEX:61974J0036:FR:HTML; last accessed 8 April 2007) (hereafter *Walrave and Koch*).
4 Arrêt de la Cour de Justice des Communautés Européennes du 14 juillet 1976, *Gaetano Donà contre Mario Mantero* (at: http://eur-lex.europa.eu/LexUriServ/LexUriServ.do?uri=CELEX:61976J0013:FR:HTML, last accessed 8 April 2007 (hereafter *Donà*).
5 Stephen Weatherill, 'Discrimination on grounds of nationality in sport', *Yearbook of European Law 1989*, 10 (1990), 55–92.
6 The following article, which also twice misrepresents Jean-Marc Bosman as Marc Bosman, gives an example of many misinterpretations on *Bosman*. Jonathan Magee and John Sugden, 'The world at their feet: professional football and international labor migration', *Journal of Sport and Social Issues*, 26(4) (2002), 421–437.
7 Stephen Weatherill, *Cases and materials on EC law*. London: Blackstone, 1996, p. 1021.
8 Jean-Christian Drolet, 'Extra time: are the new FIFA transfer rules doomed?', *International Sports Law Journal*, 6(1–2) (2006), 87–103.
9 See Alexander Brand and Arne Niemann, 'Europeanisation in the societal/trans-national realm: what European integration studies can get out of analysing football', *Journal of Contemporary European Research*, 3(3) (2007), 180–201. Arne Niemann, Borja Garcia, Wyn Grant (eds), *The transformation of European football: towards the Europeanisation of the national game*, Manchester University Press, 2011.
10 Stefan Szymanski and Tim Kuypers, *Winners and losers*. London: Penguin, 2000.
11 'Declaration on the specific characteristics of sport and its social function in Europe'.
12 Commission of the European Communities, *White paper on sport*, COM (2007) 391.
13 Andrew Caiger and Simon Gardiner (eds), *Professional sport in the European Union: regulation and re-regulation*. The Hague: TMC Asser, 2000.
14 Simon Gardiner, Richard Parrish and Robert C. R. Siekmann (eds), *EU, sport, law and policy: regulation, re-regulation and representation*. The Hague: TMC Asser, 2009.
15 Richard Parrish, *Sports law and policy in the European Union*. Manchester University Press, 2003.
16 Some illustration of this can be found in UEFA's media release 070, 9 May 2007. Other examples include: 'Report from Brussels', *UEFA direct*, 57 (2007), 10–11; Joseph S. Blatter, 'Sport must retain its autonomy', a

FIFA media release dated 18 January 2007. The International Olympic Committee also organised its first seminar on the autonomy of the Olympic and sports movement on 21–22 September 2006.

17 As summarised in Opinion of Mr Advocate General Lenz delivered on 20 September 1995, his conclusions presented to the ECJ in the *Bosman* case (at: http://eur-lex.europa.eu/LexUriServ/LexUriServ.do?uri=CELEX:61993C0415:EN:HTML; last accessed 14 May 2007).

18 Christopher Davies, 'Blatter calls for limit on foreign signings', *Daily Telegraph*, 20 December 2005.

19 Paul Morgan, 'Blatter moves to end foreign invasion of the English game', *Mail on Sunday*, 14 May 2006.

20 Davies, 'Blatter calls for limit on foreign signings'.

21 Ad Hoc Committee 'On A People's Europe', *Report to the European Council*, 1985 (at: www.ombudsman.europa.eu/historical/en/default.htm; last accessed 8 April 2007).

22 For more details about the approach explicated in this paragraph, see: Alexander L. George and Andrew Bennet, *Case studies and theory development in the social sciences*. Cambridge, MA: MIT Press, 2004 (hereafter George and Bennet 2004).

23 Robert K. Yin, *Case study research: design and methods*. London: Sage, 1994, p. 45ff. (hereafter Yin 1994).

24 Benedict Anderson, *Imagined communities: Reflections on the origin and spread of nationalism*. London: Verso, 1991 (hereafter Anderson 1991).

25 David Rowe, *Sport, culture and the media: the unruly trinity*. Maidenhead: Open University Press, 1999 (hereafter Rowe 1999) makes this point, at pp. 24ff. This idea was also expressed by Jérôme Touboul, journalist at *L'Équipe* in an interview with the author, and it has been confirmed by interviews with other journalists.

26 Henri Tajfel, *Human groups and social categories*. Cambridge University Press, 1981, p. 255 (hereafter Tajfel 1981).

27 George and Bennet 2004.

1

Understanding partisan identification

Sociology has largely provided the main paradigms that still frame most social science studies on sport and the understanding of partisanship: the critical, functionalist, figurational and interpretative approaches. These four approaches provide different answers to the central question: what prompts a partisan identification? Thorough research on the means of identification has only been conducted within the figurational and interpretative frameworks. The empirical relevance of some aspects of these theories has been shown in the works of historians, geographers, sociologists and anthropologists on factors of partisanship: class, race and gender, space and place. They have therefore provided the basis for the insights tested and the methods of investigation used in this study.

The determinants of support

Critical approaches

The critical approaches to sport belong to a wider range of sociological traditions according to which the meaning of the participation in sporting or supporting activities is not determined by the individual but is imposed on him or her. The main shared hypothesis for all critical sociologists is that sports form part of a network of institutions promoting social values that reflect the interest of the dominant classes. The subordinate groups believe in them and carry them out, though it is contrary to their interest. Sports appear to be an instrument of the domination of the ruling classes. These theories are reminiscent of Marx's own in *The German Ideology*.[1] According to Marx, the superstructure (all social and cultural forms other than the economy) is determined by the infrastructure (also known as the base): the (economic) mode of production. In capitalist societies, there is a division between the masters of production (owning the means of production, capital) and the direct producers (owning only their labour force). One of the chief functions of superstructures is to promote the key ideologies of a given capitalist society in order to reinforce the reproduction of the system.

Orthodox critical theories

The 'orthodox' critical theory of sports sociology (developed notably in France by Jean-Marie Brohm and his followers in the review *Quel corps?*)[2] is the most salient example of critical theories applied to sport.[3] In the aftermath of May 1968, Brohm's theories took on a dominant position among the sociological studies of sport in France until they were replaced by the theories of Bourdieu's school in the 1980s. Brohm and the orthodox critic theory owe much to Marx's theory of ideology. Brohm, for example, contends that the function of sport is to maintain the established order; it is seen as ideologically reproducing the social mode of production through political and ideological enrolment, the diffusion of the bourgeois order and the improvement of the working force.[4] From this perspective, supporting a club can only be seen as entirely determined by forces at work in society that the agent cannot escape.

Bourdivine theories of sport: habitus *and field*

Even if they mark a departure from the strict determinism of Marxism, the theories of Pierre Bourdieu[5] on sport can be related to critical theory, with which they share two common hypotheses. First, sport and other such leisure activities feature in an ongoing struggle for the domination of one class. Second, sport provides the lower classes with the misleading and ideological idea that upwards mobility can be attained through them. Hence it contributes to social control.

The notion of *habitus* (the shared cultural values and practices that drive the social behaviour of a group), first developed by the Frankfurt school of sociology in the 1930s, is central in Bourdivine writings. When applied to sport, it implies that the decision to take part in a sport as an actor or as a spectator is the result of an unconscious assimilation of tastes. For the ruling classes, taking part in some sport is equivalent to a badge of social distinction. For the subordinate classes, it also acts as a way of emphasising status distinctions within a class (for example between genders). *Habitus* has found an important development in the work of Christian Piocello, who has argued that there exists a 'system of sports'. Each social class has its own sport, and the choice made by an individual to play a given sport is constrained by the class to which this individual belongs. This correlation between class and the sport played (or, by extension, supported) may appear very deterministic. Yet, it also emphasises that the agent has the ability to choose between different sports and that agents of the same class may make different choices, or the same choice, but for different reasons.

A second major insight from Bourdieu is the notion of 'field' (*champ*). Sport constitutes a field. There is a 'sports world' with its own relation to time (rhythms and history), its own set of rules and values, its own organisation (limits and hierarchies). Jacques Defrance has, indeed, demonstrated[6] that in the case of France during the second part of the nineteenth century, the institutionalisation of sport led to the autonomy of the sport field. Through the development of sports institutions and their recognition by other social institutions (e.g. the state), sport became a specialised activity with a distinct social organisation. The idea that sport is autonomous has been adopted in many social sciences. For example the French historian, Alfred Wahl, has argued that sport has its own rhythm and chronology that only have tenuous links with the rhythms of general political, economic and social history. Wahl concludes that the history of sport (including football) therefore has to be studied independently.[7] Consequently, studying an agent's choice to support a given team must take into account the specific context of the sport field.

Hegemony theory

Hegemony theory has replaced the strict deterministic character of orthodox Marxist theory with the notion of hegemony, inspired by the works of Gramsci. Hegemony theory, in contrast, postulates that values are constantly negotiated between classes through their intellectuals in order to ensure the continuing domination of the ruling classes. John Hargreaves, for example, contends that dominant social classes have to fight and compromise with the subordinate classes to impose their sport-based norms, values and functions.[8]

Morgan has underlined that in Britain and North America 'hegemony theory has achieved intellectual dominion in critical considerations of sport. It is no exaggeration to refer to hegemony theory in this context as the received critical view on sport'.[9] Hegemony theory has, therefore, led to a variety of approaches. Ben Carrington and Ian McDonald have applied hegemony theory to the study of relations between dominant and dominated groups to other social categories than class, notably race and gender.[10] The works of John Sugden and Alan Tomlinson have also renewed the hegemonic paradigm as they emphasise the dynamics of agency and power (where power replaces structure as a central element of sociological study). Their methodology has also broadened the scope of hegemony theory as their critical approach intersects with five other approaches: 'historiography, comparative methods; critical sociology; ethnography; investigative research and gonzo'.[11] Hegemony theory has been used by students of the media and sport such as Alan Clarke and John Clarke, who have argued[12] that sport is one among many objects in the media discourse used to reproduce and transmit ideological themes and values dominant in our societies. Garry Whannel, for his part, examined the relationship between sport and television,[13] highlighting the way that television has remodelled sport. He also argues that representations of sport (or blackness and women in sport) are changing, as they only reflect the compromise between different actors of the society. Hegemony theory therefore puts an emphasis on the necessity to understand an agent's choice to support within changing social dynamics, and in the light of changing social institutions, like the media.

Functionalist approaches

Functionalist approaches share with critical approaches a common hypothesis: the meaning of sport is to be found at the social, not individual level. Yet, functionalists do not usually pass judgement on the values of social functions, and whether they contribute to domination. According to functionalists such as Gunther Lüschen,[14] society is a whole, a unified system within which sport is only one social institution (among others) which has functions to perform. As such, the sport institution can be said to reflect the society as a whole or it can be compared to other institutions in order to understand which functions it performs.[15] For example, Christopher Stevenson and John Nixon[16] have identified five functions sport performs. Sport contributes to the maintenance of psychological stability at societal level: it performs a socio-emotional function. As sport contributes to the inculcation of social beliefs and groups, it permits socialisation. Disparate individuals and groups are integrated by sports. Used for ideological purposes, sport also performs a political function, but it also provides an upward social mobility function for deprived individuals and groups. Following the functionalists, the individual decision of whether to support a team can, arguably, be entirely determined or simply affected by the role football plays in society. As ideology, hegemony or *habitus* for critical theorists, the relevance of social functions to the individual here provides the main elements towards an explanation of the choice of one sport to play or support.

Understanding supporters' behaviour

Interpretative sociology

In stark contrast to the approaches which state that the meaning of sport is to be found at the social level, the method of interpretative sociology posits that the understanding of behaviour must include the meaning individuals give to this behaviour. This paradigm has been used in hermeneutic studies of the media, for example, in Young's study of the themes used by the media in the coverage of the Heysel disaster.[17] The studies of subcultures (systems of beliefs, values and norms shared by a substantial minority of people within a larger cultural ensemble) is another main field for an interpretative framework in North America and Europe. The approach has been partly illustrated by the work of Loïc Wacquant in his studies on boxing,[18] Christian Pociello on rugby[19] and Charles Suaud on tennis clubs.[20] Even if the meaning that supporters give to their actions is to be taken into account in any analysis of their behaviour, figurational sociology, and the works of Roger Caillois have shown the importance of being careful in any assessment of supporters' behaviour.

Figurational sociology: Norbert Elias and the civilising process

Norbert Elias and Eric Dunning's theory of the civilising process is one of the most influential sociological work studies on sport. It adopts a figurational perspective. Instead of structures or agents, networks of interdependent humans (figurations) are the unit of investigation. Norbert Elias first developed a general sociological theory based on empirical data (published in 1939),[21] which shows that a twofold long term process took place in Europe between the end of the Middle Ages and the First World War. Manners and social standards became increasingly refined. This included, for example, the growing rejection of activities involving violence, or the lowering of the 'threshold of repugnance'. At the same time, self-control over feelings and behaviour came to take precedence over external controls: the social rules, including a mounting taboo on violence, became increasingly internalised.

In a study co-written with Eric Dunning, Elias later assessed the role played by sport in the civilising process.[22] Elias and Dunning argue that modern sport initially developed as less violent and more civilised ways for the aristocracy to enjoy themselves. For instance, since the brutality of boxing became less acceptable, it was the subject of increased codification. The prohibition of wrestling or 'hugging' marked a step in the control of violence. Elias and Dunning contend that in our modern 'civilised' societies this ban on violence has been internalised by the agent. Supporting a team therefore provides one with excitement and, accordingly, the opportunity for a controlled release of emotions. Behaviour that would not be acceptable in wider society becomes tolerable within the stadium. The Leicester school of sport sociology expanded considerably on this field. This school became famous for using the theory of the civilising process to account for the hooligan phenomenon.[23] They argued notably that hooligans were drawn from 'rougher' parts of society and remained less incorporated into the more 'civilised' society of the twentieth century. As the social control of emotions is lowered in the stadium, it is a necessity to be careful in any assessment of the supporters' behaviour – even in taking into account the value they give to their behaviour. The theories of Roger Caillois further this analysis.

Roger Caillois: paidia

The classic analysis of games proposed by French grammarian Roger Caillois also points to the difficulty of appreciating fully the meaning of a supporter's behaviour.[24] Caillois puts forward a fourfold typology of games depending on the dominance of the role of competition (*agôn*), chance (*alea*), hazard (*mimicry*) or giddiness (*ilinx*).[25] Caillois further identifies a tension between two sources of satisfaction provided by games, *paidia* 'a primary power of improvisation and ecstasy' and *ludus* 'the taste for gratuitous difficulty'.[26]

Sport is a game in which *agôn* (competition) clearly dominates. The relative elaboration of the rules of football (as opposed to the simplicity of the rules of a 100m run) implies that *ludus* plays an important part.

Caillois is also adamant that the attitude and activities of sport spectators can be likened to the playing of games: 'the multitude of spectators favour *mimicry*, exactly as collective turbulence stimulates *ilinx* and then feeds on it'.[27] These games played by supporters, with their apparent disorder, the noise and agitation may also seem characteristic of *paidia* and are independent of the gesture and decisions of ordinary life.[28] If supporters are 'playing a game', and because this game has been likened to *mimicry*, if they are playing a role (that of a supporter), it is difficult to assess the extent to which they actually believe in the gestures they make and the things they say. This is particularly pertinent when slogans and actions have been inherited from the past. They might have become void of any sense: 'A quantity of games are likewise founded on lost beliefs or vacuously reproduce rites that have lost any significance'.[29]

Understanding factors of partisanship

Apart from sociology, history is certainly the social science which has produced the largest number of academic works on sport, especially in England and France. Social historians such as Tony Mason,[30] Richard Holt[31] or James Walvin[32] have studied the rise of football and the formation of football supporters' identities since the early era of contemporary sport. Some of their explanations might still be pertinent for many of today's features of partisanship. Shifting the emphasis to place rather than time, geographers have insisted on the links between territory and support for a team. John Bale, for instance, has provided a comprehensive theory on how a ground (and its location) can shape football's partisanship. Similarly, the importance of local and national context in the perception of football and partisanship has been emphasised in sociological and anthropological studies.

Class, race and gender

David Russell[33] has identified three major elements in the long-term construction of English fans' identity in the works of social historians: working class culture, male values and different levels of territorial affiliation. He contends that football 'truly has been a major site for the reflection, reinforcement and construction of key social and political identities'.[34] Russell first focuses on the appropriation of the game by 'the people'. From the 1870s on, the working-class spectators have actively engaged with the game and been able to 'stamp their identity, value and culture on the game'.[35] Therefore, he provides arguments in favour of the theses developed by Bourdieu and Pociello: football is part of the *habitus* of the working class. Russell also insists on the fact that real control of the game (through football's governing bodies) has evaded the working class and remained in the hand of dominant groups – notably those owning the means of production.

Following other authors such as Holt,[36] Russell contends that 'the game has always been a decidedly male preserve and a location for the expression of, and experimentation with, a variety of masculine identities'.[37] Similarly, Chas Critcher views the style of play of British teams as reflecting a specifically British definition of manliness.[38] Yet, Russell argues, football also allows for the expression of a range of emotion (for example, through tears) that is normally socially unacceptable for men (a point in line with Dunning and Elias's claims on the controlled release of emotions).

Russell also argues that 'from its earlier moments, football has proved a potent vehicle for the generation of territorial loyalties'[39] and acknowledges Holt's study as a reference.[40] Yet, he fails to mention Holt's strong emphasis on the major part played by success or failure in the identification to a club: 'this kind of blind territorial affiliation must not be pushed too far. Crowds were not unconditionally loyal and support for a side could vary according to its playing success'.[41] The importance of success on the field has actually been underlined by a number of American studies in sports psychology. Supporters, they found, are prone to increase demonstration of their support ('bask in reflected glory', or 'BiRG') after victories[42] and to underplay their ties with the teams ('cut off reflected failure', or 'CORF') after defeats.[43]

However, Anthony King has vehemently criticised the stance adopted by Russell and others on class, gender and race. He contends they reflect more the position of the social scientists than that of their object:

> In particular, the contemporary sociology of football fails because it unselfconsciously assumes the views of white, male, generally working-class fans to be both representative of the football crowd as a whole and politically populist in sentiment. Recent writings have failed to situate the views of these white, male fans in a wider social, historical and gender context and have instead romanticised and exaggerated the attitudes of these individuals because they reflect the sociologist's own imagined relations with football.[44]

King's claims are vindicated by abundant examples of academics who explicitly side with the fans that they are closest to or who, by their own admission, even use academic writings to further a cause they are defending as supporters.[45] Furthermore, King argues that *the end of the terraces*, i.e. the transformation of English football stadia into all-seaters, fundamentally altered the composition of the crowd. It is now more affluent, feminine (or familial) and ethnically diverse.[46] Others have argued that masculinity is still dominant in English stadia. It has only been renegotiated (notably in fanzines)[47] and is reasserted periodically by supporters, notably of the national team.[48] Women also still seem marginalised within football in England. They are mostly seen as merely one of three elements providing entertainment to the supporter: the 'booze, betting and birds' trilogy.[49]

Nevertheless, two related insights from Russell are particularly relevant to this study. Russell contends that the local press had a major role to play in the definition of a territorial identity as 'many such representations depict football as the shared passion of a closely unified community'.[50] Russell also states that 'football certainly contributed to the articulation of a perceived 'North–South' divide within English society'. He shows that a local affiliation may merely be part of a wider issue of territorial identity. Russell pushes the argument further. He analysed the reports on the failures and success of the England side: 'from at least the early 1930s English international football clearly became increasingly politicised and to stand as a mirror for the national condition'.[51] Therefore, the tendency to see in the English game a reflection of English values and therefore to dismiss or ignore the success of other teams is a component of insularity just as the tendency to relate the decline of English football to the weakening of English position in the world. This insularity can, at worse, take the form of xenophobic nationalism.

Space and place

The stadium

Territorial factors have been identified among the determinants of identity, but geographers have undertaken relatively little research on the subject. Other themes have attracted interest instead: the identification of sport regions (through the mapping of practices or the geographical diffusion of sport and games); the relocation of sport clubs and franchises or the relocation of success between territories; the migration of sport talent and the spatial impact of sporting event. The economic aspect of the latter has been particularly studied, in France for example, by Gougnet and Nys,[52] and migration is the subject of regular publications from a dedicated academic institution, the Professional Football Players Observatory.[53] Relevant, though, is John Bale's notion of the 'topophile' triangle.[54] The three elements (or angles) of this triangle are the club, the supporter and the stadium. It is called 'topophile' as the attachment (-phile) to a place (topo-), the stadium, mediates the attachment for the club. Through memories, because of the symbols it displays or its location, the stadium becomes invested with meaning. The fan sees it at the same time as a 'sacred place' (the scene of nearly religious celebrations), as a 'scenic space' for a community (unconsciously reinforcing a sense of belonging), as 'home' and as a place for the expression of pride and local patriotism.[55]

Local patriotism

As emphasised by Holt, pride of place has proved particularly important in the history of football.[56] Anthony King claims that the stadium remains important as a medium for attachment to a local area.[57] Post-national identity, King contends, results from the identification to three elements: region, nation and supranation. Cities are particularly dynamic areas of the territories and thus 'the most important element in post-national identity will be a regional or local affiliation to a particular city'.[58] Football clubs, he concludes, traditionally represent cities and, therefore, provide a good focus for the study of these new local identifications, even if the consequence of such identifications is that the definition of the locale has to be reinvented. Giulianotti and Robertson have emphasised the importance of globalisation in this process of reinvention. It may take the form of what Robertson has branded 'glocalization', 'whereby local cultures adapt and redefine any global cultural product to suit their particular needs, beliefs and customs'.[59]

The territoriality of identities

These links between support and territory have been detailed in four articles within a collection devoted to the study of football culture and identities (edited by Gary Armstrong and Richard Giulianotti).[60] Following on studies by John Sugden and Alan Bairner,[61] Bairner and Shirlow show that the 'ethnic', religious and political (or constitutional) division of Northern Ireland between a minority of Catholics (giving preference to Ulster's integration within the Republic of Ireland), and a majority of Protestants (backing the current union of Ulster with mainland Britain) is reflected in the spatial partition of both communities as well as in the different clubs that each gives support to.[62] The change in the 'religious' composition of a neighbourhood can even lead to a club switching allegiances. Derry City left the North Irish league in 1972 and joined the league of Ireland in 1985 after Brandywell, its neighbourhood changed from being Protestant to being Catholic. Here, the local territory defines the religious identity of the club, and prompts the club to join a league which is further away but closer to its identity. Equally, Windsor Park, where Northern Ireland play, is the home ground of Linfield, the most loyalist of clubs. It is located in predominantly Protestant areas of Belfast (Donegall Road and Village). This can largely explain the decrease of Catholic support for the Northern Ireland team since the World Cup finals in 1982. Arguably, the growing success of the Republic of Ireland's national team may have also played its part.

The changing nature of the identities supported by a club

In the study of Israeli clubs by Carmeli and Bar,[63] it appears that on a territory claimed by two populations with different origins and religions, football clubs do not inevitably provide a support for the identities of both populations. Instead, all football clubs may be representative of one of these two populations only, and reflect political differences within that population. Clubs with the prefix Hapoel attract support from Labour party members or sympathisers as they originated in the Trade unions' sport organisation. Clubs with the prefix Beitar attract support from the Likud party (right-wing nationalist). Clubs with the prefix Maccabi tend to attract support from liberals.

More important, such a polarisation appears to be clearly not immutable and club identities have proved to be changeable too. The 1996 promotion of an Arab team, Hapoel Taibeh, from one of the major Arab towns inside the 1948 frontier, to the top division of Israeli football brought into the stadium the conflict between Jewish and Arab populations, and the question of the place of the Arab Israeli in Israel. Other clubs' identities have consequently changed: for example Beitar Jerusalem became the champion of hostility towards the Arab team Hapoel Taibeh.

Supporters abroad: Norwegian identity and British football

The findings of Matti Goksøyr and Hans Hognestad on British influences in Norwegian football[64] are in sharp contrast with the previous cases. Since the importation of the game by sailors, merchants and other English expatriates or anglophile Norwegians, football has become the largest participatory sport for both men and women. Still, football has always remained a 'foreign product'. It failed to deprive skiing of its position as the national sport 'because the game cannot provide the key symbols of Norwegian identity or manifest genuine national virtues'.[65] The situation now prevailing in Norway is therefore paradoxical. English football clubs attract more support than the local Norwegian clubs, largely thanks to the media (the sport press, from the 1920s onwards and television after 1969 have both reported extensively on English clubs): during the 1970s and 1980s a great number of supporters' clubs dedicated to English teams or to English football in general were established. The recent upsurge in Norway's international results seems paradoxically to have strengthened the links with England: many Norwegian international players play for English football clubs. A supporter can be attached to a club which expresses foreignness or is the place where national success is built. What does this say in terms of attachment to a locale? Can there be a conflict of attachments to different locales? Or is it possible to surmise, following Ernst Haas's pioneering works on identities in the nascent European Communities, that different levels of attachment or allegiances may coexist?[66] Haas was considering a case of shifting allegiances from national to supranational. Is it possible to extend his model to include different types of allegiances, like allegiances to the near and the far, for example?

Means of identification

A number of factors (sex, class, gender, place, space) explaining why fans follow a sport or support a team have been put forward (and criticised) by academics. How precisely they relate to their team has been given comparatively little attention. The means of identification have been most comprehensively studied by three social scientists. Owing partly to figurational sociology,[67] the works of Christian Bromberger,[68] Patrick Mignon[69] (both from France) and Richard Giulianotti[70] (from Scotland) clearly use an interpretative approach as they all emphasise the supporter's rationality and freedom in choosing whether to support a club. They underline the role played in identification by the symbolisation of identity, rivalries and the construction of communities.

The rationality of the supporters and the post-fan

Bromberger's first point relates to the rationality of fans' behaviour which, he argues, is not decided at the social level. The decision to support a club can always be argued rationally by each individual. No two football supporters will support the same club for exactly the same reasons. Bromberger insists on, and accounts for this diversity of the football crowds. Richard Giulianotti takes this assessment one step further when he identifies a new kind of fan, 'the post-fan', whom he defines as having developed a 'reflexivity, irony and participatory outlook'.[71] The 'post-fan' is representative of the current postmodern context, in which money is omnipresent. Football players, once local heroes, have become media stars and commodities. The concurrent rise of the fanzine culture and football subcultures has changed the nature of the relations between the supporters and the clubs. Post-fans know that fan reputations are constructed or exaggerated by the media. They are aware of the power relationships and politics of football. 'They maintain an ironic and critical stance towards the apologetic propaganda emanating from their board of directors, and generally sympathetic relationship that exists between the latter and the mass media.'[72] Furthermore, they 'are at the epicentre of supporters movements which militate to change club policy on the players, managers or directors' while recognising their influence is limited.[73] Giulianotti links this development of the post-fan attitude to a change in the social origins of the fans (which, like King, he links to the end of the terraces). The post-fans, he argues, are educated. They hail from a middle-class background, yet show no rejection of popular culture.

The behaviour of fans towards their own club and the media has, therefore, to be interpreted cautiously since they most likely reflect a power struggle. Bromberger also puts strong emphasis on the difficulty correctly to appreciate the meaning of the 'rhetoric of the supporters'[74] against their opponents. The manifestations of the fans, the songs they sing and the slogans they refer to, reflect the intrinsic nature of the partisan logic, 'which consists in making use of any possible sign in order to discredit the adversary, to shock the Other and by these crushing humiliations, to influence the result of the game'.[75] Hence, as underlined by Dunning, Elias and Caillois, partisan behaviour should be the object of a cautious and balanced analysis, especially when it comes to analysing discourses on identity. These discourses considerably amplify the feelings and passions of one social group they represent. In particular, researchers and activists against racism in football have made similar points in order to emphasise the need to fight racist acts or words, regardless of the beliefs held by the perpetrators:

> ambiguous and contradictory expressions of racist practice get enforced because their perpetrators don't accept them as racism…Our research has found that it is the nature of the deed and not the uniformity of the doers' racism that matters.[76]

The symbolisation of identity

The choice to support a given team is rational at an individual level, but football must also be made sense of in society. For Bromberger, the success of football can be attributed to its ability to provide a mirror for the values of our democratic society (and reveals its 'symbolic horizon': uncertainty and merit for instance). This idea derives largely from Alain Ehrenberg's theorisation on contemporary societies as worshipping performance.[77] It has been condemned by critical sociologists as contentious or ideological.[78] Yet, Bromberger's work encompasses and develops most of the research done in the area up to 1998. It also provides one of the most detailed ethnographic researches on football supporters, which results from more than ten years of ethnological enquiry (1985–95 and 1998) in France, Italy and Iran.[79] It offers many major insights into supporters' process of identification with their teams.

Providing a mirror for our society, football indeed owes its position as a privileged medium for the expression of conflicts to the fact that each confrontation offers supporters the opportunity to mobilise and demonstrate their membership of a group: '(football) provides a support for the symbolisation of one aspect (local, professional, regional) of their identity'.[80] Three main means of symbolisation have been analysed in detail by Bromberger. These means all operate differently. First, the team's style of play acts as the affirmation of an imaginary identity. Second, the composition of the team acts as the allegory of a collective destiny. Third, the personality of the players makes them emblematic figures of social identities.[81] The second means analysed by Bromberger puts into perspective the very question raised by the greater presence of foreigners in the post-*Bosman* era.

Arguably, these three means have also been alluded to in the analyses developed by Chas Critcher on style, but they were not identified individually and they were lumped under the multiform notion of style (which also includes phenomena of violence).[82] In an article about football and the nation, Albrecht Sonntag has, however, developed an analysis which is similar and complementary to that of Bromberger.[83] He identified five ways in which football can symbolise identities. First, the composition of the team reflects the ethnic image of the nation (or the ethnic image a nation has of itself). Second, the style of the team reflects the stereotyped image of the nation – both in the eyes of the foreigners and the nationals, no matter what the reality is.[84] Third, football provides an opportunity to create new national myths. Fourth, it provides an opportunity for one nation to celebrate itself. Fifth, it provides an environment where nations are equal. All these means can be studied at the local level of the club and insist on the notion of community. The idea that a nation celebrates itself through football might attract attention, as it can be related to an important idea from Durkheim: 'in religious worship, society adores its own camouflaged image. In a nationalist age, societies worship themselves brazenly and openly, spurning the Camouflage'.[85] For Bromberger, though rites and myths are undoubtedly involved in football, they do not necessarily mean so much in terms of religion, as they do not always involve any belief in transcendence. Their meaning must therefore reside in the celebration of a community.

On another level, Bromberger confers special importance to the emblems of the club, and among them, especially the colours, as ways to mobilise and demonstrate, not only support for the club, but also membership of a group.[86] The example of Barcelona FC (Barça) is the most striking illustration of this point: 'the blue and ruby red (*blaugrana*) of the Barça competes with the Catalan gold and red'.[87] There were restrictions on the rights to use the original Catalan colours during Franco's era. Consequently, the colours of Barcelona FC have become not only a symbol of affiliation to the club but also of the resistance to Franco and the political claims for a Catalan autonomy. Giulianotti and Robertson usefully complete Bromberger's analysis by including the club crest and the home ground among the 'standardised emblems' of the club.[88]

Bromberger has also emphasised the importance of playing style in raising supporters' identification:

> The identification with a club is not indeed seen and conceived by the supporters as the simple (arbitrary) sign of a common membership, but as the (justified) symbol of a specific mode of collective existence, that the team's style of play embodies.[89]

Examples of this thesis have been given by authors such as Roberto DaMatta. In his analysis of Brazilian football[90] he mentions the 'golden rule of the Brazilian social system', that things should be done with so much dissimulation and elegance that they look easy. This rule is said to be embodied in the typically Brazilian art of dribbling the ball in order to avoid direct confrontation with the opposing team. In these cases, as emphasised by Bromberger[91] and Sonntag, it is once again not the reality that matters but the image a community has of its style.

Two reasons explain why this idea could be usefully tested through the newspapers. First, the commentators – including the press – are given a special, even key, role in the definition of this style and its significance: 'the style comes to represent a fate or a collective will'.[92] Second, Bromberger emphasises the importance of the styles of the team as markers of identity in the case of local confrontations: 'Each great local team also stamps its mark on the game, and thus, an important confrontation appears like a "war of styles"'.[93]

The construction of communities

Football partisanship has its origin in the capacity of a team to become a symbol of an identity. Its consequence is generally the construction of communities. Bromberger's work indeed emphasises that 'football offers itself, perhaps it needs no emphasising, as a privileged field for the expression of collective identities'.[94] One important element in the construction of communities is the dislike of another team. One constant aspect of football partisanship is therefore its 'agonistic' nature (it is defined and realised through an opposition).[95] This confirms findings from two main exponents of social identity theory, Tajfel and Turner, according to whom a group finds a source of coherence in the positive image it has of itself (the 'in-group') and the negative image it has of another group (out-group).[96] In football, the opposition may be labelled religious (Glasgow or to a much lesser extent, in the past Liverpool and Manchester), social (Turin, Madrid) or political (Barcelona). It can be mediated as well as exacerbated through football confrontations. A collection of articles on football rivalries (edited by Giulianotti and Armstrong) further state that 'the opposition to a local enemy is the most common form of this aversion, the sources of which usually lie outside of the football sphere'.[97]

Patrick Mignon uses two historiography concepts to further the analysis on the construction of communities.[98] Mignon considers imagined communities,[99] a notion first developed by Benedict Anderson in his study on the birth of nations.[100] According to Anderson, the community is '*imagined* because the members of even the smallest nation will never know most of their fellow-members, meet them, or even hear of them, yet in the minds of each lives the image of their communion'.[101] The sense of community therefore arises from a mental construction by which some people feel (rightly or wrongly) that they share an experience. This experience can be speaking a common language (in the case of nations), being in the same position towards the possession of the means of production (in the case of class) or living on a set territory (in the case of cities).

According to Mignon, when it comes to football, imagined communities build on the rituals surrounding the game, the invented traditions of football.[102] According to Hobsbawm in his work on the invention of tradition,[103] societies invent events which express a way a society thinks about itself. These events later become routine and form traditions which serve to justify, claim or emphasise the existence of the societies and the values upon which these are based. Invented traditions are a way to reinforce the identity of a community, for they root this identity in the past but nevertheless are likely to be interpreted to fit the changes in this identity. According to Mignon, the invented traditions, the rituals of football, contribute to the existence of new collectives in six ways. First, proximity in the stadium reveals the distance (say, in social status) and closeness (say, living in the same area) between people who might otherwise never meet. Second, the emblems and qualities of the team make the national or the local collective become tangible. Third, at both national and regional level, a football team provides an opportunity to tell an apolitical history of the community. Fourth, supporters share a common cyclic time, punctuated by the organisation of games and competitions. Fifth, supporters share the experience of reading reports in the press. Sixth, supporters share the interpretations of what each game offers (the style of play, the behaviour of the crowd and its meaning).

The individual and collective identities in France, England and Scotland as well as their mode of construction are probably different. As a metaphor for identity, football should reflect these differences. Patrick Mignon's approach to the comparison between France and England's differing passion for football actually insists on the difference in the building of collective identities:

> We shall oppose a society that founds collective identities, social classes for example, on a cultural mode (Disraeli's two nations) and another which founds them on the political registry (the struggle for access to citizenship), therefore giving way to two football cultures, and accessorily two kinds of extreme partisanship.[104]

It has, indeed, often been the case, for example in the works of Louis Dumont[105] or Rogers Brubaker,[106] that the French conception of national identity as a civic identity (based on Rousseau or Renan's views) was opposed to a German conception of identity as being based on ethnicity or race (originating in the works of Herder), widely adopted in the British isles.

The press and the construction of communities

Despite national differences, the media have clearly been instrumental in the construction of communities. Which part of the changing media scene is most relevant to this study? The growing body of literature on sports media and sports journalism indeed puts a strong emphasis on television and the exponential growth of the new digital media that has occurred since the beginning of the 1990s. Authors such as Rowe, Boyle and Haynes[107] have emphasised that the print media has been heavily transformed by this digital revolution. Indeed, as Boyle points out:

> Digitisation has clearly impacted on journalism in various forms. Within the arena of sports journalism, it has seen the emergence of

> an increasingly sophisticated battle for control of sports and how they are delivered, reported and made sense of for readers, listeners and viewers.[108]

Nowadays, the sports press is only one medium among others and it feeds on other media as much as the other media feed on it. The information also circulates between other media at a faster rate. This combined phenomenon of rapid reciprocal feeding has been termed 'vortextuality' by Gary Whannel.[109] It emphasises the need for the print sports text to find a new place within this 'vortex', in the face of the new media.[110] Some parts of the print media have retained their old functions: for example, 'stories' are still 'broken' in the tabloid print media. However, the sports press has also adapted to the changing environment, and successfully so, since it does not seem that newspapers have suffered in their sales from the development of web sports coverage.[111] Most likely, readers have already viewed, read or listened to or about the event that the journalist is reporting on, either on television or on one of the new media (most probably, the Internet). Boyle is adamant that the press plays new roles as it deals with the 'the scene-setting, the pre- and post-event analysis and any attendant scandal or controversy'. In other words, 'the journalists are then interpreting for the print media an already heavily televisually mediated event'.[112] Far from weakening the importance of the role played by the press, this new function of interpretation has only strengthened it. As Rowe explains, the press reports 'must be reconciled with the perceptions of a potentially huge audience which has been exposed to the event in sparkling sound and vision'.[113] Following Rowe, it can thus be argued that the press now expresses and constructs at the same time a general *consensus* among followers on the event that is reported on. Furthermore, Boyle has argued that:

> Sport as a cultural form grows and develops with its retelling. Print sports journalism is about both reliving the story and building a bridge between past and present sporting narratives: at its best, sports journalism is about making sense of the wider context within which events have occurred.[114]

The growth of television and new media has therefore reinforced the role of the press in the construction of memories through telling, retelling and the establishment of a consensus on the interpretation of events. Arguably, it nowadays plays more important a role in the construction of imagined communities. This increased role in memory building combines with an already identified role of the press in the construction of identities. In 1999 Rowe argued that 'the media can become one part of a complex relationship that helps link an individual to a larger collective grouping',[115] and insisted that the importance of the role played by the media varies according to the circumstances. He went on to suggest[116] that 'media representations are often an important factor but not necessarily the most influential in individual and collective identity-formation'.[117] Boyle and Haynes concur that identity formation does not take place solely in the media.[118] As Rowe put it, for the most part, the identities of the clubs and their supporters already pre-existed before the media 'reproduced', 'amplified' or 'reconstituted' parts of them. Whether the media creates new identities or only echoes existing ones remains to be explored.

The case for a study of the press has therefore been strengthened by the emergence of the new media, part of which also lends itself for study in its own right, on two counts. Each English newspaper has developed its own website, which hosts the archives of the printed edition. More important, fans have engaged with the new media. A significant number of supporters are young males, typically early adopters of new technology.[119] Fans have created a number of websites and blogs, which have been described as 'fanzines of the modern age',[120] as fans use them to voice their opinions. These websites (at least those most frequented) constitute an important resource that can be researched to listen directly to the voice of the fans.

A review of the literature has provided a better understanding of football partisanship, what motivates supporters to practice or follow the sport, and to support a given team as well as how (through which means) they identify with a club. The literature review has also emphasised the importance of the press in the construction of partisan identification, and leads to the design of a framework for the research on partisan identification.

Notes

1 Karl Marx and Friedrich Engels, *L'Idéologie allemande*. Paris: Éditions Sociales, 1974.

2 See for example, Jacques Ardoino and Jean-Marie Brohm (eds), *Anthropologie du sport: perspectives critiques/actes du colloque: Paris-Sorbonne, 19–20 avril 1991*. Paris: Andsha; Vigneux: Matrice; Montpellier: Quel corps?, 1991. In English, the most widely available book is Jean-Marie Brohm, *Sport, a prison of measured time: essays*. London: Ink Links, 1978.

3 An interesting presentation of the orthodox theories can be found in

William J. Morgan, *Leftist theories of sport: a critique and a reconstruction*. Urbana and Chicago, IL: University of Illinois Press, 1994, ch. 1 (hereafter Morgan 1994). See also: Bero Rigauer, *Sport and work*. New York, NY and Guildford: Columbia University Press, 1981.

4 See for example: Jean-Marie Brohm, *Le Mythe olympique*. Paris: C. Bourgois, 1981; *Sociologie politique du sport*. Nancy: Presses Universitaires de Nancy, 1992; *Les meutes sportives: critique de la domination*. Paris: l'Harmattan, 1993.

5 Mainly exposed in Pierre Bourdieu: 'Programme pour une sociologie du sport', pp. 203–216, in *Choses dites* (Paris: Éditions de Minuit, 1987); 'Les Jeux Olympiques: programme pour une analyse', *Actes de la recherche en sciences sociales*, 103 (1994), 102–103; 'Comment peut-on être sportif?', pp. 137–195, in *Questions de sociologie* (Paris: Éditions de Minuit, 1984); 'Les univers de possibles stylistiques', pp. 230–248, in *La Distinction: critique sociale du jugement* (Paris: Éditions de Minuit, 1992).

6 Jacques Defrance, *L'excellence corporelle: la formation des activités sportives et physiques modernes (1770–1914)*. Rennes: Presses Universitaires de Rennes, 1987.

7 Alfred Wahl, 'Enjeux: le football, un nouveau territoire pour l'historien', *Vingtième siècle: revue d'histoire*, 26 (1990), 127–132.

8 John Hargreaves, *Sport: power and culture: a social and historical analysis of popular sports in Britain*. Cambridge: Blackwell, 1986.

9 Morgan 1994: 61.

10 Ben Carrington and Ian McDonald (eds), *'Race', sport and British society*. London: Routledge, 2001.

11 John Sugden and Alan Tomlinson (eds), *Power games: a critical sociology of sport*. London: Routledge, 2002, p. 10

12 Alan Clarke and John Clarke, 'Highlights and action replays: ideology, sport and the media', in Jennifer Hargreaves (ed.), *Sport, culture and ideology*, pp. 62–87. London: Routledge & Kegan Paul, 1982.

13 Gary Whannel, *Fields in vision: television sports and cultural formation*. London: Routledge, 1992.

14 As exposed, for example, in Gunther Lüschen: 'The interdependence of sport and culture', *International review of sports sociology*, 2 (1967), 127–142; 'The system of sports: problems of methodology, conflict and social stratification', in Gunther Lüschen *et al.* (eds), *Handbook of social science of sport*, pp. 197–213. Champaign, IL: Stipes, 1981; 'Towards a new structural analysis: the present state and the prospects of the international sociology of sport', *International review for the sociology of sport*, 23(4) (1988), 269–285; 'On theory of sciences for the sociology of sport: new structuralism, action, intention and practical meaning', *International review for the sociology of sport*, 25 (1990), 69–83.

15 John W. Loy and Thomas Booth, 'Functionalism, sport and society', in Jay Coakley and Eric Dunning (eds), *Handbook of sports studies*, pp. 8–27. London: Sage, 2000.

16 Christopher Stevenson, 'Sport as a contemporary social phenomenon:

a functional explanation', *International Journal of Physical Education,* 11(1) (1974), 8–14. Christopher Stevenson and John Nixon, 'A conceptual scheme of the social functions of sport', *Sportwissenschaft,* 2 (1972), 119–132.

17 Kevin Young, '"The killing field": themes in mass media responses to the Heysel Stadium riot', *International review for the sociology of sport,* 21(2/3) (1986), 253–266.

18 Loïc Wacquant, 'Corps et âmes: notes ethnographiques d'un apprenti-boxeur', *Actes de la recherche en sciences sociales,* 80 (1989), 33–67.

19 Christian Pociello, *Le Rugby ou la guerre des styles.* Paris: A. M. Métailié, 1983.

20 Charles Suaud, 'Espace des sports, espace social et effets d'âge: La diffusion du tennis, du squash et du golf dans l'agglomération nantaise', *Actes de la recherche en sciences sociales,* 79 (1989), 2–20.

21 Norbert Elias, *The civilizing process.* Oxford: Blackwell, 1994.

22 Elias and Dunning started to publish on sport in 1969. Their essays have later been collected in Norbert Elias and Eric Dunning, *Quest for excitement: sport and leisure in the civilizing process.* Oxford: Blackwell, 1986 (hereafter Elias and Dunning 1986).

23 The founding work of the Leicester school is probably Eric Dunning and Kenneth Sheard, *Barbarians, gentlemen and players: a sociological study of the development of rugby football.* Oxford: Martin Robertson, 1979.

24 Roger Caillois, *Les Jeux et les hommes: le masque et le vertige.* Paris: Gallimard, 1967 (hereafter Caillois 1967).

25 Caillois 1967: 47.

26 Caillois 1967: 76.

27 Caillois 1967: 99.

28 Caillois 1967: 124.

29 Caillois 1967: 124.

30 Notably Tony Mason: *Association football and English society (1863–1915).* Brighton: Harvester, 1980; *Sport in Britain.* London: Faber, 1988; *Sport in Britain: a social history* (ed.), Cambridge University Press, 1989; *Passion of the people? Football in South America.* London: Verso, 1995.

31 Richard Holt, *Sport and society in modern France.* London: Macmillan, in association with St Antony's College, Oxford, 1981.

32 James Walvin, *The people's game: the history of football revisited.* Edinburgh: Mainstream, 1994.

33 David Russell, 'Associating with football: social identity in England (1863–1998)', in Gary Armstrong and Richard Giulianotti (eds), *Football cultures and identities,* pp. 15–28. Basingstoke: Macmillan, 1999 (hereafter Russell 1999).

34 Russell 1999: 15.

35 Russell 1999: 16.

36 Richard Holt, *Sport and the British: a modern history.* Oxford: Clarendon, 1989, p. 8 (hereafter Holt 1989).

37 Russell 1999: 17.

38 Chas Critcher, 'Putting on the style: aspects of recent English football', in John Williams and Stephen Wagg (eds), *British football and social change: getting into Europe*, pp. 67–84. Leicester University Press, 1991 (hereafter Critcher 1991; Williams and Wagg 1991).

39 Russell 1999: 18.

40 Holt 1989: 159–179.

41 Holt 1989: 172.

42 D. Todd Donavan, Swinder Janda and Jaebeom Suh, 'Environmental influences in corporate brand identification and outcomes', *Brand management*, 14(1/2) (2006), 125–136: 128.

43 Christian M. End, Beth Dietz-Uhler, Elizabeth A. Harrick and Lindy Jacquemotte, 'Identifying with winners: a reexamination of sport fans' tendency to bask in reflected glory (BIRG)', *Journal of applied social psychology*, 32(5) (2002), 1017–1030: 1019. The article refers to the following sources for the notion of, respectively, BiRG and CORF: R. B. Cialdini, R. J. Borden, A. Thorne, M. R. Walker, S. Freeman and L. R. Sloan, 'Basking in reflected glory: three (football) studies', *Journal of personality and social psychology*, 34 (1976), 366–375. C. R. Snyder, R. L. Higgins and R. J. Stucky, *Excuses: masquerades in search of grace*. New York, NY: Wiley-Interscience, 1983.

44 Anthony King, *The end of the terraces: the transformation of English football in the 1990s*. London and New York, NY: Leicester University Press, 1998, p. 13 (hereafter King 1998).

45 For an avowed example of this position, see Adam Brown, 'Introduction', in Adam Brown (ed.), *Fanatics! Power, identity and fandom in football*, pp. 1–7. London: Routledge, 1998 (hereafter Brown 1998).

46 King 1998.

47 Richard Haynes, 'Every Man(?) a football artist: football writing and masculinity', in Steve Redhead (ed.), *The passion and the fashion: football fandom in the new Europe*, pp. 55–77. Aldershot: Avebury, 1993.

48 Ben Carrington, '"Football's coming home" but whose home? and do we want it? Nation, football and the politics of exclusion', in Brown 1998: 101–122.

49 John Williams and Jackie Woodhouse, 'Women and football in Britain', in Williams and Wagg 1991: 85–108.

50 Russell 1999: 19.

51 Russell 1999: 24.

52 Jean-Jacques Gouguet and Jean-François Nys, *Sport et développement économique régional*. Paris: Dalloz, 1993.

53 Raffaele Poli, *Le marché des footballeurs*. Bern: Peter Lang, 2010. Raffaele Poli, Loïc Ravenel and Roger Besson, *Annual review of the European football players labour market*. Neuchâtel: Éditions CIES, 2010.

54 Exposed notably in John Bale, *Sport, space and the city*. London: Routledge, 1993.

55 John Bale, 'Playing at home: British football and a sense of place', in Williams and Wagg 1991: 130–144.

56 Holt 1989. Vic Duke, 'Local tradition versus globalisation: resistance to the McDonaldisation and Disneyisation of professional football in England', *Football studies*, 5(1) (2002), 5–23.
57 Anthony King, 'Football fandom and post-national identity in the New Europe', *British journal of sociology*, 51(3) (2000), 419–442 (hereafter King 2000).
58 King 2000: 420.
59 Richard Giulianotti and Roland Robertson, 'The globalization of football: a study in the glocalization of the "serious life"', *British journal of sociology*, 55(4) (2004): 545–568: 546.
60 Gary Armstrong and Richard Giulianotti (eds), *Football cultures and identities*. Basingstoke: Macmillan, 1999 (hereafter Armstrong and Giulianotti 1999).
61 John Sugden and Alan Bairner, *Sport, sectarianism and society in a divided Ireland*. Leicester University Press, 1993.
62 Alan Bairner and Peter Shirlow, 'The territorial politics of soccer in Northern Ireland' (hereafter Bairner and Shirlow 1999), in Armstrong and Giulianotti 1999: 152–163.
63 Yoram S. Carmeli and Iris Bar, 'Team selection and chosen people in Israel: the case of Hapoel Taibeh' (hereafter Carmeli and Bar 1999), in Armstrong and Giulianotti 1999: 164–175.
64 Matti Goksøyr and Hans Hognestad, 'No longer worlds apart? British influences and Norwegian football' (hereafter Goksøyr and Hognestad 1999), in Armstrong and Giulianotti 1999: 201–210.
65 Goksøyr and Hognestad 1999: 201.
66 Ernst Haas, *The uniting of Europe: political, social, and economic forces 1950–57*. Stanford, CA: Stanford University Press, 1958, p. 14 in particular.
67 The three authors make explicit references to the works of Dunning and Elias.
68 Found in two works of Christian Bromberger: *Football, la bagatelle la plus sérieuse du monde*. Paris: Bayard, 1998 (hereafter Bromberger 1998); *Le match de football: ethnologie d'une passion partisane à Marseille, Naples et Turin* (in collaboration with Alain Hayot and Jean-Marc Mariottini). Paris: Éditions de la Maison des sciences de l'homme, 1995 (hereafter Bromberger 1995).
69 Patrick Mignon, *La Passion du football*. Paris: Éditions Odile Jacob, 1998 (hereafter Mignon 1998).
70 Richard Giulianotti, *Football: a sociology of the global game*. Cambridge: Polity, 1999 (hereafter Giulianotti 1999).
71 Giulianotti 1999: 148.
72 Giulianotti 1999: 148.
73 Giulianotti 1999: 148.
74 Expression derived from the title part IV: 'La rhétorique des supporters' of Bromberger 1995.
75 Bromberger 1998: 75.
76 Les Back, Tim Crabbe and John Solomos, 'Racism in football: patterns of

continuity and change', in Adam Brown (ed.), *Fanatics! Power, identity and fandom in football*, pp. 71–87: 84–85. London: Routledge, 1998.

77 Alain Ehrenberg, *Le culte de la performance*. Paris: Calmann-Lévy, 1991.

78 See for instance Henri Vaugrand, *Sociologies du sport: théorie des champs et théorie critique*. Paris: L'Harmattan, 1999, pp. 73–74.

79 Bromberger 1998 and 1995.

80 Bromberger 1998: 59.

81 Bromberger 1995.

82 Critcher 1991.

83 Albrecht Sonntag, 'Le football, image de la nation', in Pascal Boniface (ed.), *Géopolitique du football*, pp. 31–40: 34. Brussels: Complexe, 1998 (hereafter Sonntag 1998). See also Albrecht Sonntag, *Les Identités du football européen*. Grenoble: Presses Universitaires de Grenoble, 2008.

84 These styles have been exposed for example in Astolfo Cagnacci, *Pays du foot: une passion et des styles*. Paris: Autrement, 1998.

85 Ernest Gellner, *Nations and nationalism*, pp. 55–62. Oxford: Blackwell, 1983.

86 Bromberger 1995: 105.

87 Bromberger 1995: 105.

88 Richard Giulianotti and Roland Robertson, 'Glocalization, globalization and migration: the case of Scottish football supporters in North America', *International sociology*, 21(2) (2006), 171–198: 175.

89 Bromberger 1995: 121.

90 Roberto DaMatta, 'Notes sur le *futebol* brésilien', *Le Débat*, 19 (1982), 68–76.

91 Bromberger 1998: 77.

92 Bromberger 1995: 122.

93 Bromberger 1995: 122.

94 Bromberger 1998: 59.

95 Bromberger 1998: 60.

96 Henri Tajfel and John Turner, 'The social identity theory of inter-group behavior', in Stephen Worchel and William Austin (eds), *The psychology of intergroup relations*, pp. 94–109. Chicago, IL: Nelson-Hall, 1986.

97 Gary Armstrong; and Richard Giulianotti (eds), *Fear and loathing in world football*. Oxford: Berg, 2001. This academic endeavour is indebted to the journalistic accounts of Simon Kuper, *Football against the enemy*. London: Orion, 1994.

98 Mignon 1998.

99 Mignon 1998: 31.

100 Developed in Anderson 1991.

101 Anderson 1991: 6.

102 Mignon 1998: 31.

103 Eric Hobsbawm and Terence Ranger, *The invention of tradition*. Cambridge University Press, 1983 (hereafter Hobsbawm 1983).

104 Mignon 1998: 10.

105 Louis Dumont, *German ideology: from France to Germany and back*. Chicago, IL: University of Chicago Press, 1994.

106 Rogers Brubaker, *Citizenship and nationhood in France and Germany.* Cambridge, MA: Harvard University Press, 1992.
107 Rowe 1999; Raymond Boyle and Richard Haynes, *Power play: sport, the media and popular culture.* Harlow: Pearson, 2000 (hereafter Boyle and Haynes 2000); Raymond Boyle and Richard Haynes, *Football in the new media age.* London: Routledge, 2004 (hereafter Boyle and Haynes 2004); Raymond Boyle, *Sports journalism: context and Issues.* London: Sage, 2006 (hereafter Boyle 2006).
108 Boyle 2006: 3.
109 Garry Whannel. *Media sports stars: masculinities and moralities.* London: Routledge, 2002, p. 206.
110 Boyle 2006: 27.
111 Boyle 2006: 142–143.
112 Boyle 2006: 54 and 80.
113 Rowe 1999: 107.
114 Boyle 2006: 142.
115 Rowe 1999: 14.
116 Following Raymond Boyle, 'Football and cultural identity in Glasgow and Liverpool'. Ph.D. thesis, University of Stirling, 1995. (The dissertation could not be procured.)
117 Rowe 1999: 13.
118 Boyle and Haynes 2000: 187.
119 Boyle and Haynes 2004: 138.
120 Boyle and Haynes 2004: 141.

2

Researching partisan identification

Hypotheses and framework of analysis

The condemnation, by football authorities (FIFA, UEFA), of the increase in the number of foreign football players rests on a few understated assumptions that deserve investigation. When it comes to clubs, it is assumed that they represent a national identity. When it comes to supporters, it is assumed that they identify with the club they support because they share the nationality of its players and that other grounds for identification play a more minor role. The framework of analysis adopted for this study builds on the existing literature to construct a more complete picture. The research clearly adopts an interpretative approach. It considers that supporters have a degree of freedom in the choice of a sport to follow and club to support. The approach chosen does not look at partisanship as entirely determined by the infrastructure or power relationships. However, the approach is open to the possibility that the position in society, within a class, may be a factor of partisanship among others, and that these factors are fluid. The research is, however, more concerned by the means through which supporters come to identify with a club, and support it. The framework posits that supports come to support their club because they identify with it through various means, which symbolise different aspects of their identity (the composition of the team in terms of the nationality of players is only one of these means). The framework therefore assumes that the identity of a club may integrate elements of the national, but only among other elements (such as locality, class, religion).

The framework also surmises that the press plays a central role in this process of identification. It provides accounts on the facts in the life of a club and their interpretation. Their succession defines the shared memories on a club, which build its public image (how supporters, followers of football but also complete outsiders perceive it). It is hypothesised that the role played by the press in the identification to the club may depend on how positive this portrayal is. A constructive depiction of a club would increase identification. Equally, identification would be negatively correlated to unflattering reports on the team. The press also puts an emphasis on some aspects which are considered to be more characteristic of a club than others (the club may, for example, be presented as Protestant, Scottish, Catholic, Irish, old, new or multinational) including possibly, the portrayal of its opposition to a main rival. This study therefore analyses the image the press gives of each club and how supporters react to it, notably whether they are drawn to one characteristic of the club in particular, or a combination of such characteristics. All the dimensions and components of the club are taken into account: the team (the players and the coaching staff) as well as the management and the supporters, who are therefore reacting to the image of themselves as portrayed in the press. Supporters are not understood as passive, though. It is assumed they 'negotiate'[1] both the narrative of the press and the public image of their club (including their own). Supporters can approve or reject (partly or wholly) these narratives.

Likewise, the depiction of foreign footballers in the press may also play a part in their adoption or rejection by the supporters. The printed media may therefore facilitate or discourage identification. The hypothesis is that a xenophobic press, portraying foreign players negatively or raising the question of their presence in a disapproving manner might dissuade supporters from identifying with those players. In the typology of symbols adopted here, the composition of the team (and the inclusion or exclusion of 'strangers') is only one particular mean through which supporters identify with their team.

This typology distinguishes between inanimate and animate symbols. It posits that supporters identify to clubs through people. The identification through a given player emphasises the relation between individual identities (on both sides of the identification process: the supporter and the player). It poses the question of when a player becomes symbolic of a team, and why. What are the player's characteristics that make him particularly popular with the clubs' supporters? Are all supporters identifying with the same player? Or is it possible to find groups of supporters, each of which identify with a different player?

Equally, identification with a team through its style highlights the importance of the collectives (here again, of supporters or of players). And, as a result, the press plays a major role. It simultaneously identifies the style of play of a team and constructs or emphasises its meaning. Through press reports, style comes to embody social characteristics, notably of class, gender or race, which might combine to form a complex social identity. Style can, for example, represent Britishness. The composition of the team stands in between the other two means of identification through people as it stresses the problematic inclusion of the individual within a collective. The actual collective, the team, may represent the imagined collective, the community of supporters, and reveal problems of inclusion in that collective.

Supporters also identify to clubs through their (inanimate) emblems. Colours have proved particularly potent in displaying elements of identity, notably as they appear on logos and jerseys – but also on other merchandise sold by the club. The stadium is seen here as the other major emblem of clubs. It brings to the fore both the supporters' link (real or imagined) with a locality and the game's dimension as a celebration of imagined communities through invented traditions. Consequently, it may be assumed that the importance of these symbols, especially the emblems, is never more clearly revealed than in periods of change, when traditions are threatened. These symbols indeed provide a link (real or imaginary) with the past. The attachment to a stadium, for instance, becomes all the more evident when the club alters the existing stadium, moves (or simply considers moving) to a new one.

By investigating each mean of identification, it will be possible to evaluate their comparative importance, therefore assess whether identification through players is the main mean of identification. This will provide an answer to the question on whether the influx of foreign players in the post-*Bosman* period actually poses a threat to football.

Research methods, sources and object

The press in England, Scotland and France

The study of the press has been the main method used in this enquiry. The printed media plays a double role and has been researched in both dimensions. The press reports events on and surrounding the pitch and has been the main source of information pertaining to the clubs and their supporters. The press also clearly impacts on the image of the clubs, thereby altering the relationship between club and supporters. It has therefore also been studied as an actor in the supporters' relationship with the club. Mignon's insistence on context takes all its value here: 'the structure of each national press has some characteristics wholly specific to that country', and furthermore 'among the prime determinants of the structure of each national press are the social and political structures of each country, and its associated cultural characteristics'.[2] The themes that come up in England, Scotland and France, and that impact on the supporters' identification with their club therefore vary hugely. The emphasis in the study of the Scottish press has been on how it portrays sectarianism in football, and whether the printed media (as whole, or in parts) indulges in it. The question of xenophobia has replaced that of sectarianism in the analysis of the English press. In the Parisian case, however, the problematic construction of a relationship between supporters and their club appeared to be the most important issue.

The English press: tabloids, xenophobia and jingoism

The first striking feature of the English national press is the sheer number of daily titles available: at least ten during the week, and their Sunday counterparts. The second feature is the strong divide that, arguably, still exists between the broadsheets and the tabloids.[3] The tabloid press has defining characteristics, particularly salient in its treatment of sports and football. Commenting on the tabloids' coverage of the England team, Stephen Wagg has for instance talked of 'a kind of patriotic derangement':

> Names and faces change, but the essential story does not: if England, who devised and exported the game, are beaten, then the man in charge of the England team is not doing his job properly and he must be replaced. Other countries, in this bizarre and ultimately racist conception of the international football world, play only walk-on parts.[4]

The British press has, indeed, been extensively discussed and criticised for its 'insular nature',[5] or 'the enduring power of stereotypes, the vogue for cliché journalism exploiting fictional bogies, and European excesses'.[6] The National Heritage Committee of the House of Commons even went so far as criticising the tabloids' reports on the England–Germany Euro semi-final for their 'xenophobic, chauvinistic and jingoistic gutter journalism'.[7] This report has been criticised by Jon Garland and Mike Rowe on two accounts. First, xenophobia does not affect only football reports but generally all matters covered. Second, 'much of the press', not only the tabloids, relish in it.[8] How widespread xenophobia is in the English press divides academics. They all agree that tabloids revel in it. Yet for authors such as Boyle and Monteiro:

> There has not been a convergence in sports news values in the press, as is sometimes argued to be the case in other areas of journalism. Rather,

the distance between sports coverage in the tabloid and broadsheet/compacts end of the marketplace has never appeared so pronounced.[9]

After stating that 'the "quality"/"broadsheets" newspapers tend to be more "objective" and "sober" in their reporting',[10] Poulton, Maguire and Possamai remarked that 'on closer examination, however, the divide between tabloid and broadsheet coverage is not as clear-cut'.[11]

Broadsheets may seem increasingly similar to tabloids, notably since *The Independent, The Times* and *The Guardian* have been relaunched in smaller sizes (the last in 'Berliner' format on 12 September 2005, the other two having switched entirely to a tabloid format, euphemistically called 'compact', respectively on 14 May 2004 and 1 November 2004). This has led academics of the media such as Sparks[12] to contend that all sections of the British press have become increasingly more like the tabloids. *Le Monde* has identified a general trend among broadsheets:[13] they are gradually adopting the practices of the tabloids, such as catchy (some might say shocking) titles, even in their news reports. Sport may play a part in this 'tabloidisation' of broadsheets. Because of its ability to attract a large audience, sport has long been an important feature of the popular press.[14] The new phenomenon in the past fifteen years has been the development of the sports pages in the broadsheets.[15]

In the much noted absence of any daily focusing on sport in Britain,[16] sport always is an important feature of the newspapers. Tabloids and broadsheets alike dedicate it a large portion of their editions, even those for which, like *The Guardian* or *The Independent*, it was traditionally less important.[17] It spreads over at least 12 pages everyday in *The Guardian*,[18] and up to 32 pages in *The Times* on a Monday.[19] It also always features in a place of prominence: the sports section can be found at the back of the newspapers, which acts as a second cover, especially in the tabloids. The broadsheets also create dedicated pull-out supplements when the amount of sporting events justifies it, for example on a Saturday and a Monday. Because of their appeal, pictures are omnipresent in the tabloids, while they are more discrete in the broadsheets (but increasingly less so). The comparatively low status of sports writers and reporters within the journalist's profession has led people to wonder whether this growth in writing on sports does not equal a 'dumbing down' of the broadsheets.[20] Rowe, however, has pleaded in favour of a nuanced approach. This would avoid explaining the development of the sports page simply in terms of 'consumer freedom' (the press supplies the product, here sports writing, in response to demands from the audience) or conversely of 'mass oppression' (the ruling class promotes stories about sport in order to distract the working class from thinking about political questions – notably of domination).[21] For his part, Boyle contends that the increased size of sports sections is not a dumbing down of the broadsheets: it is, rather, the consequence of an increase in the size of a middle-class imbued with working-class values and of the renewed interaction of the press with the other media (especially the new ones).[22]

Among these newspapers (and their Sunday counterparts) a selection has been made in order to research whether the xenophobia noted in the coverage of the national team is present in the reports on club football, and what impact it has had on the supporters' identification to their club (notably through their foreign players). It reflects both the number of titles and the segmentation of the English press. The bestselling broadsheets *The Times* and the *Daily Telegraph*, which have long been regarded as Britain's two newspapers of record, have provided the reference for the study. Two tabloids have also been looked into: *The Sun* (on a Sunday, the *News of the World*), which is the leading daily newspaper in Britain in terms of sales and the *Daily Mirror*, which shares slightly more left-wing leanings with the two other broadsheets investigated as complement: *The Guardian* (on a Sunday, *The Observer*) and *The Independent*. References have also been made to the *Evening Standard*,[23] London's most widely read daily and, on rare occasions, to the very local publication in Arsenal's vicinity, the *Islington Gazette*.

Scotland: the 'semi-autonomous' press of a 'stateless nation'

Though superficially similar to England's, the press in Scotland has peculiar characteristics. Alex Law has talked about 'a "stateless nation" like Scotland, served by a semi-autonomous media'.[24] The English press is available throughout Scotland in special editions but a national Scottish press exists. Law insists on its comparative weight:

> Scotland's biggest selling daily, the tabloid *Daily Record*, is read by one-third of Scots, well ahead of the one-fifth reading the best-selling English tabloid, *The Sun*. Readership of Scotland's two national broadsheets stood at 21 percent, nearly double the total for the English-based broadsheets combined (13 percent).[25]

The Scottish print media shares the major characteristics of the English press, though. A specific sports press developed in Scotland during the 1880s, and due to its popularity, football became the dominant feature very quickly.[26] Yet, the main source of daily information on Scottish football has now become the 'generalist' press. As in England, sport is one of its main features. As in England, it is also divided between tabloids and broadsheets. Studying all the titles available in Scotland, Alex Law has concluded that only three papers treat Scotland as the 'unspoken deictic national centre for organising regional content'.[27] These truly 'indigenous' newspapers are two broadsheets: *The Herald* (published in Glasgow) and *The Scotsman* (published in Edinburgh) as well as a tabloid: the *Daily Record* (published in Glasgow). Law also found the Scottish editions of two English tabloids, *The Sun* and *The Mirror*,[28] to be 'interlopers'. Though not totally 'indigenous', they are not 'Anglo-centric' either, for their 'Scottish lexical markers' are 'proximal' instead of 'identical'.[29] These five newspapers have therefore been researched here.

Regional and national press in France

The French press shows different characteristics. France has often been noted for the relative lack of readership of its national press. Conversely, a distinctive feature of the French press is also the importance of regional newspapers. *Ouest France,* which covers Brittany, Normandy and the 'Pays de Loire', sells twice as many copies as *Le Monde,* now the most widely read national newspaper. Paris is no exception to the rule and features its own regional daily newspaper (published on tabloid format). Fittingly called *Le Parisien,* it is now the second newspaper in France by sales after *Ouest France. Le Parisien* actually covers not only the city of Paris but also the remainder of the Île-de-France administrative region. It even goes as far as offering a different edition for each *département* within the borders of the region.[30]

Another feature that radically distinguishes the French and the British press is the presence of *L'Équipe,* a daily broadsheet focusing exclusively on sport. It is indeed one of the main national newspapers in France with sales slightly more than *Le Figaro* and only marginally less than *Le Monde.* It is therefore the main source of information for readers with a keen interest in sports. Despite being regularly questioned for its coverage of sporting events, it has acquired the reputation of being a quality newspaper providing an excellent coverage of sports news, with which no 'generalist' newspaper can compete. *L'Équipe* is undoubtedly the reason why French 'generalist' dailies devote so much less money and space to sports than their English counterparts.

Accordingly, *Le Parisien* and *L'Équipe* are the main sources of information on sports, football and Paris Saint-Germain. They have therefore been extensively researched together with the three better known (and bestselling) national daily newspapers: *Le Figaro; Le Monde* and *Libération*. Due to their very own nature of both 'generalist' and national newspapers, their coverage of the questions at stake is much less thorough. *L'Humanité*, the communist newspaper,[31] and *France Soir*, a daily evening broadsheet cater for the working class and write a large number of articles on sport. They would have been worthy of systematic study, if only they had not entered such a steep decline at the beginning of the 1990s. Their readership has now dwindled to a meagre fifth or tenth of *Le Monde*'s.[32] They have therefore been looked at more sporadically, mostly on occasions when Paris Saint-Germain was in the headlines of other newspapers.

Interviews, participant observation and academic sources

The Old Firm has been used as a touchstone study to adjust the framework for research on the introduction of players perceived as 'outsiders' in a club. The rivalry between Celtic and Rangers can, indeed, be seen as the fiercest in Western Europe and it has been based on the opposition between Catholic supporters of Irish origins and Protestant supporters of Scottish origins. As Bromberger himself points out,[33] Rangers' long-standing policy of not including Catholics in their team provides the most striking example of the use of team composition both to convey a sense of identity and to raise identification. If fans came to support Rangers because of its Protestant identity, and if this identity was asserted by the exclusion of Catholic players, then the introduction of Catholics in the team would have much more serious effects in this intense context than the multiplication of foreign players resulting from the *Bosman* ruling. The two other case studies build on the results of the Glaswegian study to focus on the effect of the *Bosman* ruling in widely differing settings.

In order to provide a solid basis for comparison, all three cases have been studied over the same length of time: the first ten years (or more precisely, full football seasons) following the introduction or multiplication in the number of 'strangers' (Catholics or foreigners). Rangers changed its policy in 1989 so the period studied in the case of Glasgow is 1989–2000. Semi-structured interviews could therefore be used to triangulate the findings of the press study in Paris and London. Ideally, such interviews would have been widely held in Glasgow too, but they could not be relied upon in that case. The bias introduced by the supporters' memory of a long bygone era proved too important after only a handful of interviews. Sixteen years after Maurice Johnston became the first catholic to play at Rangers, the core supporters of the day have aged, changed and memories have faded. The framework used in this work was therefore tested first in Glasgow on the basis of the press study triangulated with the writings of academics (readily available, since the social importance of sectarianism in Scotland has attracted extensive research on the Old Firm).

Because of their cost, large-scale interviews were never an option. For the other two case studies, intensive semi-structured interviews[34] were used as a complementary means of research, to triangulate the results of the press study: to provide an understanding of the relationship between the interviewees and the press and therefore to corroborate, amend or infirm the conclusions drawn out of the press study. Representatives from three kinds of audiences have been interviewed: club officials, journalists and supporters. With club officials, the main themes explored have been the club's policies on foreign players, and on raising and managing support. With journalists, the focus has been on their treatment of the clubs, in order to confirm any potentially identified bias. Two main questions have been investigated in the interviews with the supporters. Are supporters able to identify with the team through foreign players, or through a mostly foreign team? How is their identification with the team affected by their reading of the printed media? The use of semi-structured intensive interviews raises two main questions. How representative is the sample? What distortion is introduced by the situation of the interview?[35] Newspapers and football clubs are very small companies, and given the small number of club officials and of journalists in each case study, it is impossible to build a representative sample. Yet, the opinions expressed by the interviewees have proved invaluable: they belong to actors in the triangular relationship between supporters, newspapers and club. Their insights are those of insiders, even when they express the official positions of their organisation, as is sometimes the case. The major challenge has proved the impossibility to obtain interviews with journalists from all newspapers and officials from all clubs. In Glasgow one journalist (from *The Herald*), in Paris three (from *L'Équipe, Le Figaro* and *Libération*), in London four (two from *The Guardian,* two from *The Independent*) have answered questions for this study.[36] Interviews with officials have been held in Glasgow (two officials from Rangers) and at Arsenal (two officials). Celtic have provided official statements in lieu of an interview for which no official was available. Despite numerous attempts to contact Paris Saint-Germain's officials, it proved impossible to interview anyone from the club. Its instability (it has known four different presidents and a change of major shareholder during the time the study was conducted) and a corporate culture of secrecy may have contributed to this reluctance. In their stead, two members of the Paris council, which is heavily involved in the club (notably former President of the Assemblée Nationale, the late Philippe Séguin, whose work in 1973 has shaped the structures of French football)[37] have been interviewed.[38]

The interviews with the supporters created a different challenge. Representativity was less an issue than it might seem at first sight. It is possible to distinguish different categories of supporters, depending on their level of involvement with their club. For example, Giulianotti does this in his 'taxonomy' of football supporters.[39] Yet, this is not really an issue as the ones which are more readily available for interviews are also the most committed, who have greatest relevance in the study of identification with a club.[40] It was also relatively easy to recruit fans from different categories for interviews. Fans with a maximum involvement in their club have been contacted through organised supporters' groups. Distant fans, with more limited involvement, were contacted through supporters' forums on the internet. The supporters with limited involvement acted as a 'control group' to check the relevance of the problems raised by the other supporters. The issues for which they shared the same concerns as the most committed supporters have emerged as the most important for the community of supporters as a whole. It was possible to interview thirty-eight supporters of Arsenal and forty-three supporters of Paris Saint-Germain. Though arguably small, the samples appeared large enough. Supporters were fairly repetitive, since they were asked about fairly general issues on which there is a general level of agreement. The interviews indeed only served to triangulate (or cross-check) the findings made through the study of the press and of available media from the supporters (fanzines, internet, etc.).

Yet the methodological challenges posed by fans of both clubs were different. Arsenal supporters were very responsive to enquiries for face-to-face or email interviews. Parisian supporters have proved more difficult. They commonly feel misrepresented in the media, and are suspicious of anyone who wishes to interview them, even though all of them knew the purpose of the enquiry was an academic endeavour. Only three agreed to a formal interview (including two by phone). 'Participant observation', a method first developed by anthropologists to study distant cultures, where the researcher becomes immersed in the activities of the groups and people studied[41] proved the key to gaining the confidence and obtaining the answers needed for this study. A number of games were attended in Paris and the contacts made allowed for a 'snowball sampling'[42] (interviewees pointed out to other informants who could be interviewed). The supporters were asked questions casually before games, at games or after games, sometimes in groups, sometimes individually. Most Paris Saint-Germain fans interviewed requested not to be named in print. All fans' contributions, including those from individuals holding public positions in supporters' clubs, therefore appear anonymously. Participant observation and the attendance of games in Paris and London have allowed the behaviour and declarations of fans to be put into perspective. In order to limit the risk of bias, the research exposed gives value to the point of view of the supporters but refuses to adopt it. This point of view has always been cross checked through interviews with other informants.

The interview technique used also aimed at limiting the bias introduced by the interviewer, whose questions may have forced interviewees to reflect on issues that they had not considered themselves. Indeed, asking a supporter bluntly whether he or she identifies with foreign players was unlikely to be conducive to any conclusive answer. For a start, supporters very seldom think their attachment to a team in terms of identification, but rather in terms of likes and dislikes for some of the features or characteristics of the team. Fans may not have a clear understanding of their own behaviour. Asking the question in terms which were alien to them created a risk of misunderstanding and biased answers: notably over-thought answers or theoretical positions which did not correlate to their behaviour. More important, the supporters may have given the answer that they believe was expected of them, taking into account such factors as the nationality of the interviewer. Also, beyond discourse, acts matter. The insistence has been on whether the supporters show signs of identification with their team through one means or another (especially through players foreign or native).

The structure of the interviews has therefore been to start with very general issues. They were articulated in the way that supporters express them. The interview moved to the research topics as they were raised by the interviewee(s). At the start of the interview, supporters were asked successively whether they were 'happy' with their club, their team and their players and why. The supporters themselves therefore raised the matters of importance. Unless they had raised the presence of many foreigners as a motive of unhappiness with the team, the supporters' ability to identify with foreign players has been assessed through asking them which was their favourite player in the team (currently and all-time), whether they had a favourite era in the history of the club (including today) and who best embodied it. It was only in last resort that the question was asked of whether they objected to the level of presence of foreign players in their clubs. Questions on the supporters' relationship with the newspapers were structured in a similar manner in the second part of the interview. They were first asked a general question on their appreciation of their club's treatment in the print media as a whole. They were then asked to elaborate on the motives of discontent, and more rarely content, they had themselves identified.

To control the bias that was still introduced by the presence of the interviewer, and the arguably limited number of interviews, a great deal of attention has been paid to sources where supporters express themselves freely. Supporters write extensively in places such as fanzines[43] (often now prolonged or superseded by websites and internet forums) and in private messages sent to mailing lists which, following the method of limited participant observation, have been subscribed to whenever possible, but not written to. All this written material has been studied to establish whether the questions that had most relevance for the framework were raised.

Structure of the work

The next three chapters are each devoted to a case study. Glasgow provides a touchstone for those on Paris Saint-Germain and Arsenal. All three are structured in the same way. An introduction exposes the situation at the beginning of the study (sectarianism in 1989 for Glasgow, the development of the identity of Arsenal and Paris Saint-Germain until 1995). Since this background introduction falls out of the scope of this research, it is based on secondary materials (academic writings in the case of Glasgow, commercial publications in the other two cases – the findings of which have always been checked by cross examining sources). The questions raised by the press in the study are analysed in a second section, since they explain the findings exposed in the next two sections on how identification to a club is raised through its emblems (which provide a focus for the identity of the club or of its supporters) and through people (the style of the team and its composition emphasise the collective that the club represents, whereas the social identities of players link with the identity of the supporter).

Notes

1 Stephen Wagg, 'Playing the past: the media and the England Football team' (hereafter Wagg 1991), in Williams and Wagg 1991: 220–238.
2 Both quotes from: Neil Blain, Raymond Boyle and Hugh O'Donnell, *Sport and national identity in the European media*. Leicester: Leicester University Press, 1993, p. 55 (hereafter Blain 1993).
3 Blain 1993. This is particularly emphasised in Liz Crolley, David Hand and Ralf Jeutter, 'National obsessions and identities in football match report', in Brown 1998: 173–185.
4 Stephen Wagg, 'Introduction and acknowledgements', in Stephen Wagg (ed.), *Giving the game away: football, politics and culture on five continents*, pp. xi–xii: xi. London: Leicester University press, 1995 (hereafter Wagg 1995b). It has been exposed in detail notably in Wagg 1991.
5 Raymond Boyle and Cláudia Monteiro, '"A small country with a big ambition": representations of Portugal and England in Euro 2004 British and Portuguese newspaper coverage', *European journal of communication*, 20(2) (2005), 223–244: 228 (hereafter Boyle and Monteiro 2005).
6 Beck, Peter J., 'The relevance of the irrelevant: football as a missing dimension in the study of British relations with Germany', *International affairs*, 79(2) (2003), 389–411: 410 (hereafter Beck 2003).
7 National Heritage Committee (House of Common), *Fourth report: press coverage of the Euro '96 football competition*. London: Stationery Office, 1996.
8 Jon Garland and Mike Rowe, 'War minus the shooting? Jingoism, the English press, and Euro 96', *Journal of sport and social issues*, 23(1) (1999), 80–95.
9 Boyle and Monteiro 2005: 240.
10 Joseph Maguire and Emma K. Poulton, 'European identity politics in Euro 96', *International review for the sociology of sport*, 34(1) (1999), 17–29.
11 Joseph Maguire, Emma Poulton and Catherine Possamai, 'Weltkrieg III? Media coverage of England versus Germany in Euro 96', *Journal of sport and social issues*, 23(4) (1999), 439–454: 446.
12 Colin Sparks and John Tulloch (eds), *Tabloid tales: global debates over media standards*. Lanham, MD and Oxford: Rowman & Littlefield, 2000.
13 Marc Roche, 'La presse britannique de qualité s'inspire des très contestés tabloïds', *Le Monde*, 8 August 2003.
14 Boyle and Haynes 2000: 24–30.
15 Boyle 2006: 1 and 49; Boyle and Haynes 2000: 177–178.
16 Boyle 2005: 226.
17 The point made strongly in Boyle and Monteiro 1995: 226, was confirmed in a phone interview with John Brodkin, journalist, *The Guardian*, 12 December 2006.
18 Confirmed in an interview with Matt Scott, journalist at *The Guardian* on 12 December 2006.

19 Confirmed in a telephone interview with Matt Denver, journalist at *The Independent* on 5 December 2006.
20 Rod Brookes, *Representing sport*. London: Arnold, 2002. Cf. Boyle and Haynes 2000: 167; Rowe 1999: 42; Boyle 2006: 1.
21 Rowe 1999: 24.
22 Boyle 2006: 180.
23 Between 2 and 29 October 2006, the average sales were as follow: *The Times*, 620,085 copies; *Daily Telegraph*, 851,902; *The Sun*, 2,930,512; *News of the World*, 3,198,784; *Daily Mirror*, 1,476,682; *The Guardian*, 332,867; *The Observer*, 432,833; *The Independent*, 214,892; *Evening Standard*, 281,915; (all certificates retrieved on www.abc.org on 5 November 2006).
24 Alex Law, 'Near and far: banal national identity and the press in Scotland', *Media, culture and society*, 23(3) (2001), 299–317 (hereafter Law 2001).
25 Law 2001: 303.
26 Bill Murray, *The Old Firm: sectarianism, sport and society in Scotland*. Edinburgh: John Donald, 1984, pp. 48–50 (hereafter Murray 1984).
27 Law 2001: 305.
28 *The Herald* was known as the *Glasgow Herald* until 1 February 1992; *The Mirror* was known as the *Daily Mirror* until 6 January 1997.
29 Law 2001: 304.
30 Namely Oise (60), Paris (75), Yvelines (78), Essonne (91), Hauts-de-Seine (92), Seine Saint-Denis (93), Val-de-Marne (94), Val-d'Oise (95); Seine-et-Marne (77) even has two editions: Seine-et-Marne nord and Seine-et-Marne sud.
31 Still officially known as 'L'organe central du Parti Communiste Français'.
32 The average daily sales of the newspapers were: *Ouest France*, 762,857; *Le Monde*, 380,812; *Le Parisien*, 351,700; *L'Équipe*, 358,562; *L'Humanité*, 70,477; *France Soir*, 47,835 copies (all figures according to Diffusion contrôle – association pour le contrôle de la diffusion des médias, last accessed from www.diffusion-controle.com; 9 October 2004).
33 Bromberger 1995.
34 Fiona Devine, 'Qualitative analysis', in David Marsh and Gerry Stoker (eds), *Theory and methods in political science*, pp. 137–153. Basingstoke: Macmillan, 1995 (hereafter Devine 1995).
35 According Gary King, Robert O. Keohane and Sidney Verba, *Designing social inquiry: scientific inference in qualitative research*. Princeton, NJ: Princeton University Press, 1994, pp. 27–28.
36 In chronological order: Daryl Broadfoot from *The Herald* was interviewed on 14 June 2001; Blaise de Chabalier from *Le Figaro* on 21 December 2003; David Revault d'Allonnes from *Libération* on 28 December 2003; Jérôme Touboul from *L'Équipe* on 29 December 2003; Sam Wallace from *The Independent* on 26 November 2006 (by phone); Matt Denver, from *The Independent* on 5 December 2006 (by phone); Matt Scott from *The Guardian* on the 12 December 2006; John Brodkin from *The Guardian* on 12 December 2006 (by phone).

37 Rapport à Monsieur le Secrétaire d'État auprès du Premier Ministre, chargé de la Jeunesse, des Sports et des Loisirs, sur certaines difficultés actuelles du football français, établi par Monsieur Philippe Séguin, Auditeur à la Cour des Comptes, 12 February 1973 (hereafter Séguin 1973).

38 Carol Patton (press officer) and Laurence McIntyre (security chief) from Rangers were interviewed on 12 June 2001; Stéphane Le Floch (Paris councillor) on 9 September 2003; Philippe Séguin on 25 September 2003; Michael O'Brien (assistant club secretary) and Jill Smith (supporters' liaison officer) from Arsenal on 9 November 2006. Iain Jamieson from Celtic could not be interviewed but sent documents.

39 Richard Giulianotti, 'Supporters, followers, fans and flâneurs: a taxonomy of spectator identities in football', *Journal of sport and social issues*, 26(1) (2002), 25–46.

40 As explained by an unnamed Celtic official: Richard Giulianotti, 'Sport spectators and the social consequences of commodification: critical perspectives from Scottish football', *Journal of sport and social issue*, 29(4) (2005), 386–410: 392.

41 Devine 1995: 138.

42 Devine 1995: 142.

43 Fanzine in the pre-*Bosman* era were studied in Richard Haynes, *The football imagination: the rise of the fanzine culture*. Aldershot: Arena, 1995.

3

Glasgow: the Old Firm

Introduction

The Glaswegian derby between the Celtic and Rangers Football Clubs, collectively known as the Old Firm, has become one of the most commented on football games on the planet. Yet, the Old Firm is anything but a world-class sporting event. Indeed, the Scottish league is a comparatively weak one. In 2010, it is ranked 16th in Europe by UEFA[1] and, apart from Celtic losing the final of the UEFA Cup in 2003, none of the two Glaswegian teams have had any remarkable success at the European level since the 1970s. Although both are among the twenty-five richest European clubs, they are ranked below their wealth by UEFA.[2] The interest the media and scholars have shown in the Old Firm has thus little to do with the sporting achievement. The intensity of the support both clubs have received from their fans, and, moreover, the reasons for that support, justify the otherwise unexpected attention received by the Old Firm. Since the end of the nineteenth century, the clubs have been the symbol of two distinct communities of Scotland in general, and of Glasgow in particular. The Catholic minority from Irish descent have backed Celtic, and the Protestant majority, from Scottish, or sometimes English, descent have backed Rangers. The very frequency of the games between the two clubs have become the occasion for each group to reaffirm their existence and beliefs.

Such has been the intensity of the confrontation (whether branded a religious or a nationalist one), that it has been an issue not only for the fans, but also for the clubs themselves. Celtic have always used the services of Protestant footballers (without them, success in Scotland might have been elusive). But Rangers decided only after the First World War, when the crisis in Scotland led to widespread sectarian discrimination at work, that they would not employ a Catholic. Such a policy came to an abrupt end on 10 July 1989. Graeme

Souness, Rangers manager since 1986 (and, crucially, the first one to be married to a Catholic), signed a Catholic player, Maurice Johnston, formerly from Celtic and Nantes (France). Johnston had been shown to the crowd in Celtic Park, wearing a Celtic jersey, just a few days before. Protests arose on both sides. Some Celtic fans felt betrayed by Johnston. Some Rangers fans protested against the surrender of what they saw as a century-old tradition and burned their season tickets in front of TV cameras.[3] (Apparently many of these supporters later called the club in order to know how they could get a replacement for the season book they had 'lost' or 'accidentally damaged').[4] Today, most of them seem to have accepted the presence of Catholics in Rangers' first team. And, following the 1995 *Bosman* ruling, they even seem to have accepted the fact that many Celtic and Rangers players could be foreign as well, and thus completely alien to the Glasgow traditions, the very reasons for the rivalry that is contained in the Old Firm. Yet, the intensity of the support both communities each give to their team seems not to have decreased.

The opposition between Rangers and Celtic therefore provides a particularly salient case to study how the introduction of players deemed 'strangers' to a club's identity affects its support – the main reason why the *Bosman* ruling has been criticised. The meaning that the Rangers vs. Celtic rivalry has retained is investigated in the eleven football seasons since Rangers abandoned its sectarian policy. This period (1989–2001) also includes five complete football seasons since *Bosman*. The processes of identification can therefore be studied and the model adopted tested, following the two successive introductions of 'strangers' in Glasgow's rivalry.

A history of the Old Firm: the religious and sectarian issues

The religious issue and the foundation of Celtic

The change the signing of Maurice Johnston in 1989 brought to the Old Firm rivalry can only be understood with regard to its history.[5] The religious issue has been present in the identity of Celtic since the foundation of the club but it took some time before sectarianism became part of the confrontation. Rangers' sectarian policy was maintained for more than eighty years and it went largely unnoticed for sixty years. Sectarianism was so deeply rooted in the club's culture, that it was ended very late: twenty years after it first came under attack.

During their early years, the games played between Rangers and Celtic did not take on any particular significance. Most academics agree that, at the time, Rangers could not be considered to be a Protestant team.[6] Their founders, their membership and their support were certainly recruited from the Protestant majority of Glasgow but this was the norm for almost every team in Scotland.[7] At the time, Protestantism was not yet an issue, and even less an identity, for Rangers. It is therefore through Celtic, that the religious issue is said to have been present in the Old Firm from the very beginning. It is a view commonly held among academics that Celtic has been a Catholic club since its foundation in 1887: it was founded by Catholics,[8] for Catholics, and was logically supported by the Catholic community of Glasgow.

Yet, the very name of the club, Celtic, does not refer to religion and was chosen as 'a reflection of both its Irish and Scottish roots',[9] and the colours (the emerald green and white hoops) and the emblems of the club, the shamrock and the harp, relate to their links with Ireland. Moreover, since the very beginning, the crowd has displayed symbols of their attachment to Ireland. They have been waving the tricolour flags of a dreamed of independent Ireland and then the Republic of Ireland. Officials from the clubs were also deeply involved in Irish politics.[10] This involvement was informal, 'through prominent players and officials, rather than officially through the club itself'.[11] G. Finn has argued, though, that those all Protestant clubs de facto excluded Catholics, and that this sectarian behaviour prompted Irish-Scots (Scots born from Irish descent, or recently emigrated from Ireland) to found their own clubs, like Celtic, in order to take part in the activities of Scottish society.[12] Following Finn's reading, it is possible to contend that the founders of Celtic were as much concerned with expressing their Catholic identity as they were with reacting to their exclusion as Irish migrants. Campbell and Woods have also insisted that at the time the two words Irish and Catholics were actually synonymous in the west of Scotland:[13] Celtic might have self-defined as Irish, and be considered as Catholics by the Protestant majority. The assumption central to this work has been that the Scottish Catholics are Irish migrants, who were established a long time ago but are still rejected on grounds of being migrants as much as on grounds of religion.

However, as Murray shows, relations between the clubs remained friendly until Celtic achieved outstanding success between 1892 and 1897.[14] This attracted them a stronger and wider Irish Catholic following and, arguably, jealousy from the Scottish Protestant majority. During this period, Rangers beat Celtic in the final of the Glasgow Cup:[15] it then replaced Queen's Park as Celtic's main challenger and became the focus of most Scottish Protestant pride. The polarisation on ethnic and religious lines had clear consequences on relations both on the field between the two teams, and in the stadium between the fans. These relationships began to deteriorate in 1896,[16] and reached hitherto unknown heights of violence in 1909. The managements of the two clubs, which had both been incorporated before the new century (Celtic 1897, Rangers 1899), quickly understood the profit they could derive from a hostility that was able to fill the stadia and organised the game to their benefit. This attitude did not go unnoticed, and earned the clubs the nickname 'Rangers, Celtic Ltd, The Old Firm'.[17] Yet, for all the income they could get from the religious and ethnic nature of the opposition (hence the fervour of the fans and their dedication to follow the confrontation), there is little evidence to suggest that the clubs positively or directly encouraged any sectarian feeling at that time, although they were clearly content to earn money from it.

Sectarianism

Sectarianism made its appearance in the Old Firm between 1908 and the 1920s. It is undeniably derived largely from the attitude adopted by Rangers. Celtic's board decided as early as 1895 that the club could sign Protestants, without any limits on the numbers.[18] Rangers realised after 1908 that they could field an all-Protestant team, yet win. From then onwards and until 1989, Rangers never knowingly signed a Catholic for its first team.[19] Yet, it is only in the 1920s that the absence of Catholics apparently became an established practice or policy, when the players refused to see a Catholic join the team against the manager's wish.[20] Murray has argued that the context of the period helps to explain their attitude: the depression led to an upsurge of violence in the form of organised rival gangs, and the further deterioration of relations between supporters of Celtic and Rangers. Also, within the context of high unemployment, Protestants were commonly assured they would get priority for jobs. In this environment, the adoption of a sectarian policy by Rangers went largely unnoticed. Murray also believes that the creation of the Irish Free State in 1922 'took the heat out of the sectarian question in Scotland'.[21] He contends that from this point onwards, Catholic Scots became more concerned with Scottish affairs than Irish ones. This is arguably further proof that the opposition was first and foremost between Scots of Irish descent and 'native' Scots, rather than between Catholic and Protestant.

Rangers' sectarianism did not come under attack for another forty years. The economic boom of the 1950s and 1960s (and according to Murray, the opening of the Catholic Church following the second Vatican council) eased the tensions in Glasgow and weakened the sectarian employment policies. With regard to football, the decisive factor was the change in fortunes of the clubs. Celtic seems to have been widely disregarded in the 1950s and 1960s as its poor results often resulted in crowd troubles.[22] But those troubles ceased to be a regular feature of Celtic matches after 1966. Moreover, Celtic's 1967 win over Inter Milan in Lisbon, made them the first non-Latin club to win the European Champions' Cup. The 1967 team developed into a celebrated symbol for the whole of Scotland: the 'Lisbon Lions'.[23]

In contrast, Rangers started to come under serious criticism after 1969, when its results started to suffer from Celtic's domination and crowd troubles proceeded to grow.[24] The Scottish press (most notably the *Daily Express* and the *Daily Record*) consequently denounced, for the first time, Rangers' sectarian practices, as they were seen to encourage hatred and bad behaviour on the part of their fans. Between 1969 and 1986, many other attacks on Rangers' policy, in the newspapers as well as in the radio and TV, would regularly re-emerge after any hooligan incident.[25] Meanwhile, Rangers' attitude became more and more widely condemned, not least by the Scottish Protestant clergy.[26] As a result, during the 1970s and 1980s, the club issued statements that the managers could enrol Catholics if they wanted to. These statements were only to be contradicted sooner or later either by the lack of Catholic signings, or by other statements, occasionally from incautious Rangers directors,[27] and sometimes by former players.[28] Other events also undermined the club's declarations. For example, the board refused to elect David Hope to the chairmanship, because of his marriage to a Catholic.[29]

Thus, Rangers' practice of excluding Catholic players only ended in 1989. The revolution began with a coup on the Rangers' board. The signing of Graeme Souness, who was not a Rangers man and most importantly married to a Catholic, as the new Rangers' manager followed. During the first three years, Souness practised a policy of big spending on the transfer of players, which was then uncommon in Scotland. Souness hired English stars, and even a black English player, Mark Walters in 1987, without stirring any emotion among the fans. But he had to wait until 10 July 1989 to sign a Catholic player, Scottish international Maurice Johnston.

The persistence of the opposition

A previous weakening of identity and modernisation?

> Barely a decade on from the arrival of Souness at Ibrox and Rangers could parade a team of foreigners most of whom are Catholics.[30]

Bill Murray's statement of 1998 shows the importance and the rapidity of the transformation that followed the signing of Maurice Johnston and was furthered by the 1995 *Bosman* ruling. Still, the support Rangers and Celtic receive does not seem to have either decreased or fundamentally changed. It is possible to wonder whether the relative weakening of links between each club and its respective community that had taken place before 1989, plays a part in the continuity of the support Celtic and Rangers have received. According to Murray, the Catholic charities that Celtic supported already played a smaller role than they used to. The role of the club in organising the social life of the Catholic community had declined in even greater proportions in 1989. At the time, Rangers had also become detached from the organisations with which they had been affiliated: freemasonry (of which there has always been very little proof) and Orangism (Murray has shown how Rangers let Orange Lodges use Ibrox for their marches).[31] Therefore, if the official links between both clubs and their respective communities through official organisations had already weakened and the rivalry between the fans have continued, the signing of Maurice Johnston may have been less a revolution than the final stage of an evolution.

H. F. Moorhouse offered the idea of a dissociation between the clubs and their traditional fans when he contended that unlike a Celtic club stuck in the past, Rangers was the only modern and business-minded club in Scotland.[32] Further research has emphasised the difference that must be made between the claims of the management about the modernity of the club, and the attitudes of the supporters. The emphasis put on tradition by Celtic's management was not necessarily shared by supporters.[33] Equally, Rangers' insistence on modernity has not entirely eradicated traditional behaviours from all sections of the supporters.[34] Also, analyses in terms of modernity and archaism are very often dated. Since Moorhouse wrote in 1991, Celtic's management has made the transition to a more business-oriented way of running their club following the 1994 takeover by Canadian businessman, Fergus McCann.[35]

A Catholic or an Irish identity?

Under new ownership, Celtic has clearly underplayed the Catholic identity of the club. Its social mission statement of the club, written around 1995, states that *from its foundation,* Celtic 'was a football club that Scottish and Irish, Protestants and Catholics alike could support'. It makes no further reference to a Catholic identity. The club has also launched a 'Bhoys against bigotry campaign' which condemns and discourages any sectarian attitude among their own fans. The club has further stated that:

> Celtic has a proud history as a non-sectarian club. It is disappointing that some people cannot distinguish between religious bigotry and the positive connections that Celtic has with Ireland.[36]

Many of the club's publications state that the club is 'proud of its joint Scottish and Irish identity'.[37] At the level of the fans, the Irish element in the club's identity has certainly remained important. Symbols of the Republic of Ireland still fill the stadium, from the Irish tricolour to the green and white of the jersey. However, Celtic does not officially back any political cause in Ireland. Following Finn's idea that the club was founded as a reaction against exclusion, and taking into account that Celtic claims its identity has been first and foremost Irish, it is possible to argue that the Catholic identity of Celtic Football Club has been to a large extent externally assigned by its opponents. Bradley is adamant that, more than their faith, their experience of immigrants has shaped the identity of the Irish Catholics.[38] Even Murray (who takes the point of view that the opposition between Rangers and Celtic is above all sectarian) states that sectarianism in Scotland has an 'underlying appeal to nationalism on both sides'.[39] Finally, the distinction between Catholic and Protestant which in Ireland is between respectively 'natives' and 'settlers' (most of whom were from Scottish origin) is reversed in Scotland where the Protestants are 'natives' and the Catholics and Irish are migrants. Bradley calls them the 'Scottish-Born Irish'.

The Glaswegian case provides a touchstone study of partisans identification for two main reasons. The exclusion of Catholics from Rangers' line up was the clearest example of the composition of the team as a means to display the club's identity and raise identification among the fans. Although expressed in religious terms, this exclusion had fundamentally to do with the rejection of migrants who, if not foreigners, were at least strangers to Glasgow. The hypotheses of this work can therefore be tested to study the significance football partisanship retained in Glasgow between 1989 and 2001, after the withdrawal of Rangers' sectarian policy led to the abandon of the composition of the team as a means of identification for supporters. The other means which remain have been studied too. The press provides a narrative, or produces a discourse, that may polarise the rivalry and reinforce the identity of the clubs and maintain the exclusion of Catholics, at least symbolically. People and emblems also come to symbolise identities and act as a support for fans' identification in Glasgow.

The broadsheets, the tabloids and the Old Firm

Statements on the role played by the press with regard to the rivalry between Celtic and Rangers have often been contradictory. On the one hand, the classic statement from one writer on religious issues (Callum G. Brown), insists that the press 'has long tried to play down the sectarian division',[40] in the hope that this would make it disappear. He has been given support by two students of the Old Firm. Joseph M. Bradley does so implicitly[41] as he does not question the position of Brown on the press, but does question his use of the word sectarianism. Bill Murray insists on the silence of the press with regard to sectarian issues in 1965 and its discretion until the 1969 riots in St James's Park.[42]

However, other views have been expressed. Laurence MacIntyre (responsible for safety at Rangers Football Club) is far from supportive of the idea that the press had either been trying to play down the religious divides between the clubs or had simply remained neutral.[43] He has accused the press of 'making a fuss where there was none'. Carol Patton (press officer at Rangers) has confirmed this view. For her, the press was guilty of 'hyping it up' – according to Laurence McIntyre, because the press has a 'vested interest' in the rivalry which 'sells their copies'.

How do Scotland's three major daily newspapers (*The Herald, The Scotsman* and the *Daily Record*)[44] report on the rivalry between Celtic and Rangers? To what extent do they try either to 'play down', or to 'hype up' the antagonism? Is it still possible to say (Brown's quote and Murray's position respectively date from 1987 and 1984) that they kept on ignoring the issue of sectarianism in society as well as in football?

A close analysis of the *Glasgow Herald, The Scotsman* and the *Daily Record* between 1989 and 2001 shows a complex pattern. Positions have evolved slowly since 1989 and the signing of Maurice Johnston. Indeed, it appears that sectarianism (and its relationship with football) is not ignored by the press at large any more, as it was until 1975.[45]

On the contrary, it is dealt with in most newspapers quite frequently, usually in special issues or reports. In the much narrower field of daily sports journalism, though, there appears a marked difference of treatments between the tabloids and the broadsheets, which may explain the opposition between the statements from Brown and the Rangers executives. Although the tabloids seem to be playing on the opposition by adding some fuel to the fire, the broadsheets (and especially *The Herald*) in contrast tend to be playing it down.

Sectarianism and football in the press

It is impossible to say any longer that the press ignores the sectarian issue in relation to football as it used to. Gone are the days when players' comments on Rangers' sectarianism were largely ignored by the Scottish press as in 1965 when Ralph Brand, a former Rangers player, heavily criticised the club for its sectarian policy in the *News of the World*.[46] Nowadays special reports on sectarianism, written by news journalists, are published frequently though irregularly (between about once a year and once every two years) by the newspapers, most usually in their Sunday edition. For instance, in the *Sunday Herald* dated 11 March 2001,[47] published after Donald Gorrie, Member of the new Scottish Parliament, decided to raise the issue of sectarianism and proposed a bill on 'Harassment aggravated by sectarianism'. These special reports can even occasionally take the form of a whole centrefold distributed with the journal. They are also published in other Britain-wide newspapers,[48] and very seldom deal with the sectarian issue only in football. They usually adopt a broader point of view and try to encompass, if not all, at least some of the sectors of Scottish life in which sectarianism can be an issue, such as personal life (with typical stories of a family broken by bigotry), life at work (usually with a token story of religious-based discrimination in the workplace).[49] They more rarely raise the question of the roots of sectarianism or of the state-funded Catholic schools[50] to which both Murray (in all his works) and Laurence MacIntyre, like other Rangers' officials,[51] make several references. Still, football is usually given a preponderant place in those reports – and in some cases is its main focus: the behaviour of the fans, and their songs are largely commented on.[52] Occasionally, the articles will try to establish that the activity of political parties such as the British National Party or the Scottish National Party have been witnessed outside the stadia of teams such as Rangers, Motherwell, Hearts and Dundee.[53] Furthermore, these articles are usually opinionated: they take up a position against sectarianism, denouncing bigotry and the wrongs it causes.

Conversely, sports journalists seem more reluctant to raise the issue of sectarianism in relation to football. It is only on some rare occasions that they adopt a comparable point of view and denounce the bigoted attachment to a given team – thus even directly or indirectly refer to sectarianism. In *The Herald*, for example, this does not seem to have happened more than twice during the first half of the 1990s. It happened first before an International game against Portugal, scheduled at Hampden on 14 October 1992. In many previous games, supporters in some sections of the crowd, those that included a majority of Celtic (the East terracing) or a majority of Rangers supporters (the West terracing) had whistled some Scotland players, or on the contrary had given support to some players of the foreign team because of their belonging to either Rangers or Celtic. The most striking example of this was the friendly international against Poland on 19 May 1990. Celtic fans had cheered Poland and Celtic players Dziekanowski and Wdowczyk, who were booed by other large sections of the crowd. This was given some publicity by the press.[54] James Traynor, then chief writer of *The Herald* raised the question of any united support for the Scottish team. He claimed this was dented by Rangers supporters' allegiance to the Union Jack, and the Irish identity of the Celtic fans,[55] a claim also supported by academic studies showing Old Firm fans gradually ceased to support the 'Tartan Army' (the name colloquially given to supporters of Scotland's football team) through the 1990s.[56] In 1994, it happened a second time. After a relatively successful Champions' League campaign in 1993 by Rangers,[57] James Traynor suggested that when competing in Europe,[58] all Scottish football fans should support Rangers. His point was made with reference to the probably distorted memories of the support that the famous Celtic team labelled 'The Lisbon Lions' (and now celebrated all throughout Scotland) received when winning the European Champion Clubs' Cup in 1967.

Nevertheless, articles of this sort from sports journalists are rare. In their post-match reports, they even seldom mention sectarian singing or abuse.[59] According to Laurence MacIntyre, this fact can be easily explained. 'Sports journalists are trying to stay away from that', he says, if only because they do not want to 'get abuse in the stadia', and do not want to smash 'their links with the football clubs'.[60] Hence, a first major difference in the treatment of the question of sectarianism and football appears to be that news journalists raise sectarian issues relatively often whereas sports writers very seldom do. A second major difference is in the treatment the Celtic v. Rangers rivalry get from broadsheets on the one hand, and the tabloids on the other hand.

Broadsheets and tabloids

The bias in favour of the Old Firm

In their daily report on Scottish football, the tabloids and the broadsheets adopt very dissimilar attitudes. These can explain the opposition between the statements from Brown and Murray, on the one hand, and Laurence MacIntyre as well as Carol Patton from Rangers on the other. The ways both categories of newspaper deal with the Glaswegian rivalry at first presents some similarities. In their sports section, the three newspapers regularly publish previews and reports of the matches written by sports journalists. These are part of the daily, or weekly, information on sports that can be expected from any British newspaper. As such, they form only part of the articles on the Scottish Premier League. Yet, as Rangers and Celtic are Scotland's top teams, and as they certainly have the biggest group of fans, they tend to attract more focus. This is reflected in the three newspapers. On the one hand, their regular participation in European Cups,[61] which happens practically every year, and their ability generally to progress further than other Scottish clubs in those competitions, attracts them more media attention. On the other hand, no matter which team, or in what competition they are playing, Celtic and Rangers seem certain to be given more coverage than, say, St Johnstone or Dunfermline.

This disproportionate attention for the Celtic or Rangers games, which is common to the three newspapers, is most striking in the *Daily Record.* Any news item, even the trivial, on the Old Firm is given an exaggerated importance. Over the three months, January to March 1995, there are 617 references to Rangers, 501 to Celtic, 121 to St Johnstone.[62] Pieces on games involving an Old Firm team are also typically longer and usually cover a much bigger space than any other report, on any sport. The choice of the iconography that illustrates the articles reinforces the bias in favour of the Old Firm.

The report in the *Sunday Mail*[63] of 22 April 2001 gives a good illustration of all those three points. First, except for one half of a column dedicated to the national team, anecdotal stories on both Celtic and Rangers' players cover the entire back page (the main page of the sports section). Second, the report on the Dundee–Rangers game of the previous day is given the penultimate double page minus two columns. In comparison, the reports of the three other games played on the same day are all squeezed into a double page. Moreover, the written report on Dundee–Rangers is actually three columns long (which is slightly longer than the one and a half to two columns dedicated to each of the three other games). Third, and not least, the report is accompanied by four pictures (the summary of Aberdeen–Dunfermline is not accompanied by any, and the other two games only by a total of three pictures). Three of the four pictures are in colour, the biggest of which shows three Rangers players celebrating a goal. Players from Dundee appear only on the two smaller colour pictures. In each of those, Dundee defenders are shown being surpassed by a striker. Thus, not only are Rangers given a disproportionate coverage in the text, but pictures tend as well to suggest either its superiority over its opponent, or that they are the sole focus of the article.

Even though it is less obvious, *The Herald* and *The Scotsman* also both give a disproportionate attention to Rangers and Celtic. In the Glasgow-published *Herald*, games involving Celtic or Rangers typically get the main headlines on the back page, over any other sporting event. The reports on those games are usually twice the size of the report on any other game; they may even include an occasional picture. *The Scotsman* shows only a little less bias in favour of the Old Firm teams, especially as news items concerning them do not always get pre-eminence over any other sports news. For example, the Celtic vs. Rangers confrontation of Saturday 4 November 1989 fails to make the main headline of the sports section of their edition dated Monday 6 November 1989: the Old Firm game only gets the third headline, behind Formula One. Still, the Old Firm remains the main focus of the football pages. Published in Edinburgh, *The Scotsman* could be expected to devote most of their attention to the local teams. This is even the opinion of Daryl Broadfoot,[64] journalist at *The Herald*, that 'they are more concerned with Hibernian and Heart of Midlothian than Rangers and Celtic'. However, a database search reveals that in the year 1999, 259 articles in *The Scotsman* contained references to both Hibernians (or Hibs) and Hearts and 989 to both Celtic and Rangers.[65] It appears that, as a general rule, between 1989 and 1999, games involving either Celtic or Rangers are given more importance in *The Scotsman* than any other game is. The Edinburgh derby (when 'Hibs' confront 'Hearts') is the only game which is regularly given more coverage than a normal football game involving either Celtic or Rangers.

'Hyping it up'

Despite the similarities, an analysis in terms of the contents of the two different kinds of press confirms the findings of Boyle, Monteiro and Haynes as it shows a marked difference between tabloids and broadsheets. The first are hyping up the rivalry, the second are playing it down. On no occasion do the similarities and differences show more clearly than in the run-up to the day of the Glaswegian derby. In both kinds of press, the exaggerated importance given to the Old Firm is even more amplified. Both start mentioning the Old Firm game to come as soon as they report the last game, which usually takes place about a week before.[66] These reports usually conclude on an assessment of both teams' chances the following week. Then all through the week, both tabloids and broadsheets devote articles to the forthcoming encounter. An analysis of a typical week (for example 22 to 29 April 2001)[67] before an Old Firm match shows that in *The Herald* as well as in *The Scotsman* and *Daily Record* or the Scottish edition of *The Sun*, one or the other Old Firm team (and usually both) makes the sports headline everyday through three different kinds of articles. The first kind of articles includes previews of the game, and the forces in balance at the beginning of the week (Monday or Tuesday) then, on the eve of the Old Firm encounter (Saturday). A second kind of article is a midweek special focus on the story of one player (Henrik Larsson in the three newspapers during the week 22–29 April 2001 as he had scored 49 goals in the season so far). The third kind of articles includes more anecdotal stories about both teams, such as shared or repeated rumours of transfers to come (e.g. between 22 and 29 April 2001, Pierre-Yves André and Claudio Caniggia were presented as Rangers' possible signings, Mahon as Celtic's). The Old Firm game to come becomes the main focus of the sports pages in the three newspapers, which clearly feed on the rivalry – thus probably strengthening it.

Yet, the treatment of the news in tabloids and broadsheets is different and the content of the articles is poles apart. First, the tabloids clearly focus on football and on the Old Firm much more: between 22 April and 2 May 2001, articles related to the Old Firm made it to the front page of the *Daily Record* and *Sunday Mail* on six occasions, and to the back page in every occasion.[68] Football in contrast very seldom makes it to the front page of the broadsheets. (This happened only twice between 1989 and 1995 in the case of *The Scotsman* and three times in the case of *The Herald*.)[69] The treatment of the same event in *The Sun* or the *Daily Record* is also comparatively more substantial. A transfer rumour would only get a few hundred words in the broadsheets. In the tabloids, whole articles (up to a few columns) are devoted to the same rumour. Any such story is always followed the next day by a sequel detailing every actual or possible change in the situation – or more probably explaining that there has not been any substantial change.

Second, it is striking that tabloids very regularly raise the more contentious issues that the broadsheets in general shy away from. The article on Caniggia's possible signing in the *Daily Record*[70] explicitly plays on the opposition between Rangers and Celtic. A picture of Claudio Caniggia's 8-year-old son, Alexander, wearing a Celtic jersey covers half of Friday 27 April 2001's front page. The headline reads: 'You're signing for who Dad?' and the caption of the insert picture of Claudio Caniggia reads 'Clash? New Rangers Claudio'. The article mentions that Claudio Caniggia was once linked to Celtic and reads 'Picture exclusive – It looks like World Cup winner Claudio Caniggia faces a family feud over his summer signing for Rangers'. It adds that Claudio Caniggia's son 'clearly does not share dad's passion for the blue half of the Old Firm'.

Furthermore, the *Daily Record* often launches a polemic between the two clubs that is normally unheard of in either *The Herald* or *The Scotsman.* They usually quote and emphasise the verbal attacks of Rangers' players on Celtic players or fans and vice versa. For example, the back page of the edition dated Monday 23 April 2001 is covered in half by a picture of Rangers' players. It includes a very small text square which headline reads 'Jorg blasts champions'. This caption reports comments made by Rangers' Jorg Albertz, according to whom Celtic's victory in the league is only due to Rangers' poor performances. Thereafter, new events related to this initial story are commented upon throughout the week. They culminate on the day before the Old Firm encounter, when a back page article entitled 'Don't get shirty with my lads – O'Neill backs celebration' sums up the whole affair of the week. Albertz's comments were met with the Celtic players sporting T-shirts with a 'No excuses' message below an icon representing its double win in the League Cup and in the League Championship. This in turn 'provoked outrage at Ibrox'.[71] During a press conference on Friday night, the Celtic manager finally backed the sporting of the T-shirts by his players, and put an end to the story.

Some polemics can take bigger proportions. The incident that took place in the first fortnight of February 2001 has been pointed out by Laurence MacIntyre as a good example of the influence of the press on the rivalry. The Irish Prime Minister postponed a trip to Scotland,[72] at a time when two confrontations between Rangers and Celtic had been scheduled. This caused a storm in the newspapers.[73] According to Laurence MacIntyre, 'if there hadn't been a fuss [in the media], there would not have been a problem'. Having been the Chief Constable of the Glasgow region between 1992 and 1997, he believes that any risk was less due to the trip in itself than to the articles in the press. These articles made the more anti-Irish elements of the population aware of the trip and its timing, and they presented the trip as a danger to public order. In the case of the Irish Prime Minister, there was only the potential for trouble. The actual boos accompanying Celtic's Neil Lennon when he made his first appearance for Northern Ireland at Windsor Park (its national stadium) after signing for Celtic,[74] is, according to Carol Patton, an example of real – though relatively minor – trouble that was only caused by media hype.[75]

These two affairs show clearly that the tabloids are not only hyping up the rivalry between the two teams, but also stressing the political antagonism this rivalry is associated with – at the certain risk of bolstering it, or even raising real troubles. The tabloids undoubtedly appear to be emphasising the potential for opposition between the teams. First, they affix elements of antagonism in events that should be relatively neutral, such as transfer rumours or news. Second, they give birth to and echo a war of declarations between the teams. Third, they point, and probably stress political aspects of the antagonism. The broadsheets are, on the contrary, totally exempt from such an attitude.

Were it not for the wider context of Rangers–Celtic opposition, such an attitude on the part of the tabloids would probably not merit further comment. These articles can especially be seen as traditional means by which the tabloids increase their sales. For example, the fact that a rather suggestive picture of the young and scantily clad Mrs Caniggia covers half of the Saturday 28 April 2001 front page tends to show the *Daily Record* has a tendency to exploit any means to increase its circulation. The difference between tabloids and broadsheets would thus only reflect a difference in the conception of journalism. This is the claim made by Daryl Broadfoot, football journalist at *The Herald* in an interview with the author.[76] Yet, the attitude of the broadsheets also reveals a willingness to play down the antagonism – and to confine it strictly to football.

Playing down the divide

The comparison with the tabloids may give the idea that broadsheets are just maintaining a more neutral attitude towards the Old Firm. Actually, they play down the sectarian divide. This has appeared most clearly on two particular occasions. The first one is the signing of Maurice Johnston and his progressive integration into the Rangers team. *The Herald* depicts quite clearly the situation at Rangers, and the shock that this 'first non-sectarian signing'[77] by the club had created. Yet, when comparing the story's treatment by *The Scotsman*, it is equally clear that *The Herald* omitted a great deal in order to try to minimise the religious divide. Indeed, the religion of Maurice Johnston only appears after the first third of the *Herald* article. Also, it only appears in a reported speech from David Miller (then general secretary of the Rangers supporters' association and a staunch opponent of the signing). The signing was given front-page treatment in *The Scotsman* with the headline: 'Storm as Catholic Johnston signs for Rangers',[78] as well as that of the English paper *The Independent*.[79] Also, nowhere is it mentioned that Celtic have a Catholic and Irish identity. Thus *The Herald* omits to give a clear vision of what the signing of Johnston means in its wider context, less so, indeed, than, for example, the English weekly journal *The Economist,* whose readership in England but more particularly in the United States, may be less familiar with the Scottish football scene, and which wrote (not without some exaggeration):[80]

> Glasgow's Protestant football team, Rangers, signed up a Roman Catholic, Maurice Johnston, who at one time played for Celtic, Rangers' traditionally Catholic rivals. Fundamentalists on both sets of terraces were furious.[81]

Moreover, the statement from Tom Connolly, spokesman for the Catholic Church in Scotland, who is quoted in *The Herald* article appears to be truncated. In *The Herald,* Connolly says: 'If this is instrumental in breaking down the senseless, ignorant bigotry, then I would welcome it. Definitely'. These are the only words published in *The Herald,* but in *The Scotsman* his statement is completed with more cautious comments: 'This signing is obviously, as far as I can see, a purely financial deal'. It seems that these omissions tend either to empty sectarianism of its meaning (by only alluding to the religion of the player, or by presenting only one side of the opposition) or to present Catholic reaction in a more favourable sight.

It is striking as well that after Maurice Johnston scored his first goal in an Old Firm game[82] (the second in which he played), *The Herald* as well as *The Scotsman* stopped presenting him as either a Catholic player or a former Celt in their following reports of Old Firm games. This is something they had never failed to do in all previous reports on him. On the occasion of that goal, *The Scotsman* even went so far as to publish an article,[83] separated from the report of the match, which asserted that on that day, Maurice Johnston had conquered the Rangers fans and become for them a true Rangers' player – regardless of his religion. Reality was certainly a bit more complicated. There are for instance testimonies[84] that after more than a year, some supporters would still come to the stadium with a wreath signalling the death of the 'True Spirit of Rangers'.[85]

Second, on another occasion, the sectarian aspect of the troubles that took place in Celtic Park on 1 January 1994, was considerably downplayed by *The Herald*. Both the sports pages (in a special article) and the news section put forth the belief that the violence was the result of poor sporting results.[86] Although the protests from the fans actually seemed to be aimed at the Celtic board, the report may seem biased. *The Scotsman* shows the same bias.[87] By depriving the rivalry of its historical background, both *The Herald* and *The Scotsman* succeeded in avoiding any mention that the divisions between Celtic and Rangers were usually thought and felt to be based on religious or national (ethnic) criteria.

Hence, it appears that journalists adopt three kinds of attitudes when looking at the issue of rivalry in the Old Firm. News journalists in any kind of press willingly deal with it in reports on sectarianism as a general issue. Sports journalists of the broadsheets tend to ignore it or downplay some of its aspects (e.g. the religious content). Finally, sports sections (articles in tabloids are often unsigned) of the tabloids rarely hesitate, not only to emphasise the rivalry, but to insist on some of its aspects (e.g. the political link with Ireland), at the risk of being accused of hyping up the rivalry and stirring real troubles.

Markers of identity

The differentiated attitude of the two categories of newspapers appears in a new light when it is linked to a study of how people and emblems come to symbolise identities and foster identification. Indeed, an analysis of the Scottish press tends largely to confirm but also to extend the hypotheses tested here. On the one hand, it does certainly confirm and emphasise the importance of colours, which is pointed up in the secondary literature on the Old Firm. Moreover, it clearly shows that an additional kind of emblem, the very names by which Celtic and Rangers are called, takes on an equivalent importance to that of colours in the Scottish context. On the other hand, the same analysis confirms the importance of the value assigned to the style of the team.

Symbols: emblems, colours and names

Colours, emblems and flags

The profound importance of the colours (and to a lesser extent, the other emblems) as a focus of identification in Scottish football has been emphasised on many occasions. First and foremost, although Celtic use no emblems which are explicitly Catholic, the club's association with the Irish colours (green and white) and emblems (the shamrock) has been a permanent subject of comment by all writers on the matter, and the club itself. Celtic has indeed shown a remarkable consistency in the use of these colours and emblem (notably as it appears on the crest of the club). Nowadays, they can be found in all the publications of the clubs, their website and even in the design of their shops. Celtic's pride of its Irish origins does not seem to have raised much criticism. More controversial has been their waving of the Irish tricolour on the mast over Celtic Park, over which the Scottish Football Association threatened Celtic with exclusion from the Scottish League in 1951.[88] After the troubles in Ireland in the 1970s, criticisms were heard again, especially on the part of journalists and authors. Bill Murray, for instance, saw the Irish tricolour as a symbol of the IRA.[89] Some of them suggested that Celtic should revert to the Green flag with a golden harp that they had waved before 1922. That was seen as the symbol of Ireland's cultural rather than political identity. The political and the religious problems that the flag has come to symbolise has been summarised in a letter to the *Glasgow Herald* where it was presented as:

> The flag of a foreign and frequently hostile state, whose constitution impudently claims sovereignty over part of the United Kingdom, and whose land and people the present Pope has declared to be 'Mary's Dowry'.[90]

Nevertheless, Celtic has reaffirmed many times its determination to keep on flying the Irish tricolour as it takes on a totally different meaning for them:

> The Club has stated on many occasions that it views the colours of the tricolour standing for the white of peace between the orange and green communities of Ireland. Certain journalists have made ignorant remarks such as suggesting that the tricolour is the symbol of the IRA and it is this type of damaging remark the Club is working against.[91]

The club's official support for the Irish tricolour goes as far as to sell its own version of it, whereon is stamped the four-leaf shamrock. The fury surrounding the flag points to an important aspect of the Rangers–Celtic rivalry: arguably, the real divide is between those perceived as 'Scots' and those perceived as 'Irish'; rather than between religious factions.

Rangers' case is a little different. The blue is as omnipresent in Rangers' case as the green and white in Celtic's, and it has never left the team's home jersey. The club uses it in all its publications and production (shop, bags, etc.) as well. It is so central to the club identity that its disappearance from some of the club's business suites prompted articles in the press.[92] There are differences, though. Rangers make a very limited use of its crest (a red lion rampant): it does not appear on the jersey (which only sports the interlaced RFC), and it can only be found in some Rangers' publications (i.e. in 2001 it was barely decipherable on the top-left corner of the club's website). Also, Rangers' association with blue happens to be fortuitous. At the time of its foundation, the choice of blue certainly carried no religious or political connotation then and Rangers have always officially denied that it carried any. The growing opposition between Rangers and Celtic supporters has charged the blue with significance. For the fans, it has become a symbol of loyalist and Protestant identity. Murray states, most vividly that 'it is the proud boast of many Rangers fans that theirs is the bluest of blue, most staunch and loyal protestant club in Scotland'.[93] Here the expression 'true blue' is indeed used to show their attachment to the crown and the Union, and their protestant identity. Murray has remarked how Rangers' supporters use the Union Jack rather than the saltire and sing God Save the Queen in preference to Flower of Scotland as the flag and the song symbolise the oppression of Ireland for Celtic fans.[94]

The blue and the emerald therefore demonstrate two different ways in which football colours can take on additional meaning, whether social, religious or political. Celtic's green and white have carried the Irish question into football. In contrast, Rangers' blue has come to represent more than was the intention of the founders. (This suggests that a football symbol has been charged with extra political and religious meaning by supporters.)

Two rather anecdotal stories make the importance of colours in the Scottish case quite clear. A supporter recalls in *Voices of the Old Firm*,[95] that in the early 1970s, a city council refused to fly a green flag awarded as an environmental prize. The city council was afraid of the troubles that could arise if the green flag was seen on its own, without a blue counterpart. On a more sombre note, the death of Mark Scott also testifies to the perceived importance of colours.[96] In 1995, this 16-year-old Celtic supporter had his throat cut at Bridgeton Cross, inside a Protestant area of Glasgow, by a man who picked him out at random among the group of Celtic supporters with whom he was walking home. Tragic though the episode was, it is not an example of usual behaviour between supporters of Celtic and Rangers. People can be found wearing colours from both teams in the same street within the very heart of Glasgow without inflicting violence on each other. Yet, before he left home, Mark's mother had warned him about the risk he ran if he wore Celtic colours in that part of town. This maternal advice and the fact Mark Scott is commonly (though not always) presented in the press as having been killed for wearing the wrong jersey reveals the significance people in Glasgow can attach to colours.[97]

A further confirmation of their importance as a symbol of identity can be found in the way the sports sections in the Scottish press deal with the subject. Trying to play down the division and what colours stand for, the broadsheets constantly and consistently avoid any reference to colours. *The Herald* has contained the fewest references. Between July 1989 and May 1995, only three explicit references to the colours of either Celtic or Rangers were found.[98] In *The Scotsman,* references to Old Firm colours are only a little less scant. They still remain the exception. However, the *Daily Record* makes much more common use of expressions such as 'the Hoops' to designate the Celtic team, and the adjective 'blue' to qualify Rangers – even in their headlines.[99] Yet, this use of the colours became less common throughout the 1990s. This, according to journalist Daryl Broadfoot, followed the arrival of former *Herald* sports editor James Traynor at the *Daily Record* in 1997 after a spell at the *Express*. The direct or indirect references to the teams' colours, which could be read in both tabloids in almost every article no longer appear on a daily basis. This trend may indicate that the tabloids are trying to soften their positions on what the rivalry stands for. Equally, it could simply indicate an improvement in the quality of writing in the tabloids.

Indeed, according to Daryl Broadfoot,[100] the use of words such as the Blues, the Greens or the Hoops should not be given too much importance as it only reflects the 'sloppy writing' typical of tabloids. Yet, comparisons with the British and French press shows that the periphrastic use of colours to name a team is relatively common, even in quality newspapers. Calling a team by reference to its colours (in terms of style, a periphrasis) seems to be considered 'sloppy' writing in Scotland only. The taboo surrounding colours in the press establishment only provides further evidence of how much they mean in terms of rivalry and identity.

Names

In the Scottish context, other markers of identity, names, particularly appear to take on comparable significance as colours. The only circumlocutions used on a regular basis by journalists of both *The Herald* and *The Scotsman* to designate Celtic and Rangers refer to the stadium or its location. In the same article, expressions such as 'the Parkhead defence' or 'Parkhead team' or the 'Ibrox duo', 'Ibrox goalkeeper' or 'Ibrox team' can appear on more than two occasions each.[101] The Edinburgh-based *Scotsman* may occasionally employ more generic terms, and talk about Celtic and Rangers with reference to their location in, respectively, the east and the west of Glasgow.[102] One difference with the tabloids is noticeable here. Circumlocutions aim at avoiding repeating the words 'Celtic' and 'Rangers'. The name of Celtic's stadium, Celtic Park, is therefore not very useful for journalists, who use 'Parkhead' (the name of the stadium's neighbourhood) instead. Broadsheets journalists also avoid using the stadium's colloquial name, 'Paradise' (the origins of which may lay in Celtic Park's proximity to a cemetery) in all probability because of its religious denotation. Conversely, tabloids use it on a very regular basis (albeit not on a daily one).[103]

The overuse of circumlocutions related to the location of the stadium is revealing only by comparison to the expressions that could be used instead. Sometimes, but very rarely and only on the occasion of an Old Firm game, the broadsheets designate Celtic or Rangers in relation to each other, by their opposition. Expressions such as 'their opponent of the day', or even 'their arch rivals' can be found in *The Herald* or *The Scotsman*.[104] Once again, it is the comparative abuse of these expressions in the tabloids that is very revealing. The circumlocutions relating to the location of the team appears to be only there to prevent the journalist from using a name bearing more significance in terms of identity. Other idiomatic names are completely banned from the broadsheets as well, but find their place in the tabloids. There, Celtic are quite often designated as 'the Bhoys' and Rangers as 'the Gers'. The latter can hardly be assigned any religious or political meaning: it is just an abbreviation of the team's real name. On the other hand, in the west of Scotland, the expression 'the Bhoys' commonly refers to Scots of Catholic religion and Irish descent.[105]

Some names are so loaded with controversial meanings that they have become a taboo and cannot find a place in either the broadsheets or the tabloids. The name 'Billy Boys', for example is used by Rangers' fans to denote themselves. It appears notably in a song that Joseph Bradley presents as one of the most popular 'football' songs in Scotland:

> Hello! Hello! We are the Billy Boys
> Hello! Hello! You'll know us by our noise
> For we're up to our knees in Fenian Blood

> Surrender or you'll die
> For we are the Bridgeton Billy Boys[106]

This name makes reference to two different strata in Glasgow's memory. It is, first, a reference to William of Orange (Billy) and the troops (the Boys) he used in his victory over the Irish at the Battle of the Boyne, on 12 July 1690,[107] which marked the defeat of Catholic King James II, and ultimately the end of an independent Ireland as well. Second, it is a reference to the most prominent, certainly the biggest and the best-known 'razor gang' that, in the troubled inter-war years, gave Glasgow a bad reputation.[108] The 'Bri'g'on Billy Boys' became famous for their involvement in numerous riots, especially those surrounding any game by Rangers, or on Orange walks on 12 July, to which they always used to turn up in masses. When Rangers' fans call themselves 'the Billy Boys' nowadays, they therefore conjure up memories of Protestant–Catholic (Scottish–Irish) opposition, of riots and violence associated with football, and of sectarian organisations (Orange orders). The importance of the sectarian songs is attested throughout the history of the club. There were suggestions that they should be forbidden as early as 1972. Also, Rangers' Vice-President, Donald Findlay had to resign after evidence surfaced that he had sung sectarian songs after his club's victory over Celtic in the Scottish Cup final of 1999.[109] In June 2006, UEFA recognised the sectarian nature of the song and asked Rangers to make a formal announcement before every game, explicitly forbidding supporters to sing it.[110]

The word 'Fenian', which can be found in the 'Billy Boys', is a second example of names entirely banned from newspapers.[111] 'Fenian' has become a colloquial and pejorative term to designate Catholic Scots of Irish descent. It also conjures up memories of the failed Fenian uprising of 1867 in Ireland. In both cases, an identity which contains facets of violence is channelled through a name by reference to the past (and especially the troubled political history between the British and the Irish). Yet, the meaning these names have taken must be evaluated carefully. Bill Murray, for example notes that the Pope supported William of Orange and not the Irish and King James during the Battle of the Boyne.[112]

Names have certainly been misused, or their meaning has been distorted to fit the contemporary situation. However, symbols do not deal with historical veracity. In this case, the reference to history is only valid to the extent that it deals with present-day identity. The process of selecting an event and some aspects of this event to the detriment of others, which are forgotten, is quite common in the formation of memory, especially collective memories. It has notably been analysed by Benedict Anderson on Michelet's writings.[113] Therefore, in the light of the Scottish case, names are identity symbols which should be added to those already identified in previous literature (colours, jersey, crests and logos).

The team and the players

Symbols related to football can crystallise identities, and the game itself, by its very nature, can do the same. Three main characteristics of a football team foster identification: its composition, the personality of the players and the style of the team. Rangers' policy, constantly enforced from the 1920s up until 1989, of not signing Catholics made it the archetype of a team whose composition reflects the image a group had of itself. The Rangers team, indeed, reflected the image of an ideal Scotland for some of its supporters: a Scotland freed of Irish (Catholic) migrants.

The collapse of Mario Jardel's signing in 1996 is probably the last example of a player whose Catholicity might have prevented him from playing for Rangers. He admitted in an interview that he crossed himself before every game.[114] Officially, his transfer was cancelled because he did not get a work permit (he was not fulfilling one of the prerequisite conditions of playing regularly for his national team). However, making the sign of the cross was a highly contentious issue at the time. A few days before Jardel's interview, a Partick Thistle player was booked for crossing himself in a game against Rangers. The referee probably wanted to sanction and prevent the repetition of what could be interpreted as a provocative sign in front of an assembly of Rangers' fans. There are also testimonies that 'Basile Boli had been warned by the Rangers management to desist from making the sign of the cross when entering or leaving the playing area – while playing for Rangers'.[115] There was no official denial from Rangers at any time. Both incidents, and the limited confidence that the Rangers management showed in their own fans, therefore tend to indicate that, in 1996 at least, Rangers' supporters had accepted the fact that Catholics could play for the team, as long as they did not show any outward signs of their faith.

It is the last time, though, that the religion of a player, and the symbols of his faith, have stirred some emotion in the press. Today, Laurence MacIntyre of Rangers reckons 'we suspect that more than half our players are Catholics', an estimation shared by Carol Patton. Sectarianism also stopped at the highest levels in the club: Rangers hired a Catholic executive in 1998.[116] Furthermore, following the *Bosman* ruling, the Rangers squad has become global in origin. In 2001, it included 36 players: 11 Scots and 16 different nationalities from three continents. Moreover, this 'multiculturalism' of the Rangers team does not seem to have decreased the support that Rangers receive. There are examples to the contrary, showing that foreign signings are not especially resented. When Frenchman Lionel Charbonnier, fresh from winning the World Cup, made his first appearance with Rangers in 1998 the whole stadium stood up to sing 'La Marseillaise' in his honour.[117] Moreover, the Scottish press is, in general, surprisingly silent on the nationality of the players (except, perhaps, when they are English). This is especially clear with comparison to the English press, where the number of foreigners playing in the Premier League seems to be a subject of recurrent concern. The Scottish Premier League has also probably showed more openness to the world than the English League (in 1987 only 1.9 per cent of the professional players in England were foreign, which compares to 24.5 per cent in France in 1990).[118] The transition to the *Bosman* era has therefore arguably been smoother.

Even though it found a striking confirmation at Rangers before 1989 and seemed to have played a part at least until 1996, it is therefore difficult to see how the presence of 'strangers' to the team identity is resented by fans of the Old Firm any more. This clearly strengthens the case for a study of whether fans can identify with teams which, following the *Bosman* ruling, are full of foreigners.

The idea (best expressed by Bromberger) that: 'each player provokes more or less favours in the different sections of the public depending on the specific qualities that he demonstrates'[119] did not really find confirmation in either the Scottish press or the secondary literature, which mostly focused on star players, for the most part successful forwards. It proved impossible to test with interviews, since fans' distant memories are too distorted: what they have to say on the matter in the middle of the 2000s might well provide an inaccurate picture of what they thought for the period 1989–2001. It is interesting to note, though, that the departure of Rangers' manager Paul Le Guen at the beginning of 2007[120] (more than seventeen years after the signing of Maurice Johnston) was partly motivated by his ongoing conflict with Barry Ferguson. The Scotland and Rangers captain had become emblematic of the club where he had been trained as a youth and to which he had returned; thus the fans clearly sided with him against the club manager.[121] Twelve years after the *Bosman* ruling, some players clearly maintain a link between the locale, the supporters and the club.

The Glaswegian case provides salient confirmation of most of the insights on markers of identity. Since 1989, Glasgow Rangers can no longer appear as the archetypal example of a team whose composition reflects the imagined identity of the community it represents. Still, until 1996, fans seemed only to tolerate the presence of Catholics within Rangers FC. They did not agree to their displaying symbols of Catholicism, which would give the image of Rangers as a Catholic or Catholic-filled team. Emblems have actually proved to be the more enduring markers of identity in Glasgow. Irish (but not Catholic) identity has been channelled into football through colours and emblems. Conversely, those of Rangers, which were originally devoid of religious or political significance, have become symbols of Scottish, loyalist and Protestant identity. Furthermore, the study of Celtic and Rangers has shown that, in addition to those emblems previously studied, names as they convey some aspects of collective memory, could take on a very similar value as symbols of identity.

Questions of style

In the context of the Glaswegian derby and its echoes in the Scottish press, one variable proves particularly important: the idea that the style of the team reflects and embodies the imagined identity of the group that it represents. Students of the Old Firm have insisted on a difference of style between the 'Rangers tradition' and the 'Celtic spirit': 'the most obvious image of the clubs is that which they portray on the football field, their style of play and their reaction to victory and defeat'.[122] Rangers are, according to Murray, 'a proud, dour and uncompromising machine',[123] and display 'ruthless efficiency which emphasises teamwork, strength and commitment rather than skill and delicacy.[124] Conversely, Murray says of Celtic that they 'could not boast of their consistency in those years, and indeed made a virtue of less polished performances which relied on individual cheek and artistry'.[125] The wide acceptance by the public of these contrasts, summarised as 'virtues of efficiency on the one hand [Rangers] and inspiration on the other [Celtic]' [126] is reflected by the fact it carries through, not only to the sports press and books on the Old Firm, but also to wide-selling novels such as Gordon Williams' *From Scenes Like These*.[127]

A second contrast with regard to style is that commentators from Rangers relate to the stereotyped style assigned to their team, whereas commentators from Celtic do not. The Rangers style is commented upon in most publications on the team which typically dedicate a whole chapter to the 'Iron Curtain' teams of the post-war years.[128] These teams defined what was to become Rangers style. They had a tough defence (the 'Iron Curtain'), intercepted the ball early, played in the opponent's half to maintain the pressure on them, and worked tirelessly as a team. Large sections of the same books are devoted to Billy Struth, Rangers manager for more than three decades, who developed this Rangers style. The books insist on the discipline he imposed on the team, his insistence on (some would say obsession with) details such as the standard of dress. He had prescribed the order in which the players should put on their shorts and jersey to look as neat as possible when entering the field. He had also demanded that players wear a suit and a bowler hat whenever going to the stadium.[129]

In contrast to Murray's assessment (who throughout his writings shows a certain preference for Rangers), references to a Celtic style are much scarcer when Celtic fans write about their own club. In most stories or books on the club, forward playing and attacking style seem to be in favour. And the great Celts that are remembered more fondly (such as Charlie Tully) are without doubt great individual personalities, if not great individualists. But Rangers histories or handbooks also celebrate (even though probably not to the same extent) their share of players who present the same kind of characteristics (for instance 'Slim' Jim Baxter). Actually, any club would probably do the same. Furthermore, the most celebrated Celtic team of all time, the 'Lisbon Lions' of the late 1960s and early 1970s shares many characteristics with the Iron Curtain teams. A Protestant, Jock Stein, was manager of this Celtic team. The style of play that he encouraged in most games was based on solid defending and rapid counter-attacks. The qualities he wanted to see in his team, strength, physical engagement, tireless commitment to the team, were actually very close to that developed by Struth for Rangers earlier. However, it is the case that writers on Celtic do not stress those qualities as much as writers on Rangers do.

The situation on style is therefore complex. On the one hand, observers can see a definite contrast in style between the two Glaswegian teams, and writers on Rangers usually insist firmly on the style of their team. On the other hand, writers on Celtic who are sympathetic to the team rarely put as much stress on the style generally referred as being their team's own, as is to be expected. For example, Joseph Bradley, an academic who seems to show more sympathy for Celtic, barely mentions it. So, to a large extent, the views on the style that Celtic is expected to show seem to be imposed on Celtic fans and players by commentators who are not Celtic supporters.

A last major difference with regard to style is that the press shows a bias. When Rangers won nine consecutive league titles between 1989 and 1997, the tabloids insisted on many occasions on Rangers' ability to play like a machine, and win everything, in conformity with the club's usually recognised style of play. The broadsheets showed more balance in their treatment of the Old Firm, but their analyses of the games conformed to the stereotyped image of Rangers' and Celtic's style of play. Celtic's play is still considered as brilliant but the 'fragile condition of defence',[130] and the lack of team spirit prevents it from becoming fruitful on all occasions: 'Some of his [Paul McStay's] moves and touches had the mark of genius, but … it was never going to be enough'.[131] The club's 'traditional' inability to show consistency is also insisted on regularly: 'Many of their fans will be wondering why their team cannot produce performances like Saturday's with increased regularity'.[132]

Rangers' traditional qualities are once again put forward: Rangers 'battled for every ball … reshuffled and closed their back'.[133] Also: 'there was nothing fancy about their work, but it was effective … The evening belonged to Rangers, who will not be concerned about the lack of football. When they had to produce more basic qualities like fighting spirit, they came through'.[134] The contrast between the Rangers and Celtic style becomes all the more obvious when they play each other:

> They [Celtic] needed to do something against Rangers but without McStay, their midfield lacked the creativity required to overcome the tenacity of Terry Hurlock and Nigel Spackman, who were operating on both sides of the promising Sandy Robertson.[135]

Over-reliance on one man (whose absence then becomes all the more disruptive) and a tradition of inventiveness are contrasted term by term to the obstinacy showed by many Rangers players who could be substituted for one another.

It is striking that in most occasions, Celtic's style is associated with an insistence on the poor results that accompany it and that, on the contrary, Rangers' ability to win is always insisted upon. This becomes all the more clear in *The Herald* dated 4 January 1993. In this article, James Traynor insists on the opposition between a Celtic team which plays well but misses a good finish (they do not score enough) and a Rangers team which 'played dreadfully' but 'have developed a habit of winning, regardless of how many of their players are having bad days'.[136] This idea is repeated and emphasised on many occasions in the article: 'Rangers can't help winning, even when they play badly, as they did on Saturday', he says and adds, just a few lines later:

> A team cannot challenge for honours without scoring goals, something Celtic have difficulty doing. There have been times this season when their football was a joy to watch, but without front-line punch, they will be remembered only as failures ... Sometimes it seems as though Celtic are more of an exhibition team, in that they look good, but lack the drive required to win prizes.

In this article, Traynor goes so far as to insist on the stereotyped image of Celtic's style as being the club's true style of play: 'That, of course, is Celtic'.[137] On the other hand, the insistence is always on Rangers' ability to win. This relative bias in favour of Rangers can easily be explained by the success they have actually achieved.[138] Criticisms of Celtic's constant failures, especially when compared with its glorious past, can sometimes be justified. Yet some other criticisms are more difficult to understand, as they are counter-factual – something some articles mistakenly acknowledge by contradicting themselves within a few lines. As in early 1994:

> Again the heart of their [Celtic's] defence was no more than a gaping hole, and even before many of the ticket holders had filed into their places, Rangers had exploited the negligence and flatness of Celtic's defence ... Until Hateley struck, Celtic had not conceded a goal at home since the arrival of Macari at the end of October.[139]

There were clearly problems in Celtic's defence during this game (which they lost by four goals to one) but it is striking that these were presented as merely one episode of a long series of failures in defence, even though the team had presented a clean sheet at home during three months, quite a remarkable feat by football standards.

Some preference for the Rangers style of play appears clearly when reading a number of articles. Celtic's style is always accompanied with negative comments, whereas Rangers' style is always evoked in a positive manner; and writers may distort the facts to make them conform to the stereotypes. In only one occasion, in *The Scotsman*, a style that presents the basic characteristics of Rangers' is clearly presented as the one favoured by the writer:

> Then against Celtic, [Rangers'] sleeves were rolled up, brows became fevered, and no-one could have mistaken this gritty domestic performance for a European-style display ... Indeed, over the 90 minutes, Celtic probably had more possession and made more passes though Rangers' return to the kind of direct style suited to the

> swingeing action of the Premier Division created more clear-cut chances ... A gifted and intelligent organiser of the midfield [Rangers'] Wilkins did not expect to embroider the play with subtlety. He was not disappointed ... It might not have been pleasing to the eye but it was the kind of leadership Rangers needed.[140]

The reference to a European-style display is anything but anodyne. Rangers' style shares many characteristics with that which is usually presented as 'indigenous' in Great Britain (and is presented as 'suited to ... the Premier division'). It might even be suggested that Rangers' style has to do with the values of hard labour and seriousness often depicted as Scottish Presbyterian values in the tradition of Knox. Celtic's style, conversely, is much closer to a style that can be described as 'continental'. It is therefore difficult not to assume that the opposition between Celtic's and Rangers' styles can be likened to an opposition between a 'foreign' team and a 'local' and 'protestant' team, reflecting the respective Irishness and Britishness of the teams. The stereotypes about styles have developed quite early (at least before the Second World War) and the very nature of stereotypes is that they endure. It is difficult therefore to tell whether they reflect a current perception of Celtic as being a 'foreign body' in Scotland. Equally, many commentators have noted progress with regard to the integration of Celtic in Scottish life after its 1967 victory in the European Champion Clubs' Cup (with a team whose style, as already noted, was 'native').

As in Bromberger's analysis, Glasgow's derby appears to be a confrontation of styles. Moreover the style of Rangers seems to represent its Scottish destiny, and the style of Celtic its destiny as immigrants (emphasising again, if needs be, that they are mostly seen as 'strangers', foreigners without the name, rather than heretics). Yet, this fact raises two comments. First, the framework adopted here did not envisage the case where commentators or writers were dealing not only with those that they perceived as 'us' (in the Scottish case: Rangers) but also with those they perceive as 'them' (in the Scottish case: Celtic). Therefore clichés on style do not only reflect the 'community of destiny' Bromberger has talked about. Their use can also reflect an exclusion from a community of destiny. The style assigned to Celtic, is largely (though not completely) externally imposed on them. It can also be likened to a 'foreign' style of play. This appears to be a means of symbolically excluding Celtic from the wider community of the Scottish nation even at a time when the presence of 'strangers' and foreigners is accepted in the Rangers' team.

Conclusion: symbols, religion, rites and celebration

The role that the press plays in the creation of a collective memory is complex. First, journalists adopt three kinds of attitudes when confronted by the issue of rivalry in the Old Firm. In both broadsheets and tabloids, news journalists willingly deal with it in the reports on sectarianism as a general issue that they publish relatively frequently (though irregularly). In the broadsheets, sports journalists tend to ignore the rivalry or try to downplay some of its aspects (e.g. the religious content). In the tabloids, journalists of the sports sections do not hesitate, not only to emphasise the rivalry, but to insist on some of its aspects (such as, for example, the political link with Ireland), at the risk of being accused of stirring real troubles.

Second, the presence or, conversely, the absence, of identity symbols in the two categories of press, the tabloids and the broadsheets, provides significant confirmation of the role played by markers of identity. An Irish (but not a Catholic) identity has been channelled into football through the colours and emblems of Celtic. Conversely, those of Rangers, which were originally devoid of religious of political significance, have become symbols of a Scottish, loyalist and Protestant identity. Furthermore, the Glaswegian case has brought to light a new category of identity symbols, which should be added to the framework of analysis. Names (those used to designate the clubs as well as those used to designate their supporters) can take on a very similar value as that carried by emblems and colours. They can indeed convey some elements of collective memory as well (this is why some names are banned in the broadsheets, which are trying to play down the divide).

Third, with regard to the idea that a team should reflect the identity of the community it is representing, it appears that quite rapidly, Rangers' fans largely accepted Catholics players. Yet, players were not really allowed to display symbols of their faith or religious identity such as crossing themselves – as it could have blurred the image of Rangers by associating them with Catholic symbols.

Fourth, the idea that the role played by the style of a team needs to be reassessed in the light of the Scottish case. The aspect of identity carried by style can be a religious identity. Also, Celtic's style is not self-defined and it has also been used to deprecate Celtic. Far from expressing a 'community of destiny' (as does Rangers' style), Celtic's style expresses its exclusion from the national community. Rangers' style seems to represent its Scottish, British and probably Protestant legacy, just as that of Celtic represents its status as immigrant. This provides salient confirmation to the reading of the Old Firm rivalry in terms of an ethnic (or political) rather than a religious opposition, and the interpretation of the Catholic identity as being externally imposed in lieu of an Irish identity.

Nevertheless, some of Bromberger's insights on football and religion[141] find a striking confirmation in the Glaswegian case. The idea that there is some 'consecration of the places associated with football'[142] is confirmed in the case of both clubs' stadia.[143] Celtic's Park's colloquial name is 'Paradise'. In Ibrox, the consecration may be less obvious, but it is certainly not less true. Ibrox has become a 'gigantic altar':[144] a statue commemorates all the people that died in the three disasters that struck Rangers throughout its history.[145] Furthermore, fans can now buy bricks stamped with their names, which are affixed to walls dedicated to past Rangers' players and which look like the walls of a sailor's chapel covered with *ex-votos* (though dedicated to persons alive).

The idea that there are some: 'temporal and cyclical affinities…' with religious time can be given emphasis in the Glaswegian derby. In most leagues throughout the world, teams meet twice, for a home and an away game; Rangers and Celtic meet twice as often. Moreover, their four encounters follow the cycle of the seasons. Between 1894 and 1996, the winter Old Firm was played, originally on 1 January, and later on the closest Saturday or Wednesday of the New Year. Furthermore, the idea that the football game marks a break in the ordinary flow of time finds further confirmation in the Old Firm. The time of the Old Firm marks a rupture with the real time of football. All the Scottish newspapers always insist on the peculiarity of the Old Firm encounters. The Old Firm encounters therefore appear as a competition of their own where the first appearance of a player is compared to an 'initiation test'.[146]

Yet, the comparison with religion must be made cautiously. For all the insistence on the religious nature of the Old Firm opposition (very often merely described as an opposition between Protestants and Catholics) very few emblems in the stadia have a religious meaning.[147] In his descriptions of the game, Murray makes only one reference to 'chants of an uncomplimentary nature about the Pope'[148] (where religion is once again mentioned to discredit the opponents rather than being brandished by Celtic supporters) and fails to describe any evidence of the celebration of anything religious (a transcendence).

Those insights even relate to a more wide-ranging debate, which cannot be resolved here: the nature of the religious aspect of identity in the west of Scotland, especially if compared with Durkheim's insights on religion: 'In religious worship, society adores its own camouflaged image'.[149] Religion in the case of Celtic and Rangers may very well appear as the means to camouflage the image of the group that is celebrating itself, a camouflage that, obviously, falls apart in most occasions.

New light can therefore be shed on the main disagreement between Joseph Bradley,[150] who thinks that there is sectarianism (and especially anti-Catholicism) in Scottish society as a whole, which football only reflects, and Callum G. Brown,[151] to whom, in reverse, sectarianism has largely disappeared from Scotland and remains important in football only – a position which finds some echoes in Laurence MacIntyre's description of Rangers' and Celtic's supporters as 'ninety-minute bigots'. Both positions indeed start with the, understated, assumption, that the rivalry in the stadium is very much based on religion, even though Bradley tries to correlate religious attachment and political opinions. Bromberger's insights correlated with Durkheim's may tend to indicate that religion is not the basis of the rivalry, but just another medium through which identity is channelled.

Notes

1 On 20 August 2010, the Scottish League was ranked 16th by UEFA, after Spain, England, Italy, France, Germany, Portugal, Romania, the Netherlands and Russia (source: www.xs4all.nl/~kassiesa/bert/uefa/data/method4/crank2010.html).

2 Valuations of football clubs according to Forbes (at: www.forbes.com/lists/2009/34/soccer-values-09_Soccer-Team-Valuations_Rank.html). On 20 August 2010, Rangers was ranked 31 in Europe by UEFA, and Celtic 53 (source: www.xs4all.nl/~kassiesa/bert/uefa/data/method4/trank2010.html).

3 Reported in both *The Herald* and *The Scotsman*, 11 July 1989.

4 Bill Murray. *The Old Firm in the new age: Celtic and Rangers since the Souness revolution*. Edinburgh: Mainstream, 1998, p. 45 (hereafter Murray 1998).

5 The narrative of the Old Firm's history in this introduction is mostly derived from: Murray 1984; Bill Murray. *Glasgow's Giants. 100 years of the Old Firm*. Edinburgh: Mainstream, 1988 (hereafter Murray 1988); Joseph M. Bradley, *Ethnic and religious identity in modern Scotland: culture, politics and football*. Aldershot: Avebury, 1995 (hereafter Bradley 1995); Tom Campbell and Pat Woods, *Dreams and songs to sing: a new history of Celtic*. Edinburgh: Mainstream, 1996 (hereafter Campbell and Woods 1996); Stephen Halliday, *Rangers: the official illustrated history*. London: Arthur Barker, 1989 (hereafter Halliday 1989).

6 This position is well illustrated in Bradley 1995; Murray 1984: 84–86.
7 Murray 1998: 33.
8 Campbell and Woods 1996: 10–14.
9 According to the club's short history published on its website (at: www.celticfc.net/ifyouknow/history.htm).
10 Bradley 1995: 35.
11 Murray 1984: 70.
12 G. P. T. Finn, 'Racism, religion and social prejudice. Irish Catholic clubs, soccer and Scottish identity I: the roots of prejudice', *International journal of the history of sport*, 8(1) (1991); G. P. T. Finn, 'Racism, religion and social prejudice. Irish Catholic clubs, soccer and Scottish identity II: social identity and conspiracy theories', *International journal of the history of sport*, 8(3) (1991).
13 Campbell and Woods 1996: 12.
14 Campbell and Woods 1996: ch. 1.
15 Ferrier and McElroy 1996: 27.
16 Murray 1988: 135.
17 Cartoon reproduced from the *Scottish referee*, 15 April 1904 in Murray 1984: 11.
18 Murray 1984: 63.
19 Although *The Scotsman* published a list of Catholic players Rangers had signed either by mistake or for its second team on 11 July 1989. It was probably derived from Murray 1988: 123–124.
20 Murray 1984: 86.
21 Murray 1984: 126.
22 Campbell and Woods 1996: 127.
23 The first three chapters of Gerard McNee deal with Celtic's success in Lisbon ten years earlier; *The story of Celtic: an official history, 1888–1978*. London: Paul, 1978 (hereafter, McNee 1978).
24 Murray 1984: 218.
25 Murray 1984: 223.
26 Cover reproduced in Murray 1984: 238.
27 Murray 1984: 223 and 227.
28 As did Ralph Brand in the *News of the World*, 26 September 1965, 3, 10, 17, 24 and 31 October 1965 (as reported in Murray 1984: 213).
29 Bradley 1995: 39.
30 Murray 1998: 189.
31 Murray 1984.
32 H. F. Moorhouse, 'On the periphery: Scotland, Scottish football and the new Europe', in Williams and Wagg, *British football and social change*, pp. 201–219 (hereafter Moorhouse 1991).
33 Raymond Boyle, '"We are Celtic supporters…": questions of football and identity in modern Scotland', in Richard Giulianotti and John Williams (eds), *Game without frontiers: football, identity and modernity*, pp. 73–101: 82. Aldershot: Arena, 1994.
34 Richard Giulianotti and Michael Gerrard, 'Cruel Britannia? Glasgow

Rangers, Scotland and "hot" football rivalries', in Gary Armstrong and Richard Giulianotti (eds), *Fear and loathing in world football*, pp. 23–42. Oxford: Berg, 2001 (hereafter Giulianotti and Gerrard 2001).

35 Brian Wilson, 'Ready to rival Rangers again; Celtic are under new management', *The Independent*, 7 March 1994.

36 Celtic's press media release 12 September 1995.

37 For example in a publication from the club around 2000–2001 (no ISSN or ISBN), whose cover reads: 'Celtic – Social Charter; Celtic – Charity Fund'.

38 Bradley 1995: 189.

39 Murray 1984: 99.

40 Callum G. Brown, *The social history of religion in Scotland since 1730*. London: Methuen, 1987, p. 244 (hereafter Brown 1987).

41 Bradley 1995: 1 quotes (and misquotes) Callum G. Brown.

42 Murray 1984.

43 In interviews with the author that were conducted on 12 June 2001 at Ibrox.

44 According to Darryl Broadfoot in an interview with the author on 14 June 2001.

45 According to Murray 1984.

46 The *News of the World*, 26 September 1965, 3, 10, 17, 24 and 31 October 1965 (as reported in Murray 1984: 213).

47 Other examples of articles on sectarianism can be found in the *Daily Mail*, 19 May 1991 and in *The Herald*, 15 May 1992. See also for a small selection: Kirsty Scott and William Clark, 'Demands for new Monklands inquiry', *The Herald*, 5 March 1993. On the same very high-profile scandal tainted with sectarianism, see Joy Copley, 'Smith scornfully silent over new Monklands attack', *The Scotsman*, 25 January 1994. Denis Campbell, 'Monklands upstarts scent victory in an uncivil war', *Scotland on Sunday*, 6 March 1994. Other articles include for instance: Denis Campbell, 'Another silly season of orange and green', *Scotland on Sunday*, 28 May 1995. 'I've nothing against Catholics', *The Herald*, 30 November 1996. Meg Henderson, 'Born into a black and white world of orange and green', *The Scotsman*, 10 October 1997.

48 As in *The Times*, 16 December 1989.

49 E.g. see two articles on the same event: 'Soap girl fired for scribbling no surrender: soap factory worker June Reilly was sacked after doodling sectarian slogans on a production line worksheet' (*Daily Record*, 19 March 1998). Fiona Davidson, 'Woman was sacked over sectarian scribbles', *The Scotsman*, 19 March 1998.

50 A rare example is Gerry McSherry, 'Act that sows the seeds of bigotry', *The Herald*, 9 May 1995. Even though the subject is rarely treated, there was a great number of articles following proposals to reform the school system in 1998, including: Tom Little, 'Peer calls for end to state cash for Catholic schools', *The Scotsman*, 4 February 1998. Peter Lynch, 'Church's mission to explain separate schools', *The Herald*, 16 February

1998. Michael Fry, 'It's for their own good', *The Herald*, 18 February 1998. 'Lib-dems in school bigots blast', *Sunday Mail*, 29 March 1998.

51 Moorhouse 1991: 205.

52 See for example the reports in *The Glasgow Herald*, 5 August 1989. 'Attack on racism at football', *The Herald*, 1 July 1992. For a slightly different angle, see: Jack McLean, 'Old Firm game with a difference: No hatred and no bigotry', *The Herald*, 22 March 1993. Bill Leckie, 'Attitude – tackling sports big issues; the time is right for Gers to boot bigots', *Daily Record*, 16 December 1996.

53 Examples of this can be found in *The Herald*, 1 July 1992 and *The Mail*, 15 May 1992.

54 Mentioned in most newspapers (20 May 1990), it raised protests in letters from the readers that were published in the *Daily Record* (21–26 May 1990).

55 See James Traynor's article in *The Herald*, 12 October 1992.

56 Joseph M. Bradley, 'The patriot game: football's famous "Tartan Army"', *International review for the sociology of sport*, 37(2) (2002), 177–197. Richard Giulianotti, 'Scoring away from home: a statistical study of Scotland football fans at international matches in Romania and Sweden', *International review for the sociology of sport*, 29(2) (1994), 172–200. Richard Giulianotti, 'Football and the politics of carnival: an ethnographic study of Scottish fans in Sweden', *International review for the sociology of sport*, 30(2) (1995), 191–223.

57 Rangers finished third, following Champions' League Winner Olympique de Marseille (from France) and Italian Giants AC Milan.

58 See James Traynor's article in *The Herald*, 22 August 1994.

59 A very rare instance can be found in Kevin McCarra, 'Brown's passion pierces Hearts', *Scotland on Sunday*,13 March 1994.

60 In an interview with the author at Ibrox Stadium on 12 June 2001.

61 European Champions Cup (C1), called Champions League after 1992; European Cup Winners' Cup until 1999 (C2); UEFA Cup (C3).

62 Database search made thanks to Lexis-Nexis (web.lexis-nexis.co.uk/professional; 21 April 2007).

63 This actually happens to be the Sunday edition of the *Daily Record*.

64 In an interview with the author conducted on the premises of *The Herald* in Glasgow on 14 June 2001.

65 Using Lexis-Nexis (web.lexis-nexis.co.uk/professional; 20 April 2007).

66 As noted by Carol Patton in an interview with the author.

67 Analyses of the same newspapers in the weeks preceding the Old Firm games on 14 November 1996, 1 September 1997 and 12 April 1998 show similar results.

68 The *Mail*, 22 April; the *Daily Mirror*, 23, 27, 28 April; *The Mail*, 29 April; the *Daily Mirror*, 30 April and 1 May.

69 On the occasion of Maurice Johnston's signing (*The Herald and The Scotsman*, 11 July 1989), troubles that followed the Old Firm game on the 1 January 1994 (*The Herald and The Scotsman*, 3 January 1994), and a fire

attack which happened at Graeme Souness's home near Edinburgh, then occupied by Maurice Johnston (*The Scotsman*, 15 October 1989).

70 The *Daily Record*, 27 April 2001.

71 The *Daily Record*, 28 April 2001.

72 Scottish edition of *The Sun*, 8 February 2001.

73 Articles between 1 and 10 February abound, but summaries can be found in: 'Why Scotland turned its back on its sectarian past', *The Scotsman*, 10 February 2001. Jack McLean, 'The shame that football brings on our nation', *The Herald*, 10 February 2001. Dave King, 'Reid backs Labour MP over Ahern call-off', *Daily Record*, 10 February 2001.

74 On the occasion of a World Cup qualifier against Bulgaria on 28 February 2001. See: Keith Jackson, 'Lennon: I'll beat the bigots; Celtic star refuses to bow to Ulster death threats', *Daily Record*, 28 February 2001. Mike Wade, 'Lennon defies hate campaign', *The Scotsman*, 28 February 2001. Keith Sinclair, '£6m Celtic star appalled by sectarian threats', *The Herald*, 28 February 2001.

75 'Neil hopes for a good reception', *Daily Record*, 16 February 2001. *The Scotsman* ignored the question before the game and *The Herald* devoted it very little space in an article which insisted on Lennon's hope for a good reception: 'Lennon's' home wish', *The Herald*, 16 February 2001. A long article on Lennon the next day does not even mention the fact: Ian Paul, 'Lennon is set for yet another nerve test', *The Herald*, 17 February 2001.

76 Held on *The Herald* premises in Glasgow, 14 June 2001.

77 Alan Lang, 'Ibrox lands double-coup with Johnson', *The Herald*, 11 July 1989.

78 Article from the front page, by Alan Dron and Graeme Steward in *The Scotsman*, 11 July 1989.

79 *The Independent*, 11 July 1989.

80 Exaggeration denounced in Moorhouse 1991: 209.

81 'Britain this week', *The Economist*, 15 July 1989.

82 Game played at Ibrox on 4 November 1989.

83 Mike Aitken, 'Souness gamble on Johnston pays off', *The Scotsman*, 5 November 1989.

84 As reported in the last chapter of Stephen Walsh. *Voices of the Old Firm*. Edinburgh: Mainstream, 1995 (hereafter Walsh 1995).

85 Bromberger 1995.

86 James Traynor, 'Celtic's back-line is found to have a weak heart', *The Herald*, 3 January 1994. Duncan Black, 'Celtic fans fear action replay of violence', *The Herald*, 3 January 1994.

87 Hugh Keevins, 'Celtic count the cost of sorry start to new year', *The Scotsman*, 3 January 1994. Hugh Keevins, 'Champions make fast work of sluggish Celtic', *The Scotsman*, 3 January 1994. Hugh Keevins, 'Dignity, and direction, lost in poisoned Paradise', *The Scotsman*, 3 January 1994.

88 Campbell and Woods 1996: 127–128.

89 Murray 1984: conclusion.

90 *The Glasgow Herald*, 6 May 1990.

91 In a publication from the club circa 2000–2001 (no ISSN or ISBN), whose cover reads: 'Celtic – Celtic's Social Charter – Bhoys Against Bigotry – Information Pack'. Fourth page (not numbered).

92 Melanie Reid, 'The man taking the blue out of Rangers', *The Herald*, 1 August 2001. Lesley Roberts, 'The model professionals; Mols and Amo put on the Euro style', *Sunday Mail*, 5 August 2001. Also some fans have apparently asked for condoms in Rangers' blue at the club store: 'Truly blue fans', *Daily Record*, 12 June 2001.

93 Murray 1984: 75.

94 Murray 1984: 230.

95 'A collection of fans' testimonies', Walsh 1995.

96 A good summary, still relatively close to the event can be found in: Ron MacKenna, 'Terrible end to brief encounter', *The Herald*, 15 March 1996.

97 A selection of articles stating that Mark Scott was killed for wearing the wrong jersey includes: 'The Maze and the minister's duty', *The Scotsman*, 8 October 1997. Meg Henderson, 'Born into a black and white world of orange and green', *The Scotsman*, 10 October 1997. Hugh MacDonald, 'Evolution rather than revolution', *The Herald*, 22 May 1999. Magnus Gardham, 'Student Cara battles bigotry in memory of murdered Mark', *Sunday Mail*, 20 February 2000.

98 The 'colours' of Celtic are mentioned in *The Herald*, 3 January 1991; Hampden is described as a Blue Heaven in *The Herald*, 1 April 1991; Rangers as the players 'in blue' in James Traynor, 'Simon says it all when playing the game', *The Herald*, 2 May 1994.

99 A small selection for the first half of 2000 includes: Iain Campbell, 'Slip-ups to give a hoop the hump', *Daily Record*, 6 March 2000. John Docherty, 'Jumping through hoops', *Daily Record*, 10 April 2000. Keith Jackson, 'Bhoyz in the hoops to lose their leader', *Daily Record*, 8 May 2000. Mark Guidi, 'Football: hoops fans won't be a pain to Danes', *Sunday Mail*, 14 May 2000. Mark Guidi, 'Mark's so hoop-set to leave fave fans', *Sunday Mail*, 21 May 2000. 'Football: no hoop of Izzett signing', *Daily Record*, 31 May 2000.

100 In an interview with the author in Glasgow, 14 June 2001.

101 For instance in Ken Gallacher, 'Penalty makes it a foregone conclusion', *The Herald*, 8 November 1999.

102 See for an example: Tom Lappin, 'Manager too late to repair shoogly peg', *The Scotsman*, 10 February 2000.

103 A few examples include: Garry Owen, 'Wonder horse or talking horse… Savill's in no doubt', *Daily Record*, 23 December 1994. Gerry McNee, 'Gerry McNee, the man who never shirks a tackle', *Sunday Mail*, 15 January 1995. Keith Jackson, 'Only Celtic can stop us lifting the Cup', *Daily Record*, 1 November 1995. Iain King, 'Celts close in on £1m McGinlay', *Sunday Mail*, 12 November 1995. Keith Jackson, 'Celts have just saved £3m by holding onto Tom Boyd', *Daily Record*, 2 July 1996. 'Paradise bride for Mike', *Sunday Mail*, 12 November 1995. Tony Roper, 'Jamesie in fury over Paradise!', *Sunday Mail*, 24 August 1997.

104 See for example *The Herald*, 22 March 1993.
105 A database search gives 586 mentions of the word Bhoy (singular or plural) in the *Daily Record* between 1995 and 1998. During the same period there were barely 25 references to same word in *The Scotsman*, apart from those used to refer to Celtic's campaign 'Bhoys against bigotry' (using Lexis-Nexis: web.lexis-nexis.com/professional; 20 April 2007).
106 Bradley 1995: 41. Bill Murray adds that it must be sung to the tune of 'Marching through Georgia', Murray 1984: 145.
107 In the Gregorian calendar – the date in the Julian calendar (in use at the time) is 1 July 1690.
108 Murray 1984: 145.
109 Giulianotti and Gerrard 2001: 27–30.
110 Gordon Parks, 'UEFA ban Billy Boys; Gers told to warn fans at all games', *Daily Record*, 10 June 2006. Tellingly, *The Scotsman* and *The Herald* is silent on the subject.
111 Between 1995 and 1998, there are thirty-seven uses in the press of the word in connection with Celtic, all of which denounce its use.
112 Murray 1984: 146.
113 Anderson 1991. Further and very detailed historical evidence on related concepts has been provided in Pierre Nora (ed.), *Les lieux de mémoires*, 3 vols. Paris: Gallimard, 1982–1986. R. Girardet, *Mythes et Mythologies politiques*. Paris: Seuil, 1986.
114 *Daily Record*, 7 February 1996.
115 'Cross about such religious intolerance', *The Herald*, 12 February 1996. A former player from OM, and one of the best defenders in the world at the time.
116 Cameron Simpson, 'Sectarian barriers continue to fall at Ibrox; top post for whisky chief', *The Herald*, 17 March 1998.
117 Jim Kean, 'Rangers ease into gear', *The Scotsman*, 28 September 1998.
118 Bromberger 1995: 156.
119 Bromberger 1995: 165.
120 Alan Pattullo, 'Le Guen admits defeat after 198 days', *The Scotsman*, 5 January 2007.
121 As is obvious from the letters to the editor in *The Herald*, 8 January 2007.
122 Murray 1984: 194.
123 Murray 1984: 195.
124 Murray 1984: 195.
125 Murray 1984: 194.
126 Percy M. Young, *A history of British football*. London: Arrow, 1973, p. 190.
127 Gordon Williams. *From scenes like these*. London: Allison and Busby, 1980, p. 42.
128 See, for one example: Ferrier and McElroy 1996.
129 Anecdotes from Willie Henderson, *Forward with Rangers*. London: St Paul, 1966.
130 *The Herald*, 6 November 1989.

131 *The Herald*, 29 October 1990.
132 James Traynor, 'Hesitant Rangers punished by Collins and Payton', *The Herald*, 22 March 1993.
133 The Scotsman, 1 April 1991.
134 *The Herald*, 1 April 1991.
135 *The Herald*, 26 November 1990.
136 James Traynor, 'Celtic's forwards again fail to supply winning punch: lucky Rangers – but Smith must be worried', *The Herald*, 4 January 1993 (hereafter Traynor 1993a).
137 Traynor 1993a.
138 This is Daryl Broadfoot's opinion (n. 44).
139 James Traynor, 'Celtic's back-line is found to have a weak heart', *The Herald*, 4 January 1993.
140 *The Scotsman*, 28 August 1989.
141 Bromberger 1995: part 5, 'Le match: une sorte de rituel religieux?'.
142 Bromberger 1995: 321.
143 Bale 1993.
144 Bromberger 1995: 320 uses this expression to describe Anfield after the Hillsborough disaster.
145 Tragedy described in Murray 1984: 223.
146 *The Scotsman*, 28 August 1989.
147 Murray 1984: 59.
148 Murray 1984: 59.
149 Ernest Gellner, *Nations and nationalism*, pp. 55–62. Oxford: Blackwell, 1983.
150 Bradley 1995.
151 Brown 1987.

4

Paris Saint-Germain*

Introduction

Compared to the fervour that is common in England and Scotland, the support that French clubs receive may give the impression of being subdued. For Alfred Wahl, this comparative lack of backing originates in different sociability uses (centred around the café, rather than the stadium) and the extended offer of leisure activities after 1945.[1] All the attention on the lower attendance figures should not conceal the real trend since the beginning of the 1970s of a long-term increase in the number of spectators attending football games, and which can be attributed to increasingly good results of a few clubs (Saint-Étienne in the 1970s, Marseille in the early 1990s) and a renewed interest in the national team (after victories in the 1984 European Championship, the 1998 World Cup, the 2000 European Championship).[2]

The Paris Saint-Germain Football Club (PSG)[3] exemplifies the need for French clubs to build up an audience and the subsequent ability of some to do so. Founded in 1970–73, PSG is a relatively new club. In the 1970s, other clubs throughout the rest of Europe could already boast a history full of memorable successes, written by legendary players in order to attract new followers. However, PSG had to start afresh and attract a Parisian audience deprived of much football competition in the highest division since the demise of the Racing Club de Paris in 1964.[4] Also, as Patrick Mignon pointed out: 'Paris pushes to the extreme the distance that characterises the French

* Elements of this chapter have already been presented in: David Ranc, 'Le Paris Saint Germain dans la presse quotidienne française: une relation tripartite ambiguë', in Evelyne Combeau-Mari (ed.), *Sport et presse écrite en France au XXe siècle*. Paris: Le Publieur (Bibliothèque Universitaire Francophone), 2007; David Ranc, 'Local politics, identity and football in Paris', *Modern and Contemporary France*, February, 2008.

passion for football'.[5] For years, PSG indeed struggled to catch the attention of a significant audience. They played in a gigantic but often rather empty stadium during much of the 1970s and 1980s, when the average attendance oscillated between 16,960 in 1971–72 and 24,740 in 1983–84.

In the 2005–6 season, the club was able to attract a regular audience of 40,486, the second largest in France (after Marseille) and a sizeable one even by European standards. PSG have also succeeded in establishing itself as one of the major clubs in French and European football.[6] In 2003, PSG was unquestionably the best-known French club in France, with a rate of 80 per cent spontaneous recognition.[7] Its staggering run of success at European level (five semi-finals of European cups in five years between 1993 and 1997, and two consecutive European Cup finals, including a victory in 1996)[8] has secured it massive recognition throughout Europe, and justified its inclusion in the now defunct G14, a lobby group for the major European clubs. Because of its relative newness, and its rather rapid success in a hostile environment, PSG provides an interesting case study for the significance of football partisanship and the processes of identification for football supporters. How did PSG manage to attract such numbers of football supporters in a country where attendance at football games was, at best, mediocre? Consequently, how do these supporters relate to their club and through which means do they identify with it? In recent years, what has been the evolution of the supporters' relations with their club? Did the *Bosman* ruling and the subsequent change in rules regarding foreign players affect their relationship with their club?

Building up partisanship

Founding a major club in a hostile context

The very history of the club until the *Bosman* ruling is of particular relevance to this study. It can be analysed as an attempt to build a club with an identity and an audience that identifies with it.[9] As revealed by Paul Dietschy, the very foundation of PSG in 1970 can be best explained in terms of an (eventually successful) gamble: to build 'a major football club' in Paris, in a time of crisis (for both clubs and the national team).[10] The crisis was compounded for Parisian football clubs: apart from the suburban Red Star, they were absent from the elite in 1970. According to Dietschy, Parisian clubs were not able to meet the two challenges that they faced: a certain lack of sporting culture (sport was not a major leisure activity in France then); and the expectations of the Parisian audience made up of spectators (rather than supporters) which considered the game to be a show and could therefore become hostile to the home team, if it played badly.

The foundation of PSG happened in two stages. In February 1969, the Fédération Française de Football (FFF)[11] polled the Parisians: 'Do you want a major club in Paris?'. There were 66,000 people who answered favourably. It was decided that the club assets would be provided by a large number of associates holding shares: the fans themselves would own the club. A subscription was subsequently launched on 1 February 1970.[12] In order to get a place in a professional division, this virtual Parisian club merged with the Stade Saint-Germain, a club in the west Parisian suburb of Saint-Germain en Laye. The Paris Saint-Germain Football Club was born on 20 May 1970.[13]

The foundation of the club relied on a double appeal to the masses. After 1972, and a split with the professional team, which became known as Paris FC, shareholders would no longer run the club.[14] Still, from the very beginning, the history of PSG has been an attempt to build a club with supporters. It is therefore possible to follow Mignon's argument that studying PSG is about 'analysing a community of supporters and the invention of a tradition that would link the simultaneous construction of a club, an audience, a local identity'.[15] The successive management teams and shareholders of PSG therefore made a clear and deliberate long-term effort to attract supporters and to build an audience for the club.

The club's early strategy to gather support

Daniel Hechter was the first PSG President to develop a clear strategy in order to gather support. He created a very dynamic official supporters' club, Les Amis du PSG, on 22 January 1975.[16] Les Amis had headquarters and a shop in the heart of Paris. They also launched an operation to attract young supporters, which numbered 3,000 by 1977. Other operations included the organisation of a monthly supporters' party night from 26 January 1977 where members of PSG staff and management used to show up.[17] Despite a change of president, Les Amis du PSG and the club's management continued their ground-breaking efforts to attract supporters, bringing in loyalty programmes in 1980,[18] discounted away trips (in 1982),[19] free games (e.g. the April 1986 game that eventually enabled PSG to secure its first league title ever),[20] or selling tickets through a supermarket chain (Carrefour), which organised free bus trips to the Parc des Princes from its car park.[21] PSG, whose administration board included among others Bernard Brochand, a major publicity guru, were also innovative in its use of advertisements to promote the club.[22]

Colonising a hostile stadium

Les Amis du PSG were also conspicuously successful in organising a stand exclusively dedicated to PSG supporters. It was originally located in stand K, and called 'Kop K' as an homage to Anfield's supporter stand, which is called the 'Kop'. In 1978, it moved to the less-expensive end of the stadium called Boulogne, giving birth to the Kop of Boulogne (aka KoB).[23] Yet, in the 1970s and 1980s PSG were still often playing at home in a stadium where supporters of the opposing team (typically provincials who had moved to Paris) were more numerous.[24] PSG supporters invented slogans such as *'Public de merde'* ('shit audience') and *'Le Parc aux Parisiens'* ('The Park for the Parisians'). These reflected two rather different tendencies: PSG supporters' hostility towards supporters of the visiting team; their will to make the whole of the stadium theirs.

Managing the autonomy of supporters

Les Amis du PSG slowly lost its grip on supporters. In the middle of the 1970s, most of the PSG supporters were members of Les Amis du PSG.[25] By the beginning of the 1980s, most of them had left and Les Amis du PSG had lost its grip on Boulogne.[26] Some of these supporters remained independent, others organised themselves. The first autonomous supporters' group, the Boulogne Boys was founded in 1985,[27] soon followed by other autonomous supporters' group in Boulogne.[28] The intensity of the support given by supporters certainly increased with independence from Les Amis du PSG. The inspiration of the independent supporters was English: their form of support has remained fairly unorganised. Between 1985 and 1991, the Boulogne Boys introduced the highly organised Italian model of Ultra groups. The 'Boys' started to display banners, invent and sing songs following a *'capo'* (the leader of the group who directs the supporters of the group and initiates the movements and the songs). They also started to burn smoke bombs (for the first time in France), and to organise proper *'tifos'*, visual animations organised by supporters to celebrate the entry of their team on the field. These *'tifos'* were based on Italian models they had seen during European competitions. This new activity soon impressed the team and players.[29] At the same time, the club also had to discuss and negotiate with these supporters that it no longer controlled and which started to confront PSG's direction between the end of the 1980s and the beginning of the 1990s (going on strike for example in April 1991).[30]

The club management was also forced to take into account the violence generated by some of the supporters. At the beginning of the 1970s violent incidents surrounding football games developed in France, and at PSG games.[31] A new phenomenon appeared in Paris: once independent from the club, some supporters entered a 'pre-hooligan' phase. Throughout the 1980s, small-scale violent incidents following PSG games became the norm rather than the exception.[32] They triggered a number of appeals from various club officials for such troubles to stop.[33] This violence among PSG supporters became the subject of great media attention. Boulogne developed an image of a stand of independent and rather violent supporters. The media chose to focus on the presence of skinheads,[34] though according to Thierry Berthou, their number remained small, and they were driven out of the standby genuine fans towards the end of the 1980s.[35] This discrepancy between the image of the fans in the media, and the image they have of themselves, became an important issue for supporters at this point. Violent, xenophobic, racist and anti-Semitic incidents also became an intermittent feature of PSG home games and arguably led to the death of a PSG supporter in 2006.[36]

Various remedies have been sought but, as of 2010, have proved largely ineffective. At the beginning of the 1990s, the police de facto turned Boulogne into a purely 'white' stand to prevent racist acts, but this further antagonised the media.[37] Canal+, PSG's owner after 1991 turned Auteuil, the opposite end to Boulogne in the Parc des Princes, where visiting fans traditionally sat into another stand for the ever-growing number of dedicated supporters, especially the non-whites excluded from Boulogne. In 1993, Canal+ recruited two supporters and created a 'supporters' department' to foster links and control supporters.[38] However, a number of Ultra associations developed in Auteuil (the Supras and the Lutèce Falco in 1991, the Tigris Mystics and Dragons in 1992), and became no less virulent against the club than Boulogne's associations. Violent clashes between supporters of Auteuil and Boulogne have also become a recurrent feature surrounding PSG games and led to the death of a supporter in 2010.[39] Following these tragic events, the French Ministre de l'Intérieur disbanded a number of PSG supporters' groups, and PSG's management adopted a series of radical measures, including the end of season tickets in both Auteuil and Boulogne (these may be reintroduced later). The cumulative effect of these measures is impossible to gauge at the time of writing and this case study will be almost exclusively concerned with the years 1995–2006, to provide a timeframe comparable to those of the other two case studies.

As of 1995, when the *Bosman* ruling changed the rules on nationality quota in the Union, and this study started, the success of PSG in nurturing support was unquestionable. Nevertheless, the general trend has been a growing autonomy of the most dedicated supporters – accompanied by some phenomena of violence, which created a discrepancy between the supporters' image of themselves and their portrayal in the media.

National press, local press and Paris Saint-Germain

The contribution of the press to partisan identification has to be assessed with regard to both how PSG officials have used the press in their relations with supporters, and how supporters have reacted to their portrayal in the press. Study shows that the coverage that PSG receives in the French press, and most conspicuously in *Le Parisien* and *L'Équipe*, actually exhibits two striking tendencies. These have been best summarised by Philippe Séguin as *'le double parti pris de la sur-couverture et du dénigrement systématique'* ('the double choice of over-coverage and systematic disparagement').

Over-coverage

The most striking feature for anyone reading the press in relation to PSG is the enormous amount of coverage that it gets. No single day can pass without a mention of PSG in one or more newspapers, even when the club is not taking part in a competition. This is all the more apparent if one focuses on *L'Équipe* and *Le Parisien* but is nonetheless true of other papers. As it is a regional newspaper, it may be expected that *Le Parisien*'s main concern with sports is with the premier professional club in the region. In a normal edition, half the sports pages is typically dedicated to the club. Until 2004, there was barely a day that *Le Parisien* failed to publish a column called '*PSG Express*' which goes over the latest news about PSG (injuries, next game, etc.), even to state that there was no news to report.[40]

The newspaper has more significantly taken on a habit of always putting PSG first in sports news, dedicating it more coverage than events of generally perceived more importance (e.g., even, at times, the Olympic Games).[41] *Le Parisien* also gives a PSG twist to every other news on football, especially news of the French team. For example, between Friday 10 and Friday 17 November 1995, the headlines of just about every article on the forthcoming France–Israel game featured a PSG player, or an Israeli player with a tenuous link to the current PSG manager. Additionally, all the PSG players in the French team were named with reference to their belonging to PSG (e.g. *'le milieu de terrain du Paris Saint-Germain'*), whereas other players were referred to as players of the National Team (e.g. *'l'attaquant de l'Équipe de France'*).

The only Parisian newspaper which routinely puts sports on its front page, *Le Parisien*, dedicated roughly two-thirds of all its sports covers to PSG between 1995 and 2006.[42] It is not unusual for PSG to be on the cover of *Le Parisien* several days in a row, as a main or secondary headline.[43] Consequently the first few pages of the newspaper, usually on the *'Fait du jour'* ('today's main news') are often replaced by a *'Spécial PSG'*,[44] if the news about the club (good or bad) is deemed the most important item on that day. All these devices contribute to the impression (as summed up by a journalist in *Le Point*) that the readers of *Le Parisien* only hear about PSG.[45] No other major French generalist newspaper dedicates so much space to just one team to the detriment of every other. Teams from the lower divisions are only mentioned in articles within pull-outs on local issues which vary depending on the edition of the newspaper (in Paris, *Le Journal de Paris*). In contrast, *Ouest France* (France's bestselling newspaper) dedicates equal coverage to the two to three first-flight teams in the area where it is mostly read.

The case of *Le Parisien* is certainly extreme and the same bias clearly affects other newspapers less. Still, it no doubt exists there too. *L'Équipe*, for example, has a tendency to dedicate headlines and front pages more readily to PSG than any other team, apart perhaps from Olympique de Marseille (OM). Two particularly telling examples can be taken close to both ends of the period studied. In March 1995 PSG was referred to at least thirteen times on the cover of the newspaper, every other day and more than any other team. In the week beginning 18 October 2004, low-ranked PSG was on the cover of the newspapers three times.[46] At exactly the same time, the league leaders, and three times reigning champion Lyon only figured twice. In other newspapers, the attention received by PSG seems huge and disproportionate too: it bears little relation to its actual results or the attention received by other clubs. This impression is vindicated by a keyword search through the archive databases of the three main national newspapers for the year 2000. *Le Figaro, Libération* and *Le Monde,* included respectively 273, 238 and 139 articles featuring the acronym PSG and 246, 198 and 158 featuring OM. They included only 37, 22, and 80 articles for Girondins de Bordeaux: 9, 7 and 6 for ASSE (Association Sportive de Saint-Étienne), 10, 1 and 9 for FCNA (Football Club de Nantes-Atlantique).

What can explain the disproportionate attention that PSG receives? Three main arguments are put forward: sales (the covers of *L'Équipe* on PSG and OM sell best);[47] budget (PSG had the largest budget of the league for most of the 1990s); and the presence of all the national media in Paris, which makes following PSG comparatively easy. As with Rangers and Celtic, PSG is given disproportionate attention in the media. The trend is strengthened by the existence of a regional newspaper, *Le Parisien*, a newspaper wholly dedicated to sport (*L'Équipe*) and by the presence of PSG in the very town where all national papers are published. Yet, there is at least one major difference: this disproportionate attention seems to be coupled with a bias against PSG, that Philippe Séguin termed systematic disparagement.

Systematic disparagement

The three journalists interviewed all disagreed that they, or their newspaper, show any bias against PSG. They have insisted in their own words that their coverage only reflects the club's results, good or bad. It is true that the press certainly reports positively on the PSG when its results are unquestionably good. For example, PSG's success in the 1996 Cup Winners' Cup certainly warranted a number of constructive reports in all sections of the press (all the more so, evidently, in *Le Parisien* and *L'Équipe*). The journalists therefore claim that any perception that PSG get a bad press, is due to PSG's own tendency to be in crisis more often than other clubs. Skimming through the newspapers, it is, indeed, easy to believe that the history of PSG is littered with *'affaires'* ('scandals') and that the club is perpetually in *'crise'* ('crisis'). Yet, partiality has been pointed out not only by Philippe Séguin, but also in a history of the club,[48] or by managers and players. PSG, coach Vahid Halilhodzic said in an interview with *Le Monde*:

> C'est bizarre, ce jacobinisme footballistique dans les médias : tout ce qui vient du Paris Saint-Germain n'est pas bon, même quand il n'y a pas de conflit.
>
> (This football Jacobinism in the media is weird: everything that comes from Paris Saint-Germain is no good, even when there is no conflict.)[49]

A close study of the *'affaires'* and *'crises'* indeed tends to suggest that most of them were creations of the media which blew out of proportion incidents that may actually appear quite common in the life of a football club.

'C'est la crise au PSG'

PSG has indubitably been through highs and lows in the last ten years. It has even been through crises: in 1998–99, the club changed president twice and coach three times. In 2000–1, the club changed coach mid-season. During the 2006–7 season, the club president fired one of the team's star players, French international Vikash Dhorasoo mid-season, then the coach. Following the period 1991–8, when PSG was the most successful French clubs, these crises largely justify the claims by the journalists that they are treating PSG fairly. Yet it appears quite clearly that on many occasions the newspapers have singled out the negative aspects of the club's existence to capitalise on shock value. There is a wide gap between the crises described by the newspaper and the reality of the club's situation.

A good example of a crisis blown out of proportion – if not out of nowhere – is the February 1996 crisis. *L'Équipe* gave its front page to PSG's surprising defeat against low-ranked Montpellier on 11 February 1996.[50] *Le Monde,* devoted not one but two articles to the matter.[51] One article recalled PSG's blunders throughout the season. Both newspapers wrote alarmist follow-ups in the following days, as a string of poor results ensued.[52] The vocabulary used could be dramatic: *L'Équipe*'s front page headline mentioned a 'crise' on 26 February. With a remarkable sense of measure, *Le Monde* called a committee put into place by the club to assist the coach, a *'comité de salut public'*, in reference to the committee of sinister memory established during the French Revolution.[53] *Le Parisien* joined in the concert and dedicated half of its cover and three pages to the topic.[54] All of this would certainly suggest a very deep crisis at the club. Yet, the complete picture is rather different. PSG remained on top of the league table throughout the whole month, and was still competing in the European Cup Winners' Cup, which it eventually won. This victory made 1996 the most successful season in the history of the club.

This occurrence is not isolated. *L'Équipe* famously described the 1997–8 season as *'une dégringolade sans fin'* ('an endless tumble'),[55] and *Le Parisien* asserted dramatically that *'Paris, c'est fini'*, complaining bitterly that the Parisians *'ne remporteront encore pas le titre cette année'* ('once again, are not going to win the title this year').[56] Eventually, PSG won the two national cups (Coupe de France and Coupe de la Ligue) in 1998. On at least one occasion, *Le Parisien,* actually admitted to some exaggeration: contrary to what its article had said on the day before, PSG was not yet facing relegation.[57]

'Les affaires'

Similarly, many of the scandals which shook PSG over that period were remarkably short-lived and their grounds seemed rather shaky.

PSG has indeed had its fair shares of scandals, not least the transfers affair that saw two former PSG presidents sentenced to jail in 2010.[58] Yet, most of the affairs seem to have been somewhat exaggerated by the newspapers to the detriment of the club. For example, in *'l'affaire du double contrat'* Vahid Halilhodzic was accused by *L'Équipe* of being illegally contracted to both his former club Rennes and PSG.[59] The 'scandal' eventually faded as the situation was common and due to administrative procedures within the league. Other examples include *'l'affaire Anelka'*, the subject of a number of articles including a front-page story in *Le Parisien*,[60] which extended to scarcely supported rumours of a disagreement between a star player and the coach. This is hardly extraordinary in a football club, as its 2001–3 follow-up *'l'affaire Ronaldinho'* would show.[61] The subsequent *'l'affaire Yakin'* can be summed up as the failed transfer of a player because of a medical condition. It was nevertheless the pretext for about thirty articles in five different newspapers throughout July and August 2003.[62] It is doubtful if, had all these *'affaires'* happened in another club, they would have been given but a fraction of the coverage that they enjoyed in Paris. This was often denounced by PSG officials.[63] Blaise de Chabalier, journalist at *Le Figaro*, has acknowledged this when he stated that 'everything that happens at Paris Saint-Germain is amplified'.

According to *L'Équipe*'s Jérôme Touboul this amplification is the result of a competition between newspapers. According to Touboul – and Chabalier – *Le Parisien* and *L'Équipe*, which belong to the same shareholder (Amaury), are always competing for scoops. PSG suffers as it is the only one that both newspapers cover extensively. Other hypotheses have been advanced to elucidate this bias from the press. Blaise de Chabalier pointed out that PSG was until 2006 the only French club owned by a major television network (Canal+), itself part of Vivendi-Universal, one of the major media companies in the world. Philippe Séguin added that *L'Équipe* possesses its own TV channel (L'Équipe TV) and is one of the main competitors of Canal+. Jérôme Touboul also explains that the national newspapers (including *L'Équipe*) are all based in Paris. However, it does not want to alienate its provincial readership, and is keen to show that it can adopt a critical attitude towards the club of the capital, even if this means being excessively critical. This may also extend to *Le Parisien*, which publishes a national edition (*Aujourd'hui en France*), even though the sports pages is the main difference between the two editions.[64] Philippe Séguin adds that, like most Parisian dwellers, journalists do not come from Paris, where they simply moved for their professional life. Journalists therefore feel no loyalty (if not some hostility) towards PSG. Thierry Berthou[65] and many of the supporters interviewed share the same opinion. As a young male member of the Gavroches remarked: 'journalists are all provincials, they hate PSG'.[66]

There are similarities with the case of Glasgow: even the smallest element of information can be amplified. Yet, three major differences appear. First, all newspapers join in the amplification, even *Le Monde*. Second, the presence of a regional and dedicated sports press adds to the volume of coverage dedicated to PSG. Third, the reasons behind the 'hyping it up' process are rather different. What is at stake is not a major society issue as in the case of sectarianism in Scotland. It is mostly a competition between newspapers and media groups.

Supporters and PSG–OM

In addition to reports on the club and team, the newspapers also devote a small fraction of their articles to PSG supporters. The coverage by all newspapers follows a similar pattern. PSG supporters are only talked about in the three occasions that supporters most naturally come under the spotlight: when supporters publicly show their discontent with the club's management;[67] when violence erupts;[68] when PSG confront their arch rival Olympique de Marseille (OM). The difference between newspapers is one of degree. *Le Parisien* is the only newspaper to cover the supporters' situation at times of memorable victories or spectacular defeats,[69] or even in the absence of particularly 'hot' news. This limited coverage has taken on a major importance: it has largely shaped both the image of the club and the reaction of the supporters towards the media. Supporters have become very critical of the press, which is particularly perceptible in their written productions (fanzines, internet forums) and in interviews. Resent revolved chiefly around the question of violence.

Violence

Within the French context, violence has long been a unique feature in the behaviour of some PSG supporters and has, therefore, attracted particular interest from the journalists. Periods of relative calm (1993–2004) with the occasional upsurge of violence (PSG–Galatasaray in 2001) have been followed by more widespread fights. As of 2010, there have been ongoing fights between Parisian supporters from the Auteuil and Boulogne stands since 2004. Culminating in the death of a supporter in November 2006 and another in March 2010, they have commanded extensive coverage in the press. The perceived inaccuracy of the reports on such outbreaks of violence, and the prominence they were given, have sparked considerable resentment from supporters towards the press. Supporters are quick to cite the example of factual errors, which they claim are always to their detriment. For example, a supporter would quote the fact that, except for *Le Parisien*, no mention was made in the newspapers that a supporter of Marseille injured by a seat thrown at him, was actually hit by a seat from his own stand – as evidenced by the colour of the seat. If this PSG supporter is to be believed, the seat was 'merely' returned to the 'sender' by the Parisian supporters. This claim has actually been difficult to confirm but is representative of the feeling that PSG supporters have of the coverage of violence. To them, the press is at worse biased, at best incompetent. Before being broken up by a decision of the Ministre de l'Intérieur, the supporters' group called the Boulogne Boys expressed in two press releases its belief that it was unfairly blamed for all troublesome behaviour that occurs in Boulogne, which is often caused by people who are not members of the group. The group had an explicit policy of forbidding any action that can be detrimental to the image of the group, including violence.[70] Quite clearly, some members refused to follow this policy, though, and were individually involved in violence. Equally, there is no doubt that, as claimed by supporters in interviews, the printed media very commonly confuses the Boulogne Boys with other supporters' associations from Boulogne or independent supporters.[71]

More important, the reports on violence clearly outnumber any report on other supporters-related issues (especially in the generalist newspapers whose reporting on supporters is scarce). For example, the 2003 incidents with Galatasaray sparkled no less than an article every day for a week in *Libération*,[72] several articles over a six months period in *Le Monde*,[73] and innumerable articles in both *Le Parisien* and *L'Équipe*. The picture given of PSG supporters therefore appears to be largely inaccurate: it focuses on the violent few (between 50 and 300 people in the stadium according to a French intelligence agency, the Renseignements Généraux)[74] instead of the majority.

PSG–OM

The question of supporters has been treated most clearly on the occasion of PSG games with its arch rival, OM, which Jérôme Touboul calls 'their game', the game of the supporters. Arguably no other game in France is invested with as much emotion on behalf of the supporters as PSG–OM. The opposition has some specific features. Unlike in Glasgow, the opposition between the clubs from Paris and

Marseilles have been largely set up and fed by the media. Journalists Jean-François Pérès, Daniel Riolo and David Aiello have shown that the rivalry was by and large a creation of Canal+ and Bernard Tapie.[75] Canal+'s choice to buy PSG was essentially motivated by the importance of football in its clients' decision to subscribe to the encrypted channel. By funding PSG, Canal+ hoped to offer OM (then dominating the league) a competitor, make the league more attractive and increase subscriptions. Pérès *et al.* argue that the press was used extensively to develop this opposition. The common opinion among Marseilles supporters seems to be that the rivalry is largely fed by the press, an idea normally shared by PSG supporters.[76]

Yet the role of the press has appeared to be rather more complex, and exhibits contradicting traits. Truly, newspapers try to cash in on the rivalry, devoting much coverage to it. *Le Parisien* is the most conspicuous case, as it commonly starts to build the pressure a week ahead.[77] The head of the sports section at *Le Parisien* has explained that the game is always the main front-page headline on both the day of the game and on results' day.[78] Other newspapers follow the same trend. *L'Équipe* allocates its whole front page to the game on a regular basis. Furthermore, the head of the football section at *L'Équipe*, has reckoned that newspapers also reprint very willingly the declarations of players, coaches and managers from one side or the other that can be seen as provocation.[79] On the one hand, newspapers therefore appear to 'hype up' the game, *Le Parisien* and *L'Équipe* arguably more than the national newspapers.

On the other hand, the newspapers are 'playing it down': they try to minimise the opposition between supporters. *Le Parisien* only once reported solely on an episode of the rivalry between the supporters of the two clubs.[80] Newspapers frequently insist that the rivalry is no longer what it used to be. Notably, they underlined the lack of sporting stakes when the teams ranked averagely in the league. Newspapers also regularly insist on the security measures taken to avoid confrontations and on how unlikely it is that these are going to lead to any serious troubles. But even this is not without ambiguity. In the same issue, *L'Équipe* recalled the recent troubles and the history of the opposition, probably throwing some oil on the fire,[81] and how unlikely these troubles were likely to be repeated. Newspapers exhibit a duality that is not entirely dissimilar to those in Glasgow but for two facts. The first is that the divide is between the generalist and specialised newspapers *L'Équipe* and *Le Parisien* instead of broadsheets and tabloids. The second is that each newspaper also exhibits this duality, up to a certain extent.

A troubled triangular relationship

All these elements contribute to the settling of a troubled relationship between the club, its supporters and the press. First, relations between the newspapers and the club have been uniquely tense. On a number of occasions, the club or its players has, indeed, stopped communicating with the press. In May 1995, the coach (Luis Fernandez) asked his players to refrain from talking to the press.[82] On the eve of their first European Cup final, a year later, all players stopped talking to the press, citing the atmosphere of crisis created by the press.[83] At the beginning of 1999, the newly appointed president of the club forbade his players to talk to the press.[84] Such silences do not usually last for long, but on one occasion,[85] the club captain (Frédéric Déhu) stopped talking to the press for nearly two years.[86] Arguably, such behaviour has hardly been conducive to a more positive outlook from the press. And the coverage of the week preceding their European victory included articles on the crisis between the players, who remained silent, and the press.[87]

Supporters too have reacted strongly to the press.[88] Most hard-core supporters have admitted to an attitude of defiance, and to selecting their sources of information, preferring fanzines, general websites on sports or electronic fanzines, or 'sources from the club' to newspapers. Supporters have not stopped reading the press altogether but many have confessed to selecting articles according to their very definite idea of how a given journalist (especially in *L'Équipe* and *Le Parisien*) is disposed towards PSG. A female supporter, who works as a secretary, was adamant that: 'Some of them, I don't even read any more. I know all they are going to say about PSG is really rubbish'.[89]

The most complicated of those relationships is certainly between the club and the supporters. Capitalising on the well-known ill-feelings of supporters for the press, club officials have been prompt in recent years to blame the newspapers for some of the team's bad results. As Blaise de Chabalier mildly puts it, when listening to PSG officials, one might actually get the impression that the press manages the club. For example, the coach (Luis Fernandez) angrily exploding against the press on 21 November 2002.[90] Another coach (Vahid Halilhodzic) selected which journalists were allowed to attend the training sessions, and refused entrance to *L'Équipe*'s Jérôme Touboul.[91] This high-profile conflict prompted Rémy Lacombe to write in *L'Équipe*: 'Paris is mistaken when it tries to blame its bad results on the press'.[92] These strategies have had poor results. They did not provide either coach any long-lasting backing from supporters. At best, according to Blaise de Chabalier, they have left the supporters in disarray, as they did not know who were to blame for the bad results: the press or the club.

Despite the negative bias in the disproportionate coverage received by PSG, and despite the troubled relationship between the press, the club and the supporters, PSG still enjoys a positive public image. Blaise de Chabalier pointed to a study published by *Le Parisien* in March 2003: 51 per cent of the population polled declared that they have a positive image of PSG.[93] The role played by the press reports on PSG in raising identification is therefore complex. Even if the reports are negative, the large exposure the club is given has in all probability helped in recruiting supporters, since it resulted in a positive image. Furthermore, distrust of the press has appeared as a shared experience among supporters, one that they bond over. The press has, to some extent, provided an 'enemy', against which supporters define themselves, and thereby encourage identification with the club.

Symbols and names

Newspaper material on PSG supporters that does not deal with either PSG–OM or violence is scarce. It is all the more remarkable that it has mainly focused on three subjects: the new designs of the club jersey and of the logo as well as the possible change of stadium. They have been the source of much protest from the most vocal of supporters. This provides great support for the idea that emblems are essential in carrying facets of supporters' identities,[94] even when, as in the case of PSG, the meaning assigned to these symbols needs to be defined.

The 'original' or 'historical' jersey

The design of the jersey has generated the most opposition from PSG supporters and certainly the most articles in the press. Supporters have protested in hostile banners,[95] or displaying their own banner upside down.[96] They went on 'strikes': they stopped going to the stadium, or when they did, they refused to sing and dance to support their team.[97] Small-scale demonstrations were even organised in Paris: one blocked access to PSG's main shop, on the Champs Elysées, tracts were distributed, stating: *'Ici, on brade l'histoire du PSG'* ('PSG's history is sold cheaply here').[98] The actual content of the objection to the new jerseys oscillated wildly between two poles. The most uncompromising of supporters, and their associations, demanded that the players wore again the *'maillot d'origine'* ('original jersey'), the one designed by Daniel Hechter. The most easy-going only insisted that the design includes not only blue and red but also some white.[99]

The Hechter design can be called the 'original' design only by a stretch of the imagination. PSG footballers originally played in red, and the Hechter design was only invented three years after the club's foundation. Faced with this fact, supporters have (often but not always) altered their terminology and decided to call it the 'historical' jersey. In the words of one member of the PSG supporters' group called Rangers: 'Perhaps it's not the original jersey, but for us it's the one which has a history, the one which is linked to the history of the club'.[100] Yet, the 'historical' jersey was worn for just about one-third of the total existence of the club. When used, the 'historical' design was never firmly settled either. The main features (the central large red stripe surrounded by two thin white stripes on a blue background) remained but there were yearly changes in the design of the collar, sleeves, cut and in the actual hues of the three colours. It is patent that the presence of the Hechter design at the beginning and the end of the perceived foundation period (the Hechter and Borelli presidencies) created a false sense of continuity for supporters, through selection and transformation, two processes usually identified in the creation of collective memory. PSG's tradition of playing with the so-called 'original' or 'historical' design, clearly appears as an invented tradition, to use the concept popularised by Eric Hobsbawm.[101]

Invented traditions and realms of memory

According to Hobsbawm, traditions are invented in order to justify, claim or emphasise the values that a society (or a group) is based upon. Yet, the values that the jersey is supposed to boast have appeared conspicuously difficult to identify on the basis of the written production of the supporters[102] or even in interviews. When pressed, supporters would emphasise the geographical dimension of their objection to the new jersey. The disappearance of the white is resented because this colour has long been regarded as representing Saint-Germain en Laye, while the red and blue represent Paris.[103] Further inspection reveals that this reference to Saint-Germain has little to do with the reality of the suburban city to the west of Paris. The city council for instance has never complained about the lack of a white line.

The jersey can largely be seen as a reference to the foundation myths: it emphasises the role of Hechter in 'refounding' the club after the split with Paris FC. The main value that the jersey takes on for certain can only be expressed by tautologies. It is 'historical' or 'original' because it testifies to the club's history or origins. Supporters interviewed have also associated the jersey with the idea that during the Hechter and Borelli presidencies the club was more 'like a family',[104] and there was greater closeness between the club and the fans. This notion seems barely a reflection of the realities of the period: it was likely defined as a reaction to the fear that Canal+ would be a distant owner, turning the club into a profitable company, severing links with the supporters. Indeed the first protests against the new jersey date from shortly after the takeover by Canal+. More than an invented tradition, the jersey therefore appears to be what French historians Pierre Nora *et al.* have called a *'lieu de mémoire'* (commonly, though perhaps inappropriately, translated in English as 'realm of memory'). It is a place, or an object, whose function is solely to establish a symbolic continuity and to define an identity at the very moment that a group is threatened with change.[105]

Club attitudes

The club has long recognised the importance of the jersey for supporters. In 1995, the president at the time, Michel Denisot, publicly requested that the Hechter jersey be brought back because of its importance for fans.[106] Another club management adopted a different strategy during the second jersey row (2000–1). In 2002–3, the club altered the criticised design by adding a thin white line on both sides of the red stripe. However, it justified the position of this stripe on the heart by a reference to a white jersey worn between 1982 and 1989, which was also reintroduced as the 2002–3 away jersey. The club also reminded the press and supporters that PSG won its first titles with this white jersey. Commercially speaking, the tactic was successful and the jersey apparently sold record numbers. Moreover, the club's attitude was met with supporters' approval.[107] In 2004, a replica (sold by specialist company Toffs)[108] of the wholly red jersey used by PSG (1970–73) was officially presented with the jersey for the new season, undermining the claim that the Hechter jersey was the historical or original one and giving the management more options for future seasons. Ultimately, the management has proved its ability to play on the value of jerseys as a realm of memory (even if this meant undermining the 'invented tradition' that there was a historical jersey) and even to invent new realms of memory in order to achieve their goals: appease the supporters and make commercial profits.

The study of the jersey row adds much to the understanding of how symbols work for football supporters. Symbols such as the jersey, indeed, mediate an identity. Names in the Glasgow case study have also shown that history, or memory, a reconstructed vision of the past (invented traditions), can be used to give meanings to symbols and to reinforce identity. Moreover, the jersey row showed that the content of that identity does not need to be positively defined and can simply be the rejection of new values (or the fear thereof), and the instauration of a sense of continuity through a realm of memory. More importantly, it appears that these symbols are not set in stone as they can be created and invested with meaning by at least two different actors: the supporters and the management. They do so for different purposes. The historical content primes all other matters for the fans. For the club, it is only a means to an end: generating more revenues.

Logos and names

Logos

Like the jersey, the logo or emblem of the club, has also been deemed worthy of fighting over by supporters. In 1995, Canal+ introduced a new logo for the club: a white rectangle printed with the three letters PSG, on a background which followed the coloured pattern of the 'original' jersey.[109] Supporters vehemently demanded a return to the logo designed by Hechter and invested it with the same value of 'realm of memory' as the jersey: abandoning it meant a betrayal of the club's history. Despite having been the only club logo from 1973 to 1993, it also appears largely as an 'invented tradition'. The logo very seldom adorned the jersey, and its mutations have been subtle but numerous. The new logo also proved too simple for the supporters. Interviews have shown that the Hechter logo derived its value from the meaning that could be projected into it. The Eiffel tower for example can take on strikingly different values: the international symbol of Paris, or modernity (other Parisian sports club typically show the old coat of arms of Paris), or on the contrary, fidelity to the history of Paris.

The row over the logo points to an important aspect of symbols, only hinted at in the previous literature. Much of the success of symbols with football fans is intrinsically linked to the openness of their interpretation. To use a terminology borrowed from linguistics and semiotics, their meaning is made up of denotation (the reality that they are referring to) and connotation (the emotional value that they are charged with).[110] The connotations (more rarely the denotation) of the symbol can vary from one supporter to the other and therefore the same symbol is able to carry different, if not conflicting, facets of identities.

'Nom de pays: le pays et le nom'[111]

In the new logo, the contraction of the club name to PSG was felt by most supporters to be another betrayal. Some groups, such as the Gavroches even campaigned for the name of the club to be written in full, in the 'original' way: Paris Saint-Germain Football Club.[112] Yet, the 'original' logo was initially free of text and the trend has been unquestionably towards a shortening of the name. As early as 1972, the name of the first team had been officially contracted to Paris SG.[113] The club is also commonly called PSG by journalists and supporters alike. This is coupled with a disappearance of the understanding that Saint-Germain is a reference to the city in the western suburbs of Paris. Saint-Germain en Laye is often confused with Saint-Germain des Prés. Shopkeepers there are used to being asked which way is the shortest to walk to the Parc des Princes (3 miles away in reality), or to see tourists posing with a PSG jersey under the Place Saint-Germain des Prés sign.[114] Also, when journalists and supporters actually want to refer to the town, and not the club, they only say 'Paris'. If anything, the use of the article (*'Le Paris Saint-Germain'*, as in *'Le Lille Olympique'* rather than in *'Arles-Avignon'*) seems to suggest that Paris is seen as the name of the town, and PSG the name of the club.

Discourses from the supporters indeed also emphasise their Parisian identity. One of the most famous slogans used by both ends of the stadium (Boulogne and Auteuil), *'Fier d'être parisiens'* ('Proud to be Parisian'), has been developed into a song where any mention of Saint-Germain is conspicuous by its absence as on any of the sites which reference supporters' songs.[115] The *tifos*, the visual animations made by supporters at the beginning of a game, also refer to Paris in the great majority of cases. The names of some of the supporters' groups themselves also include many direct references to Paris. In Boulogne, the Gavroches de Paris derive their name from a Parisian streetkid in Victor Hugo's *Les Misérables*. The name Titifosi (a supporters' group on a lateral stand)[116] is a pun on the word from the Italian *'tifosi'* (supporters) and the French *'titi parisien'* which designates the traditional streetkids in Paris and their (now historical) Parisian accent. The name Lutèce Falco derives from the Roman name for Paris, and the little-known fact that Notre-Dame de Paris plays host to a number of falcons.[117]

'Le choix dans la date'

Through the historical and geographical references in their names, supporters' group have tried to anchor their support for the team in the past. The quest for history has proved important for PSG supporters. A historian of the club has even gone as far as suggesting that the club was really founded in 1904 as Stade Saint-Germain, arguing that Manchester United similarly traces its roots to a club with which they have merged (or have an even more tenuous link).[118] However, due to the fact that PSG is still a young team, supporters are trying to attach the club and their support for it to the longer history of the city. Articles on the history of Paris have for example been the subject of a long series in the fanzine of the Boulogne Boys.[119] Some *tifos* have made references to Paris under its ancient appellation *'ville-lumière'*. Some of the slogans and songs that the fans sing also make reference to the great period of the cabaret and chanson in Paris: notably, 'Ça c'est Paris' by Mistinguett, or a song based on the music of 'Allez, venez Milord!'[120] sung by Edith Piaf. It appears therefore that supporters are not only creating traditions and realms of memory for the sake of resisting change and the fears to which it gives rise. Despite the emblematic reference to Saint-Germain, void of any real signification, supporters are trying to anchor the identity of PSG as the team of Paris.

The grounds: 'au Parc, on est chez nous'

The question of the location became particularly important for PSG supporters when the possibility that the club might change grounds emerged following the 1998 World Cup.[121] It was already known that the purpose-built Stade de France in Saint-Denis was to replace the Parc des Princes as the national stadium for both football and rugby games.[122] However, the economical balance of the stadium depended heavily on the presence of a resident professional football club.[123] Being the only top-division football club in the region, PSG was the obvious solution for a number of institutional actors (including the relevant ministry and the city council of Saint-Denis).[124] But PSG appeared to be rather reluctant to leave the Parc des Princes and the possibility of the club's move to the Stade de France elicited a large number of articles in all sections of the press.[125] After much hesitation (which reflected disagreements within the Club and within Canal+), PSG eventually stayed at the Parc des Princes. The supporters had campaigned strongly against the move to the Stade de France, using their traditional means: banners, *tifos* and articles in the fanzines.[126] In addition to the one-line songs that express the supporters' attachment to their city (*'Ici c'est Paris'* ('Here is Paris'), *'On est chez nous'* ('We are at home') a whole song was devoted to the Parc:

> Au Parc des Princes,
> On aime bien le PSG,
> On aime bien – qui ça? Le PSG.
> Où ça? Au Parc des Princes.[127]
>
> (At the Parc des Princes,
> We like PSG,
> We like – who? PSG
> Where? At the Parc des Princes.)

The campaign against the move was organised around the familiar themes of history as a tautological justification and local rooting. They show in the supporters' two major slogans: *'Depuis 30 ans notre histoire s'écrit au Parc'* ('Our history has been written at the Parc for 30 years') and *'Au Parc on est chez nous'* ('At the Parc, we are at home'). Given the importance supporters give to names, it certainly didn't help that the mayor of Saint-Denis expressed his opinion that the club should become known as Paris Saint-Denis once it moved to the Stade de France.[128]

The Parc des Princes certainly means a lot to supporters. Except for a few months of refurbishment, PSG has played all its home games since the club reached the top flight at the 'Parc'. It is therefore the only place where PSG supporters have memories, as evidenced in interviews. The stadium is, de facto, a realm of memory. It is even more: the development of the supporters' movement has been intricately linked to the places they have occupied, and their expansion in the Parc. The creation of a dedicated stand for supporters (in K, then in Boulogne), then the creation of Auteuil are still regarded as significant moments in the history of the club. Of the supporters' groups whose names are not enmeshed in the history of Paris, many have actually called themselves after their position in the stadium: for the Boulogne Boys, the Supras Auteuil, the Kop-A-Cabana (in stand or 'kop' A) their position in the stadium is an important part of their identity. The attachment to the club seems clearly to have been mediated by a multilevel attachment to the stadium, and even to the part of the stadium they occupy.

In deciding to remain at the Parc, the club management may seem to have given way to the claims of supporters. In 2002, the club administration expressed its own attachment to the club by moving to a purpose-built building on the side of the stadium and directly linked with it. This was even the central theme of the media releases.[129] Yet, those two decisions were clearly linked to financial considerations. With 80,000 seats, the Stade de France is almost twice as big as the Parc, and it therefore would be difficult to run it at a profit if the audience were not considerably enlarged. At the moment when it seemed that PSG had finally found an audience, this may have appeared a very risky bet. Furthermore, PSG has used the possibility that they could move to Saint-Denis as a very powerful tool to negotiate better conditions at the Parc des Princes with the Mairie de Paris, which owns it.[130] The Parc was, indeed, further modernised after the work done for the World Cup in 1998, the concession of the stadium to Canal+ and the city council seem to have paid for the building of the club headquarters. PSG's decision to sell T-shirts with the slogan *'Au Parc on est chez nous'* may at first seem like an expression of the club's attachment to its stadium but the importance of money in this matter tends to indicate that it was just another way of capitalising on the supporters' feelings.[131]

Involvement from the city council

The importance of the Mairie de Paris's involvement in the life of the club appears here. Keeping PSG at the Parc des Princes was certainly not a matter of earning profit for it. The city council barely earns money (if any) on renting the stadium. If anything, the Parc arguably costs the Mairie in building and repairing work. The city council also gives PSG a subvention, recently limited by the implementation of a European directive, but which is still the maximum allowed by the EU and the highest in France (though, given the population of Paris, the smallest per inhabitant).[132] In exchange for this subvention, the Mairie de Paris signs a contract with PSG, which sets out obligations for the club. PSG must sell a number of seats for each game to the city council who give them to people from less affluent backgrounds. The club must also contribute to help amateur football in Paris, and have a social action in Paris. It does so through its charity, the Fondation PSG, notably by sponsoring a club in each of Paris's twenty arrondissements (boroughs).

Last, but certainly not least, the club must provide the Mairie de Paris with some public relations services (*'prestations d'images'*). These include the presence of the Mairie de Paris logo on the background of every interview in the Parc des Princes and on every club publication. The club must also play in the exact colours of Paris, particular hues of red and of blue, which explain why both the logo and jersey have recently become much darker. The club is also contractually obliged to play with the Daniel Hechter logo, which sports an Eiffel tower, the most easily recognisable emblem of Paris in the world.[133] It is certainly no coincidence that the upper section of the Parc des Princes which used to be yellow became blue in 1998, leaving the stadium all red and blue, in the very hues used by the Mairie.

According to Philippe Séguin, former mayor of Épinal and unsuccessful candidate for the Paris City Council in 2002, the public relations services a football club provides to city councils are extremely good value for money, a point that has been confirmed by studies on the geographical distribution of football in France.[134] The city council, Séguin argued, has a duty to provide a sporting spectacle which can provide international visibility to the city. Much of Paris's international recognition is as the capital of France and linked to acts of the Republic (i.e., the president, government and parliament). With being a candidate to host the Olympics, sponsoring a football or rugby club (in Paris, the Stade Français) is one of the few opportunities that the city council has to increase its national and international visibility and promote a local identity of Paris (as opposed to the 'capital' identity of Paris). It is very telling: the name which appears on every item is not Paris but 'Mairie de Paris'. The city council therefore appears as another actor which has an interest in and the possibility of playing on the symbols associated with the club but contrary to the club management, its action has not been the subject of much protest by the supporters. To them, the exact role of the Mairie is rather obscure but the Mairie seems to be pushing in the direction of the supporters as it tries to favour the development and rooting of a local identity.

As in the case of Glasgow, names have proved to be of equal importance as those symbols adopted in the framework for this work (including jerseys and logos). The study of PSG also adds the stadium to the list of symbols through which identity can be conveyed. Moreover, as with names in Glasgow, collective memory has appeared crucial in the process through which all symbols (the jersey, the logo, names, the stadium) became invested with meaning for the supporters. Equally, though this did not happen in Glasgow, all the symbols in the PSG case are more than just invented traditions, they are realms of memory: they provide continuity in a time of change. Memory is not only the means through which symbols get meaning: it is an important part of such symbols' meaning. Their aim is to anchor the support for PSG in two dimensions of reality, historical and geographical and to express a quest for a local, Parisian, identity through memories of the club and the city.

Another important finding of the PSG case study is that a wide range of actors can contribute to the creation of symbols. Though, eventually, the value of a symbol is only determined by the supporters (who can refuse them), the club management and the city council can play an important part in its definition. The club, notably has proved its ability to capitalise on existing symbols, and to invent alternate symbols (new 'historical' jerseys) adopted by the supporters. It is possible to suggest, after Giulianotti who created the notion of post-fan, to describe a fan able to reflect on his own actions and distance himself from them, that PSG is a postmodern club, or post-club, able to reflect on the practices of its constituency in order to maximise its gains.

Players and game

A distinctive lack of style

In addition to emblems, elements pertaining to the game (the style) and the people who play it (the team, through its composition and the players, because of their social identities) can mediate supporters' identity.

The Glaswegian case study has shown the importance of style in defining a team's identity. In the case of PSG, only one reference to style was found, and it related to the need to create 'always more spectacle'.[135] According to Philippe Séguin, Parisians are believed to like a flamboyant game, which is therefore bound to attract an audience. Séguin offers as proof of his argument that the loss of a few thousands spectators at the beginning of the 2003–4 season was due to the arrival of a new coach, Vahid Halilhodzic, who had a reputation for playing without panache. This can be related to Dietschy's claim that Parisians used to have a culture of spectators, and not of supporters, coming to the stadium as they would to another spectacle: for the show on offer. This would indicate that some parts of PSG's audience have not developed the culture of support that the study of emblems pointed to, and may not really identify with the club as supporters do. The emphasis therefore must be on the diversity of experiences within the audience and continuity with previous experiences that have not entirely been superseded by new ones.

Three other explanations can be offered to the lack of a clearly identifiable style that is PSG's own. It seems PSG adopts any style that the current coach believes is more likely to bring victory. It might be different for each coach but also for each game. The lack of an assigned style might also be a question of how it is rendered in the media. The French press may appear to be less prone to stereotyping than its British counterparts. *L'Équipe*, a dedicated sports daily newspaper, has a greater ability to analyse games in more details. The tactical schemes they provide are arguably more complex than those found in the British press. French newspapers also use a broader vocabulary than their British counterparts. The seemingly interchangeable 'central defenders' of the English press, are designated as *'libero'* or *'stoppeur'*, depending on their specific role. Midfielders are always split into at least *'milieux offensifs'* and *'milieux défensifs'*, when not referred to as *'relanceur'*, *'récupérateur'*, *'meneur de jeu* (*central or excentré*)', *'joueur de couloir'*, etc. Importantly enough, the young age of PSG as a club most certainly means that there has not been enough time to develop nostalgia for some long-gone golden era, when the style of play (and its distorted reminiscence) can provide a point of reference. Whereas in the Glaswegian case, style proved to be important, in the Parisian case it is barely a marker of identity, merely a means to an end, that of winning and attracting an audience.

Brazilians, Portuguese and suburban boys

Foreigners: the composition of the team

While the question of style appears to have very little resonance in Paris, the two questions of the composition of the team and the social identity of players appear to have taken on major importance. They also seem to be inextricably linked. The case of PSG provides a very different, if not conflicting, perspective with the hypothesis of the framework that the composition of the team reflects the idealised image of a population. The history of PSG can largely be read as a quest to attract an audience. The composition of the team has largely reflected this quest. According to Philippe Séguin: 'in order to constitute that audience, there was also (at one time) the repeated practice of constituting the team *according to* the targeted audience'.[136] For example, the numerical importance of populations originally from North Africa in Paris and its suburbs has prompted the enrolment of players such as the Algerian-born Mustapha Dahleb in 1974 and Ali Benarbia in 1999. The importance of football to the small community in Paris from what was formerly Yugoslavia (around 30,000 people) was also a key factor in the signature of Safet Susic in the 1980s. Paris is host to a large Portuguese community, which is passionate about football (it boasts an amateur team: US Lusitanos Saint-Maur, and the final of the Portuguese Cup was held in Paris once). According to Séguin, this explains the number of Brazilian internationals (Ronaldinho, Raï, Leonardo, among others) who played at PSG, the signing of Portuguese Joao Alvès in 1979 and Pauleta in 2003. The composition of PSG teams can therefore be said to have been influenced by a vision of the population that PSG represents. However, this vision includes migrants and foreigners, whereas the vision in Glasgow excludes them. The management has played on the potential identification between a foreign player and the community of migrants it represents in order to attract or, even, create an audience.

It is not surprising therefore that the *Bosman* ruling had a comparatively small impact on PSG's signing policy. One of the major assumptions behind the idea that the ECJ ruling would alter the identification of supporters with the team was that the supporters could not identify with foreigners. In a region where many of the inhabitants have foreign origins, even when they are French too, this idea appears to be wrong from the very start. If anything, the *Bosman* ruling simply allowed PSG to sign more foreign players, even some who don't seem to come from the European Union. Many Brazilian players are actually able to claim Portuguese citizenship. Many players of North African descent have French citizenship. These cases point to the importance of a change resulting from the *Bosman* ruling that is often overlooked in the literature. Prior to the ruling, in football circles, nationality was defined according to the eligibility to a national team. A double national, for example French and Tunisian, could only claim to be counted as French in France if he had never represented Tunisia (which would bar him from representing France). Nowadays, the same player would be counted as French even if, as in the case of PSG's Selim Benachour, he had played for Tunisia. Nationality is no longer defined in football terms (eligibility for a national team) but in real or political terms (citizenship held).

The framework adopted in this work must therefore be adapted to take two new dimensions into account. First, assumptions on the impact of the *Bosman* ruling based on the idea that supporters have greater difficulties in identifying with foreigners certainly have to be revised in places where much of the population arrived as the result of migration. Many supporters identifying with the club might indeed be of foreign descent. Second, as in the case of the jersey, the football club is able to play on another medium of identification in order, this time, to build an audience.

Social identity: the suburban boys

PSG's management has also played on the ability of some players to represent social identities. Arguably, being Algerian, or of Algerian descent in Paris, is a component of one's social identity, and signing Mustapha Dahleb or Ali Benarbia relied on the players' ability to symbolise the social identity of part of the population. Following this perspective, the two issues of the composition of the team and of social identity appear to be inextricably linked. Between 2000 and 2003, the club indeed pursued a policy of 'audience gathering' explicitly based on the social identity of some of the players recruited. The management wanted to attract an audience from the suburbs of Paris (the Île-de-France, or Greater Paris) where a great number of football fans apparently supported OM.[137] PSG's management therefore decided to sign up players who came from the Parisian suburbs or were representative of the suburbs in order to attract supporters. PSG brought back two products of the club training system, and originally from the Parisian suburbs, Bernard Mendy and French international as well as Real Madrid star, Nicolas Anelka and OM's Peter Luccin and Stéphane Dalmat. All of them had in common that they were young, black and talented French players. The club management thought the suburban youth (*'jeunes des banlieues'*) of Paris, who share some of these characteristics, would readily relate to them. The club made no secret of this belief.

It is remarkable that five years after the *Bosman* ruling, a club with a tradition of boasting a number of foreign players decided to recruit almost exclusively French players. Yet PSG has always had a tradition of recruiting stars from the French national team too: Jean Djorkaeff in the club's first season, Dominique Rocheteau a decade later. Commenting on the new *Bosman* ruling in December 1995, then PSG President Michel Denisot pointed out that PSG would still aim to recruit a mix of the best French internationals and foreign players. He cited the case of the two stars of the team at the time: French international (and son of Jean), Youri Djorkaeff and Brazilian World Champion Raï.[138]

The failure of this suburban-youth policy was even more remarkable. In purely sporting terms, the coach changed mid-season after a heavy defeat and the club finished ninth in the league. In terms of personnel, Dalmat and Luccin were transferred within a year of their arrival. Nicolas Anelka lasted only another few months. In terms of identification, the results were mixed, to say the least. According to the press, hiring two players from arch rivals Marseilles did not prove particularly popular with the fans.[139] It certainly raised considerable debate, especially in the pages of *Clameur*, the fanzine of the Boulogne Boys. Nicolas Anelka's popularity with the supporters is more difficult to analyse. His return was met with some acclaim from the fans (and criticisms regarding the cost of the transaction since his contract was bought for up to forty-four times the value that it was sold a mere three years earlier to Arsenal) but he seems soon to have disappointed them. Following pretty poor match results, Nicolas Anelka saw his car bombarded during training with an industrial food specialty he was promoting in a TV advertisement at the time. Eventually, the overall failure of this policy became patent. There has been no proof that supporters identified with the players, or that their hiring had any effect on PSG's popularity in the Parisian suburbs.

It is more than likely that the *Bosman* ruling has played its part in the failure of the 2000 recruitment policy, though indirectly. Creating a European Union-wide transfer market at least for European citizens, *Bosman* has increased the number of potential buyers, and of transfers.[140] It is doubtful that, before the *Bosman* ruling, Luccin and Dalmat would have spent so little time at PSG. Transferring them would have been more difficult and certainly less lucrative because the European giants of football would not have been able to buy them. One of the criticisms most frequently heard from supporters (especially when PSG has a bad spell) is that players don't fight for their club and jersey. Luccin, Dalmat and Anelka never came close to representing PSG simply because they didn't spend enough time at the club (and, arguably, never experienced success with it). It is certainly very telling that at the time of the interviews in 2003–5, the last players who had come to represent the club included the former Brazilian and PSG captain, Raï, as well as Bernard Lama. Both were hired before the *Bosman* ruling, they also spent a long time at the club (five and eight years respectively) and played during the Denisot presidency, a particularly successful period.

The impact of the *Bosman* ruling on the composition of the team and the players as social figures has therefore shown to be ambiguous in the case of PSG. On the one hand, it proved of very little importance with regard to the nationality of players. PSG have long had a tradition of hiring foreign players in the hope that they can attract a part of the population of Paris and its area and this has not really changed. PSG has also continued to hire French stars. On the other hand, the turnover within the teams that the *Bosman* ruling has encouraged has certainly decreased the opportunity for players who don't stay for long in a given team to become really associated with it, hence become symbols of the team. The theoretical framework therefore remains partly valid. The composition of the team and the social identity of players can still represent supporters' identity, even if the players are foreign, but under the condition that they stay long enough in the club to embody it.

New figures of identification

Since current players may have difficulties in becoming identified with the team and in appealing to supporters, it may seem only natural that the supporters, and the club, are turning to other people who can mediate their identities, in a manner not envisaged by Bromberger, Sonntag or any of the other theorists. Three different groups of people have emerged to mediate the identity of the club and symbolise it: first, former players coming back to the club in a new role; second, members of the management; third, the groups that the supporters have organised themselves.

History repeated

Following the lack of identification with new players who had not stayed long at the club, PSG has adopted a policy of calling back former players to perform new roles at the club. Antoine Kombouaré, a long time player of the club, and famous for scoring the fourth goal against Real Madrid in one of the most celebrated PSG games ever,[141] was one of the first to come back as a coach for the youth and reserve team in 1999 (in 2010, he coaches the first team). He was later followed by team-mates of the Denisot era: Laurent Fournier, then Vincent Guérin. The most conspicuous return though was certainly that of Luis Fernandez.[142]

One of the first products of the PSG youth academy during the Hechter presidency, Fernandez was one of PSG's (and even France) major stars between 1978 and 1986. He made a first successful return to the club as a coach between 1994 and 1996 when he won the Cup Winners' Cup as well as the League Cup and France Cup. His second return mid-season in 2000 was much less successful and he was eventually sacked in 2003. Yet, until his ultimate demise, Fernandez was very popular with at least some of the fans, who explained in interviews that he embodies the true spirit of the club because he is 'like us' – probably meaning a 'kid' raised in Paris. For the management, calling back Fernandez in 2000, besides being a sporting choice, was therefore also a way to gather or strengthen support by playing on the supporters' identification with him, and his ability to represent the identity of the club and of part of its following.

Fernandez's second return to PSG illustrates another aspect of the policy of calling back former heroes of the club. In 2000, he was greeted as both the prodigal son and saviour. This is rather reminiscent of Raoul Girardet's famous analysis of political imagination (*'imaginaire politique'*) in *Mythes et Mythologies politiques*.[143] Girardet contends that in times of turmoil, unity of the nation and continuity in its history can be restored by calling to a figure of the past. Luis Fernandez was to a certain extent a link between the different periods of the club: trained at the club during the founding years, he played when PSG won its first league title. He coached during the most successful era of the club. He also played on this in a number of occasions (in books, *Le Parc de mes passions* and in interviews):[144] Fernandez has liked to portray himself as the son of Spanish immigrants, a kid of Paris and the suburbs, who climbed up the ladder thanks to his talent, dedication and hard work. The reality is slightly different. Fernandez was raised in Lyon and move to Paris when he joined PSG in his early teens. He was lured by money into leaving the club for its erstwhile Parisian rival, Matra Racing, in 1986. He also coached many other teams, including Cannes in France. Yet, this portrait of Luis Fernandez as a true Parisian was largely embraced by the club, the supporters and the media since it fitted in with a central theme in the story of Paris Saint-Germain: the creation of a memory and a history.

The return of Alain Roche, a PSG defender of the (successful) Denisot years, illustrates another theme important in this case study. In October 2003, he returned to PSG in order to help with the recruitment of new players.[145] Roche's comeback can certainly be interpreted as a quest for continuity and legitimacy from a new management team which had very little history with PSG. According to a member of the Gavroches, this was made more important by the fact that, at the time, a former PSG player, Francis Llacer, in judicial conflict with the team, decided to follow PSG games in the Boulogne stand which he frequented as a youngster. With Alain Roche, PSG offered their own symbol of continuity against a particularly unwelcome symbol provided by the supporters. On that occasion, and as with the jersey, it appears that the management is not the only agency that can create symbols and means of identification, or invest them with meaning. The supporters (at least those who are organised into groups or those occupying the main supporters' stand) are another. Most important, in the case of the jersey, the supporters could accept or refuse the symbols proposed by the club management. Here these two agencies compete with each other to impose their own symbols and means of identifications.

The management as new mediators of identity?

The promotion of Luis Fernandez and former players now in PSG's management team also indicates a new tendency. Members of the management may be becoming, at least partly, mediators of identity. This was obviously the case of PSG President Michel Denisot, a former star TV show host and sometimes journalist, who was previously a president of a smaller club, La Berrichonne de Châteauroux where he had become acquainted with sports journalists. Michel Denisot's place in the media also grew when PSG players refused to talk to the press: Denisot became the voice of the club and came to personify PSG as the result of a deliberate policy to overcome the club's lack of communication by the players themselves. His successors have proved less able to embody the club. There is, nevertheless, room for a president to embody the club, provided he can stay long enough, and he enjoys a modicum of success. Interviews with supporters have indicated that former presidents rank among the people who have been able to personify the club, citing mostly Hechter, Borelli and Denisot. This has mostly been because they are now part of the club's history, and because the process of selection inherent to the creation of memory has weeded out the negative aspects in their policies. These two categories of new mediators of identity which have not previously been analysed in the literature share one point. They can be suggested to (or even imposed on) the supporters by the club management. Conversely, a third category of new identity mediators is actually the result of the supporters assembling and organising themselves in groups, partly as a reaction against the management.

Supporters' groups

The supporters' groups have been analysed in detail by different authors. Mignon,[146] for example, has examined the differences between two main forms of supporters' groups in France. The official supporters' association is usually supported by the club and often made of slightly older than average supporters. The autonomous supporters' groups include younger members, and often but not always claim to be of the Ultra tendency. Mignon has also analysed how some supporters, often the violent ones who call themselves 'hooligans', 'hools' or 'casuals' prefer to remain 'independent' from any kind of organisation or are only loosely linked in casual 'firms'. Conversely, Bromberger has insisted on the high degree of organisation of the Ultras, their business-like practices in Marseilles and how their behaviour created today's *'rage de paraître'* (rage to be seen). Being part of an Ultras' group is one means of getting media exposure.[147] Giulianotti, in his analyses of violence, supporters' cultures and the emerging post-fans, has tried to show how much the Ultras in Italy differ from the 'hools' and casuals in Great Britain, especially as violence is not central to their practice.[148]

All these forms of supporters' cultures exist at PSG. Les Amis du PSG, located in an expensive lateral stand, plays the role of the official supporters' group. Among the eight other supporters' groups officially recognised by the club in 2002,[149] there were at least four Ultra groups (the Boulogne Boys 85, and three in Auteuil: the Supras Auteuil 1991, Tigris Mystic[150] and Lutèce Falco 91) and three groups influenced by the Ultras (Titifosi and Hoolicools). Two groups both claim paradoxically to be 'groups of independents' in Boulogne (Gavroches de Paris, Rangers Paris). There were many more supporters' groups than those officially recognised by the club, for example nascent Ultra groups (the Authentiks, Kop A Cabana). There were also casual firms (Ayache Family) and completely independent supporters in the Bleu Haut and R1 part of the stand. This extreme diversity among the supporters' group, and notably the cohabitation between Ultra and 'traditional' groups in Boulogne is the result of a change in the forms of partisanship at the beginning of the 1990s, a process described and analysed by Mignon who identifies 'two styles of partisanship: the English style, more sober and communitarian, and the Italian style, more spectacular and more organised'.[151] This is already quite significant about the identity of PSG supporters as it reflects the position of Paris in the north of Europe but within a Latin country.

But, in the case of PSG, the most important aspect pertaining to the supporters' groups, and especially the Ultras, has barely been adequately explored: how they have themselves become mediators of identity. Bromberger has referred to the fact that supporters join Ultra groups as a means of gaining media attention. According to Séguin,[152] one of the reasons that violent behaviour from the supporters was tolerated in the early years of PSG's history was that some supporters were actually attracted by the bad reputation of PSG supporters. Indeed, the number of season-ticket holders never ceased to rise during the period 1978–84 when supporters became increasingly independent and their reputation of being violent became more important.[153] Without necessarily taking part in violent activities, they hoped to derive an image of being tough from their frequentation of the Parc des Princes. Supporters therefore have a history as mediators of identity – in the latter case, of an identity that is aspired to rather than real. The phenomenon has only expanded and taken on new forms with the Ultra groups. The *Bosman* ruling and the relative disaffection for players who don't stay long enough at their club may simply have furthered the process.

Two aspects of the Ultra groups are relevant in this case. First, as the literature suggests, Ultra groups have become, at PSG, places where people socialise: Ultra groups are extremely active off the pitch. Football tournaments within each group and between groups are organised,[154] supporters of one group regularly congregate at their headquarters (the location of which is kept secret, even to the most junior members of the group) in order to watch football games. It is particularly telling that in a normal issue of *Clameur*, the fanzine of the Boulogne Boys, fewer than one line in every few articles is dedicated to action on the pitch: articles focus on the group's members, the Ultra supporters. Alfred Wahl's statement that football was not particularly successful in France because it didn't provide *'lieux de sociabilité'* ('places to socialise') therefore needs to be reviewed.

Second, a most striking aspect of the Ultra groups is how they are constantly competing with the club with regard to markers of identity: they are also offering their own: logos, scarves and *tifos* notably. These artefacts usually offer a mix of aspects carried by the club's markers and others with which the club may not want to be identified and which personalises the identity of the supporters' group. For example, the emblem of the Boulogne Boys sports a skull the meaning of which – perhaps a reference to pirates – is not entirely clear, not even to the members who have been interviewed for this book. This competition on emblems leads to the often-repeated claim that group members should wear neither the outfits sold by the club nor the changing sportswear brands associated with hooligans and casuals but the items produced by the group.[155] Ultra supporters' groups have therefore developed strong identities, based on their social activities, and expressed by their symbols which reuse and develop the club identities. Ultra supporters' groups have become one mediator of identity which to some extent competes with the club with regard, not only to emblems: each Ultra group very often finds itself in a position of protesting against the club's policy, claims to be the sole depository of the true spirit of the club and sometimes competes with other Ultra groups as the depository of that spirit.

Mediators of identities have therefore proved very important in the case of PSG. The impact of the *Bosman* ruling on them has been rather varied. Contrary to initial expectations, it is less the possibility of hiring more foreign players than the shortening of the period players stay at clubs which has put their status as mediator of social identity at stake. Concurrently, new mediators of identity seem to have started to develop: former players who come back to the club; members of the club management. The supporters, organised in groups or independent, have also proved to take on some of the role of mediators of identity.

Conclusion

The PSG study has provided salient confirmation of some of the conclusions of the Glaswegian case and developed others. It has also brought out a number of new elements in the process of defining, through the press, football-related identities in the post-*Bosman* era. First, some newspapers take a more important role in that process than others. Specialised daily papers (by regions, on sports), a particular feature of the French press, dedicate more coverage to sports than the nationwide generalist press. The overall trend identified in the reporting on PSG in France, over-coverage and systematic disparagement, is therefore even more bare-faced in their case. Journalists are also certainly aware that their reporting has consequences in the real world. They acknowledge it when they hesitate between giving full coverage to the PSG–OM games, in order to maximise sales, and playing down the rivalry (including past confrontations) between supporters, so as to avoid new incidents.

Second, the role of the press (as a whole) must be analysed in light of the fact that it emerges as an actor in the complex relationship between the club and its supporters. The findings here are twofold. On the one hand, supporters build their identity not simply through the press (i.e. through reading it) but also against it. Undeniably, the negative bias that the most dedicated supporters perceive in the press coverage of their favourite club has, by and large, antagonised them. To some extent, some PSG fans believe that one of the characteristics of the 'true supporter' includes a strong dislike of some parts of the press. On the other hand, comments on the press by various actors (even as echoed by the press itself) have appeared to perform an important role in the definition of identities. Indeed, in many occurrences, PSG officials have used the ill-feeling of supporters towards sections of the press in order to gather support – albeit momentarily.

Third, the *Bosman* ruling seems to have had little effect on the supporters' ability to identify with the team. The main finding here is that foreign players can truly be symbolic of a local identity. New figures through which supporters are able to identify with the club have also been pinpointed. Officials (managers, president) too can be vectors of identification, especially if they have already played a role in the history of the club and come to symbolise continuity between past and present. Furthermore, identification with supporters themselves (among whom, the independent and the various Ultra groups, each with their own characteristics and values) has proved important in the recruitment of new supporters.

Fourth, the function of symbols has appeared elaborate. Further to being 'invented traditions' which provide continuity between past and present, some of them have also appeared to be 'realms of memory', thus shaping the way the past is remembered in the present. Symbols appear to have come to provide the club with an identity (sameness between different states of one object) which is clearly a local Parisian identity.

Notes

1 Alfred Wahl (ed.), *Les archives du football: sport et société en France (1880–1980).* Paris: Éditions Gallimard/Julliard, 1989 (hereafter Wahl 1989).
2 Wahl 1989.
3 For reasons of space, the club will be called PSG hereafter; see below for discussions of the club's name.
4 Mignon 1998: 216.
5 Mignon 1998: 223.
6 www.lfp.fr/ligue1/stat/taux_remplissage.asp?saison=2005/2006
7 According to the yearly poll on football clubs recognition made by an agency that specialises in sports marketing, Sport Lab, PSG has the highest '*taux de notoriété spontanée*' ahead of OM (75 per cent) and third-placed Olympique Lyonnais (30 per cent) (Jean-François Pérès, Daniel Riolo and David AIELLO (eds), *OM–PSG, PSG–OM, Les meilleurs ennemis: enquête sur une rivalité,* p. 234. Paris: Mango Sport, 2003 (hereafter Pérès 2003).
8 On that occasion, PSG became the youngest club ever to win a European Cup.
9 The resources pertaining to the history of the Paris Saint-Germain Football Club are surprisingly scarce. This short history is essentially based on: a game-by-game chronicle of the PSG written and published by a historian and fan, Thierry Berthou, *Histoire du Paris Saint-Germain football-club (1904–1998).* Saint-Maur des Fossés: Pages de foot, 1998 (hereafter Berthou 1998); Wahl 1989; Mignon 1998; an article by Paul Dietschy, 'Le Paris Saint-Germain dans le football français et européen', *Le Bulletin des Amis du Vieux Saint Germain* 39 (2002), 273–291.
10 Dietschy 2002: 275.
11 'Fédération Française de Football', French Football Federation, the association in charge of football in France.
12 Matthieu Le Chevalier, 'Colette et Daniel font de la résistance', *Le Parisien,* 12 April 2001.
13 Or 12 August 1970, according to the official history of the club on its website (at: www.psg.fr/fr/club/history/0,, 1045, 00.html; last accessed 14 May 2007).
14 Berthou 1998: 49.

15 Mignon 1998: 223.
16 According to www.psg.fr/fr/supporters/associations.html, last accessed 2005, the Tigris Mystics later disbanded.
17 Berthou 1998: 94–96.
18 Berthou 1998: 138.
19 Berthou 1998: 159.
20 Pascal Duret and Patrick Mignon, 'Faire vivre un club en Île-de-France: le cas du Paris Saint-Germain et de l'Olympique Noisy-le-Sec', *Les annales de la recherche urbaine*, 6(79) (1998), 120 (hereafter Duret and Mignon 1998).
21 Berthou 1998: 229.
22 Duret and Mignon 1998: 120.
23 Berthou 1998: 120.
24 As pointed out by Philippe Séguin in an interview, confirming what Berthou 1998: 91 said.
25 Berthou 1998: 120.
26 Berthou 1998: 143–144.
27 A potted history of the Boulogne Boys can be found at: http://boulogne-boys.org/main/?page_id=5 (last accessed 24 April 2007).
28 Berthou 1998: 271.
29 Jean-Jacques Bozonnet, 'Les ombres du Parc', *Le Monde*, 17 March 1987.
30 Philippe Broussard. 'Les difficultés du club parisien: un plan de relance pour le Paris Saint-Germain', *Le Monde*, 14 May 1991.
31 This is treated extensively in Mignon 1998. See for particular example incidents following the PSG game against Nancy in August 1971; or the incidents following the Bastia–PSG game in 1973; or incidents at Saint-Étienne in November 1974 (reported in Berthou 1998: 40, 55, 70).
32 Notably in the 1981–82 season (reported in Berthou 1998: 159).
33 For example, in March 1982, Georges Peyroche made declarations calling for an end to the troubles (reported in Berthou 1998: 56).
34 See notably, *France football*, 13 March 1984.
35 Berthou 1998: 299.
36 Piotr Smolar, 'Un gardien de la paix tue un supporteur du Paris Saint-Germain', *Le Monde*, 25 November 2006.
37 See *52 à la Une*, a TV show on TF1 in 1995.
38 Duret Mignon 1998: 120; Berthou 1998: 327.
39 www.lemonde.fr/sport/article/2010/03/18/le-supporter-du-psg-agresse-fin-fevrier-est-mort_1320763_3242.html
40 For example: 14 November 1995 for an example of a rather empty 'PSG express', the middle of two weeks of international football. On the other hand, 20 December 1996 is probably the only occurrence when it was noticeable there was absolutely no word on PSG in *Le Parisien*.
41 Witness for example *Le Parisien*, 16 and 17 February 1998.
42 Here is a small selection of some of the most striking covers: 3 November 1995; 20 November 1995; 1 February 1996; 26 February 1996; 5 April 1996; 16 January 1997; 4 February 1997; 3 March 1997; 14 May 1997; 8 November

1997; 9 March 1999; 3 May 1999; 2 April 2000; 13 February 2001; 17 February 2001; 9 April 2001; 19 April 2001; 28 November 2001; 1 February 2002; 13 April 2002; 26 April 2002; 1 December 2003.

43 Examples include: 3 November 1995; 4 November 1995; 5 November 1995; 26–28 February 1996; 1 to 5 April 1996; 7–10 May 1996; 17–19 February 2001; 1–3 February 2002 and 7–12 February 2002.

44 This happened for example on 22 March 1996, on several occasions in the first fortnight of May 1996 and on 4 April 1998.

45 Caroline de Malet, '"Le Parisien" fait peau neuve', p. 18, *Le Point*, 4 March 1995.

46 21, 22 and 24 October 2004.

47 Interview with Jérôme Touboul.

48 Berthou 1998.

49 'Paris Saint-Germain: Halilhodzic s'explique' (propos recueillis par Frédéric Potet), *Le Monde*, 13 October 2004.

50 Front page and page 7 of *L'Équipe*, 12 February 1996.

51 'Les faux pas à répétition du Paris Saint-Germain' and 'Battu au Parc des Princes, Paris-SG est pris par le doute', *Le Monde*, 13 February 1996.

52 'Le Paris Saint-Germain dans la tourmente', front page of *L'Équipe*, 13 February 1996. 'Michel Denisot souhaite dédramatiser la situation au Paris-SG', *Le Monde*, 14 February 1996.

53 'Un comité de "salut public" pour le Paris Saint-Germain', *Le Monde*, 27 February 1996.

54 'Luis Fernandez sous surveillance', front page of *Le Parisien*, 26 February 1996 – articles pp. 14–16.

55 *L'Équipe*, 18 March 1998.

56 'Paris, c'est fini', front page and p. 18 of *Le Parisien*, 14 February 1998.

57 'Les mauvais calculs du Paris Saint-Germain', E. B. 'Pas de soucis pour le maintien', *Le Parisien*, 19 February 2001 'Paris SG: et la chute continue', *Le Parisien Dimanche*, 18 February 2001.

58 'Prison avec sursis pour deux anciens présidents du PSG', *Le Monde FR*, 30 June 2010.

59 Céline Ruissel (avec S. K. et J.-D. C.), 'L'affaire du double contrat', *L'Équipe*, 5 August 2003.

60 'Anelka: "Je reste au Paris Saint-Germain"', *Le Parisien*, 19 April 2001.

61 See for example 'Se passer des services de Fernandez serait moins préjudiciable que de laisser partir Ronaldinho' (propos recueillis par Alain Constant), *Le Monde*, 3 December 2002.

62 See among others, 'Yakin se fait attendre', *Le Parisien Dimanche*, 27 July 2003. Céline Ruissel, 'Yakin, c'est déjà fini', *L'Équipe*, 15 August 2003. Céline Ruissel, 'Paris, histoire sans fin?', *L'Équipe*, 16 August 2003. 'Le Paris Saint-Germain ne veut plus de Yakin', *France football*, 19 August 2003.

63 See for example Vahid Halilodzic in *France football*, 1 July 2003.

64 Caroline de Malet, '"Le Parisien" fait peau neuve', *Le Point*, 4 March 1995.

65 Berthou 1998.

66 'Les journalistes c'est tous des provinciaux, ils détestent le Paris Saint-Germain.'

67 See for example, 'Les supporters du Paris Saint-Germain se rebellent', *Libération*, 24 February 2003. 'Supporters: les déçus du Paris Saint-Germain', *Le Figaro*, 24 February 1999.

68 'Les hooligans, mauvais princes du Parc', *Libération*, 22 October 2002.

69 See the series published in front pages of the week starting 9 April 2001 (*Le Parisien*).

70 In addition to the two press releases, this position is often stated in the group fanzine, *Clameur*. See for a good example, 'Déplacements', *Clameur* 20 (September–October 2000), 6.

71 The two press releases on the subject, the second of which recognises the role of some members in violent events while condemning them can be found at: http://blog.psgonline.net/index.php/2005/10/24/8-communique-des-boulogne-boys and www.boulogne-boys.org/communique.php (both last accessed 27 May 2007).

72 It has attracted articles in *Libération* at least on the following days: 14 March 2001 ('Paris Saint-Germain, victoire gâchée'); 15 March 2001 ('Sanctions probables après les affrontements au Parc'); 19 March 2001 ('Drôles et méchants'); 21 March 2001 ('Le Paris Saint-Germain devant l'UEFA'); 22 March 2001 ('Le Parc des Princes trinque pour ses supporters').

73 The coverage in *Le Monde* was at first less extensive but seems to have extended over a longer period of time: Philippe Broussard, 'Graves incidents au Parc des Princes', *Le Monde*, 15 March 2001 'Les incidents de PSG–Galatasaray, version web', *Le Monde*, 28 December 2001.

74 Gérard Davet, 'Les RG s'inquiètent de la montée régulière de la violence', *Le Monde*, 25 January 2003. The core of the violent supporters is estimated to be between 100 and 200 in Jean Chichizola, Delphine Chayet and Cyrille Louis, 'PSG: polémique autour d'une mort annoncée', *Le Figaro*, 24 November 2006.

75 Pérès 2003.

76 Pérès 2003: 207–208.

77 For examples see the week before the game on 15 February 2000: *Le Parisien* dedicated many features to the possibility that one of PSG's star players would not be able to play against Marseille. See Matthieu Le Chevallier, 'Robert voterait pour deux matches de suspension', *Le Parisien*, 10 February 2000. David Opoczynski and Karim Nedjary, 'Robert pourra jouer à Marseille', *Le Parisien*, 11 February 2000. The upcoming OM–PSG game was mentioned in two articles on another game, including once in the title: Matthieu Le Chevalier, 'Un peu de sérieux devrait leur suffire', *Le Parisien*, 12 February 2000. 'Une bonne chose de faite avant Marseille', *Le Parisien*, 13 February 2000. The day before, a double page was dedicated to the game: 'PSG a tout à craindre d'un OM en crise', *Le Parisien*, 14 February 2000. Over the next two days, PSG–OM was twice on the cover and got two double pages.

78 According to Jean-Louis Pierrat quoted in Pérès 2003: 215. The fact has almost always proved true. See front page and pp. 2–5 in *Le Parisien*, 8 November 1997. See front page and ff., 2 May 1999.
79 Fabrice Jouhaud quoted in Pérès 2003: 213.
80 Pérès 2003: 213.
81 See *L'Équipe*, 11 April 1995.
82 Pierre Ménès, 'Luis veut du silence', *L'Équipe*, 2 May 1995.
83 Gilles Verdez, 'Les joueurs décrètent le silence', *Le Parisien*, 4 May 1996.
84 'PSG: la révolte des joueurs', *Le Parisien*, 9 March 1999.
85 Following publication of this article: 'PSG–OM Les vrais salaires des joueurs', *Le Parisien*, 28 November 2001.
86 Patrick Sowden, 'Le Paris Saint-Germain modeste malgré lui', *France football*, 1 July 2003.
87 Gilles Verdez, 'Les joueurs décrètent le silence', *Le Parisien*, 4 May 1996.
88 As expressed in the title of the article: 'Paris Saint-Germain: la crise, comme d'habitude', *Le Figaro*, 18 December 1998.
89 'Il y en a certains que je ne lis même plus. Je sais que tout ce qu'ils vont dire sur le PSG c'est vraiment n'importe quoi.'
90 www.psg.fr/fr/news/show.php?id=2053; last accessed 3 October 2004.
91 Vahid Halilhodzic has commented on this decision in 'Paris Saint-Germain: Halilhodzic s'explique', *Le Monde*, 14 October 2004.
92 Rémy Lacombe, 'Les mauvais choix du Paris Saint-Germain', *L'Équipe*, 5 October 2004.
93 *Le Parisien*, 24 August 2003.
94 Bromberger 1995: 60.
95 P.-E. Arno, 'Le Maillot: un long combat', *PSG Mag.*, 3 July 2003 (available at: www.psgmag.net/index.php?c=articles&p=lire&id=96&m= (last accessed 26 December 2003, hereafter Arno 2003).
96 Arno 2003.
97 H. D. 'Cédric Pioline étrenne le nouveau maillot du Paris Saint-Germain', *Le Parisien*, 27 May 2001.
98 *Le Parisien*, 16 June 2001.
99 Discussions with supporters at the exit of the Parc des Princes after the Paris PSG–Bordeaux game on 17 December 2003.
100 'Ce n'est peut-être pas le maillot d'origine, mais pour nous c'est celui qui a une histoire, qui est lié à l'histoire du PSG.'
101 Hobsbawm 1983.
102 Notably the website of the Tigris Mystics and the Boulogne Boys fanzine, *Clameur*.
103 'Le blanc je crois que c'est pour Saint-Germain mais je suis désolé: le maillot du PSG il est bleu, rouge et blanc. Un point c'est tout.'
104 'Comme une famille.'
105 Pierre Noar *et al.*, *Les Lieux de mémoire*, 3 vols. Paris: Gallimard, 1982–86.
106 'Entretien avec Michel Denisot', *L'Équipe*, 4 November 1994.
107 Arno 2003.
108 www.toffs.co.uk; last accessed 1 November 2004.

109 'La griffe d'Étienne Robial sur les habits neufs de Canal+', *Libération,* 28 August 1995
110 Bernard Dupriez, *Gradus*. Paris: Union générale d'éditions, 1980.
111 Marcel Proust, À la *recherche du temps perdu*. Paris: Gallimard, 1991–95.
112 'Le nom du club c'est pas PSG, Paris SG ou même Paris Saint-Germain, c'est Paris Saint-Germain Football Club. Les autres sports, c'est pas le club qui nous intéresse.'
113 Berthou 1998: 147.
114 Interviews with waiters at the *Café des Deux Magots, Café de Flore* and the pancake seller near to the underground exit.
115 www.psg.fr; last accessed 3 June 2003; http://perso.wanadoo.fr/psgworld/chants.html and www.chez.com/psgfriends/chants.htm (both last accessed 28 July 2003).
116 Anthony Baca, 'Les supporters: mode d'emploi', *100% PSG,* 15 September 2002.
117 http://lutece.falco.free.fr/91–93.htm; last accessed 22 December 2003.
118 Berthou 1998.
119 *Clameur.* Not dated: 29; no page numbers.
120 Respectively: words by Lucien Boyer and Jacques-Charles, music by José Padilla; words by Georges Moustaki, music by Marguerite Monnot.
121 For example, 'Que faire des 80.000 places après la coupe du monde? Le Grand Stade peine à trouver les clubs "résidents"', *Libération,* 6 September 1995.
122 Jérôme Fenoglio, 'Alors que des problèmes financiers demeurent, dix villes ont été retenues pour accueillir la Coupe du monde de football de 1998', *Le Monde,* 16 October 1994.
123 Jérôme Fenoglio, 'Le financement privé du Grand Stade reste lié à la présence d'un club résidant', *Le Monde,* 4 May 1995.
124 Some articles in the press even presented PSG's move to 'Le Grand Stade' as a certainty. See 'Du camp des Loges au Grand Stade: les 10 lieux du Paris Saint-Germain', *Libération,* 27 February 1995.
125 For a good summary, see 'M. Tiberi veut conserver le Paris Saint-Germain', *Le Figaro,* 19 February 1998. 'Le Paris Saint-Germain au Parc: unanimité municipale', *Le Figaro,* 9 December 1997. Christophe de Chenay and Jérôme Fenoglio, 'Le Paris-SG suscite l'intérêt des hommes politiques', *Le Monde,* 5 April 1995. 'Une équipe pour le Grand Stade?', *Le Monde,* 8 May 1996.
126 See various editions of the fanzine from the Boulogne Boys, *Clameur.*
127 From the website Paris Saint-Germain Friends (at: www.chez.com/psgfriends/chants.htm; last accessed 28 July 2003).
128 'Patrick Braouezec, 47 ans, maire PCF rebelle de Saint-Denis, s'est battu pour le Stade de France. Et défend les sans-papiers…', *Libération,* 10 July 1998.
129 Available at www.psg.fr/fr/club/parcdesprinces/0,, 221, 00.html; last accessed 19 February 2002.
130 Interview with David Revault d'Allonnes, journalist at *Libération.*

131 Witnessed by the author during a visit of PSG's main shop in 2000.
132 Interview with Stéphane Le Floch, councillor of Paris.
133 See document 2003 JS 036 from the Mairie de Paris, where an appendix includes the Convention de partenariat entre la Ville de Paris et le club de Football Paris Saint-Germain.
134 Loïc Ravenel, *La géographie du football en France*. Paris: presses Universitaires de France, 1998.
135 Only reference found: Rémy Lacombe, 'Le Parc de mes passions', *L'Équipe*, 15 March 1995.
136 In an interview with the author.
137 Interview with David Revault d'Allonnes, journalist at *Libération*, 28 December 2003.
138 Interview with Michel Denisot, *L'Équipe*, 20 December 1995.
139 'Luccin: "J'ai choisi le PSG"', *L'Équipe*, 30 June 2000.
140 Giulianotti 1999: 122.
141 Jérôme Fenoglio, 'Paris-SG en demi-finale de la coupe de l'UEFA L'embellie européenne', *Le Monde*, 20 March 1993. To gauge the importance of the game in the memory of supporters, see: 'Courrier des lecteurs', *So foot*, January 2004.
142 Luis Fernandez and Dominique Grimault, *Le parc de mes passions*. Paris: Albin Michel, 1995.
143 Girardet 1990.
144 'Luis dit non à l'OM', *L'Équipe*, 20 November 2000.
145 www.psg.fr/fr/news/show.php?id=3964; accessed 8 December 2004.
146 Mignon 1998: 211–222.
147 Bromberger 1995: 240–256.
148 Giulianotti 1999: 39–65.
149 Baca 2002.
150 The Tigris Mystics disbanded in July 2006.
151 Mignon 1998: 212.
152 Interview with the author (see n. 38, p. 48).
153 Berthou 1998: 191.
154 Fanzine of the Boulogne Boys: *Clameur*.
155 Fanzine of the Boulogne Boys: *Clameur*.

5

Arsenal

Introduction

In glaring contrast to PSG, a cosmopolitan team since its very inception, the identity of Arsenal Football Club was long described as unashamedly English. Yet, no club in Europe has, arguably, been more affected by the unlimited opening of professional clubs to European citizens than Arsenal. On 14 February 2005, its French manager, Arsène Wenger, used an entirely non-English squad: all the players on the match sheet were foreign. This feat was repeated more than once in the following two years.[1] Far from being exceptional, the evolution of Arsenal follows closely that of the whole of English football. The English league has attracted huge crowds since its foundation in 1888. It was once effectively closed to all foreign players for a long period of time, yet it has now become one of the most cosmopolitan professional leagues in the world. Understanding how the influx of foreign players has affected supporters and their identification with their clubs through various symbols (including emblems, players and the style of play) can therefore only benefit from a close examination of the case of Arsenal Football Club, starting with its history until the *Bosman* ruling and the development of a perceived English identity.

A North London identity and marketing considerations

For most of its history Arsenal has been a North London club,[2] where it has developed a strong local following and identity. Originally founded in Woolwich (Kent) as the Royal Arsenal in 1886, it moved to Highbury in 1913.[3] The decision to relocate more than 10 miles away from its original headquarters was overtly guided by the wish to benefit from 'a greater supporter base',[4] which could be found in a 'densely populated area' within easy reach from the centre of London by the Underground.[5] In so doing, and because the move proved successful in terms of recruiting an audience, Arsenal committed 'a clear incursion into a competitor's catchment area'[6] as another league team, Tottenham Hotspur, was located within walking distance of its new grounds. The relocation of Arsenal started a bitter rivalry between the two clubs, further fed by the 1919 decision from the league to give Arsenal the place in the First Division that Tottenham had won the right to retain before the professional competitions were interrupted by the First World War.[7] It is arguably the string of victories and the innovations brought about by Arsenal's coach Herbert Chapman in the 1930s that definitely anchored Arsenal in its new home, recruited fans and really started the history of the club.[8] Under his direction (and after his unexpected death, that of George Allison, his successor), the club won the Cup twice and the league five times.[9] In addition to changing the strip in March 1933 to that which Arsenal still wears (adding white sleeves to the original red design),[10] Chapman made two famous innovations to advertise and market the club better, which affected the very emblems of the club, starting with its name. Chapman insisted in 1925 that the club be named Arsenal. It would therefore appear on top of the Football league listings and, it was hoped, gain wider exposure.[11] More crucially, Chapman successfully campaigned to have the Tube station (then called Gillespie Road) renamed Arsenal in 1932.[12] This created the unusual situation of a location named after a professional football club instead of the contrary. The resulting confusion, publicised extensively by maps of the Tube, certainly contributed greatly to the sense that Arsenal Football Club was anchored in North London.

The all-English (or British) Arsenal

Another 'golden era', that of the all-English Arsenal, played a major role in the definition of the club's identity. Rules on foreign players were extremely restrictive in England between 1931 and 1978[13] and most Arsenal teams of that era were all British, if not all English. During the whole period, Arsenal could only sign two foreigners.[14] When, following the *Donà v. Mantero* ruling from the ECJ, every professional football team in Britain was allowed a quota of three foreign players, many English teams immediately filled their new quota. Arsenal only signed one foreigner in 1978, the Australian John Kosmina, followed in 1982 only by a second foreign signing, the Yugoslavian Vladimir Petrovic.[15] Arsenal developed the image of a very British team during these years as it only signed a very limited number of foreigners until the *Bosman* ruling: six between 1989 and 1995.[16] The team George Graham took charge of in 1986[17] was therefore entirely composed of British players. The coach's first year also saw the emergence of a generation of English players developed at the club, including Tony Adams who later famously came to captain both Arsenal and England. George Graham's league-winning team of 1989 is therefore widely remembered as the last all-English team ever to win the league[18] and his 1991 league-winning team as 'a team so full of English talent'.[19]

Yet it does not seem that the low number of foreigners was the result of an explicit policy of exclusion. Unlike what happened in Glasgow, the argument that foreigners did not belong to Arsenal was not, it seems, invoked publicly at any point. The situation was more probably a reflection on the club's self-confessed traditionalism and conservatism. At the time, the belief that foreigners would not be able to adapt to the English game was widely accepted in England, all the more so at Arsenal. This was never more evident than when it was deplored by commentators, notably following Petrovic's early departure.[20] Arsenal is still remembered as a club which once epitomised England and its virtues. Until fairly recently, it was very present even in commercial publications endorsed by the club: in 2004, *The Official Arsenal Miscellany*, reminded the reader of the last all-English teams to play for Arsenal (in the league on 19 April 1994 and in a Cup game on 21 September 1994).[21] Another example is the 1999 edition of the *Official illustrated history*, which insists that Arsenal was 'the most upright of all English football clubs, the bearer of the historical banner for the English game'.[22] Furthermore, the conclusion of the book states that 'Arsenal are different from any other football club. Why? Because the history of English football can be told through their story'.[23] Arguably, these passages were reprinted from earlier editions. It is very telling, though, that no one saw fit to rewrite them after the arrival of foreign players that followed the *Bosman* ruling. Furthermore, throughout the book, there are numerous mentions of a number of rather anecdotal records, such as the highest transfer record in 1932, or the meaningless 'highest scoring draw in any English first-class game'.[24] The only reason for their inclusion seems to be that they constantly portray Arsenal as an extraordinary (record-breaking) team within the wider history of English football. Yet, the same publications are equally ready to laud the achievements of the so-called 'French imports' or 'foreign legion', which revolutionised the club from the second half of the 1990s onwards.

The French touch, later the foreign legion

Arsenal's conversion to a policy of importing players must be set against the wider context of English football. Of all European professional leagues, the English Premier League has been the most affected by the end of the nationality clauses which followed *Bosman*. The English professional league changed relatively quickly from ranking among the less-open leagues in Europe to being the most open of them all. There were isolated examples of foreign success in England before the *Bosman* ruling. Eric Cantona won a profusion of trophies with both Leeds and Manchester United.[25] Jürgen Klinsmann won the Footballer Award of the Year in 1995.[26] However, there were only 10 foreigners among the 22 teams and 242 players in the 1992–93 season.[27] As pointed out by *The Sun* journalist Dave Kidd, ten years later, only 103 of the 220 players who started Premier League games in the weekend of 17–18 August 2002 were British.[28]

The trend of importing foreign players on a massive scale no doubt started after Euro 1996 at the end of the season that saw the *Bosman* ruling. It is reflected in the great success of some foreign players. Between 1996 and 1999, four of them won the coveted player of the year award: Cantona (1996), Zola (1997), Bergkamp (1998) and Ginola (1999). Yet, in his first few years at Highbury, Arsène Wenger made great use of the English players from the George Graham era and, arguably, only signed foreign players to complement the natives. Chelsea was a more cosmopolitan team at the time, and was the first to field an entire team composed of foreign players on 16 December 1999.[29] In the season 2004–5, no team used more players from outside the UK and Ireland than Arsenal (82 per cent). The North London team was even ahead of its immediate follower, Chelsea (67 per cent),[30] and clearly became therefore the most cosmopolitan of today's English teams.

Originally following the trend of recruiting foreign players, Arsenal was certainly influential setting another: the massive recruitment of French players in the English league. Since 1996, Arsenal has been led by a French manager, Arsène Wenger, the first foreign manager to win the league, and even a League Cup double.[31] His Arsenal teams have included many French players including 1998 World Cup Winners Emmanuel Petit and Patrick Vieira, which certainly helped to raise the profile of French players within the English league.[32] The comparatively cheaper price of French players arguably helped their recruiting too. Whereas only 9 French footballers had played in the English league in 1996, 238 were recruited in the next ten years, making the contingent from France (totalling 247) the largest historically in the Premiership.[33] Other clubs also later went on the lookout for their own French manager. Fulham found Jean Tigana, Liverpool Gérard Houllier.[34] The so-called French connection has also been essential in the image of Arsenal since Wenger's debut at Arsenal in 1999, and has justified whole sections in books on Arsenal.[35] In 2006, the French bias was still very present but not as marked as it used to be. Players at Arsenal may still be mostly recruited from the French league or French-speaking countries but they hail from many different countries. On 13 September 2006, in a Champions League game, the Arsenal team was even composed of eleven players with eleven different nationalities.[36]

How has the support for Arsenal, and its strong historical English identity, been affected not only by the lack of English players but by the internationalisation of the team? Have English supporters been able to keep on identifying with a team full of foreign players, either through those foreigners or other symbols? An analysis of the position of the press on the issue, then of the supporters' reaction to this particular change and to the changes affecting the other means through which they identify with the club provides an answer.

Xenophobia in the English press

The traditional English identity of Arsenal, and its contrast with the massive presence of foreign players in more recent times have provided the main themes for the study of the English printed media. Yet, foreign players are present throughout the whole league so although the focus of this study is on Arsenal, the feelings of acceptance or rejection of foreign football players had to be studied in the whole of the sports sections of the English press. Also, the structure of the press is the same in England and in Scotland: there is a supposedly strong divide between tabloids and broadsheets. The questions explored here therefore are: do the newspapers report differently on Arsenal than on other clubs? Do they report negatively on the massive presence of foreign players at the club, or in general? In both respects, is there a difference between the tabloids and the broadsheets? Furthermore, how do supporters react to a possible negative characterisation of the club or its recruitment policies? Does this have an impact on their identification to the club? Does it change their perception of the press?

A club like another

PSG and the two Glaswegian teams Celtic and Rangers have been clearly the subject of disproportionate attention from the press. The same does not seem true of Arsenal in England. The journalists interviewed all claim that the coverage a team gets in their respective newspapers is proportional to both their sporting success and the support they elicit throughout the country. Studying the press seems to vindicate this claim. Arsenal was remarkably successful in the years 1996–2005. It also has long had a large and faithful audience. Thus the team receives a fair share of attention from the newspapers. Nevertheless, all other title contenders (Chelsea, Manchester United, to a lesser extent Liverpool) receive a similar coverage, which may only vary according to the form they exhibit on the playing field. In this respect, Arsenal's treatment is nothing exceptional.

Furthermore, studying the press vindicates the other repeated claim made by all journalists: that their individual decision to support one team or another remains private and does not impact on their writing. Neither they in their articles, and more importantly nor their newspaper, show any obvious preference for a team in particular. A small number of Arsenal supporters have occasionally mentioned in interviews that the press favours Manchester United. Journalists Matt Scott and John Brodkin have explained that other newspapers might be wary of displeasing the Mancunian manager, who already refuses to talk to the BBC. They claim that in their own newspapers, though, the place given to 'ManU' only reflects the club's recent domination of domestic football. The press study actually indicates that no paper shows an obvious bias for or against any club, including Arsenal. Supporters generally agree with this view. They also identify themes on which Arsenal is reported favourably: the spectacle offered by the very pleasing style in which the team plays (confirmed by both the study of the press and Matt Scott)[37] and, in the broadsheets, the so-called 'intellectual' temperament of Arsène Wenger (who, for example, speaks six different languages).[38] Themes on which Arsenal are criticised are mentioned frequently too. They include the club's disciplinary record[39] and, chiefly, the current lack of home-grown players, resulting from a recruitment drive focusing abroad.[40] The critics can be harsh: 'not since mad cow disease has anyone had such an aversion to buying British'.[41] This matter is particularly important. Some Arsenal players, such as Emmanuel Petit and Nicolas Anelka, have even complained about the presence in England of a rampant xenophobia.[42] Is the press, in parts or as a whole, against the strong (and almost exclusive) foreign presence at Arsenal? Can it even be considered xenophobic?

Various forms of xenophobia

The question of xenophobia surrounding sport coverage in the English press must be assessed on a number of different levels. No newspaper has adopted a constant overtly xenophobic agenda on the question. All newspapers (even tabloids) have, indeed, debated at length both what they saw as the merits and shortcomings of the foreign presence, sometimes within the remit of an article (usually in the broadsheets),[43] sometimes through columns taking opposite points of view (more frequently in the tabloids and the *Evening Standard*).[44] This can be interpreted as the result of an explicit policy to offer a balanced view on the matter. Or, as claimed by Stephen Wagg in his research on the coverage of the English national team, tabloids may not attach any value to consistency in their sports section. Incoherence is a recurring feature in tabloids, since they are guided by sensationalism only, and bound to adopt the point of view more likely to raise sales at one given moment, even if it directly contradicts the point of view previously adopted.[45]

The foreign presence in the Premiership has truly become an 'old chestnut' for journalists. In the first years that English football was forced by the ECJ to open its gates to foreigners, columnists abundantly commented[46] upon what was, as early as February 1996 (ten weeks after the *Bosman* ruling) deemed a 'foreign invasion'.[47] For the season 2000–1, *The Independent* even ran a recurring league table of 'which teams use the most foreigners'.[48] Over time, as it appeared obvious the trend would not reverse, the topic lost most of its novelty value and articles have become less frequent. Between 2005 and 2010, the question was raised mostly when new developments make it (regularly) newsworthy again and through comments from actors of the game (managers, players, executives).

This was nowhere more evident than when Arsène Wenger used an all-foreign squad on 14 February 2005. While some journalists defended the presence of foreign players (and found help in Arsenal's storming 5–0 victory over Crystal Palace),[49] some football professionals (players such as Gary Neville[50] or the head of the Players' Football Association Gordon Taylor)[51] took the most uncompromising positions. Another series of articles was started when West Ham's Alan Pardew attacked the lack of English player in Arsenal's March 2006 victory over Real Madrid in a European game.[52] Wenger accused Pardew of racism,[53] a claim Pardew refuted[54] while managers and executives joined in the debate.[55] Yet, a slight nuance between broadsheets and tabloids emerges here. The strongest attack on Wenger's policy on foreign players came in the headline 'It's a disgrace' from the *Daily Mail*.[56] Arguably, this was a quote from former Arsenal player, Paul Merson. However, the *Daily Telegraph*, based on the same quote as the *Daily Mail*, read 'Arsenal a "disgrace" says Merson'.[57] Whereas the tabloids endorse the comments made by the actors, and therefore show a clearer hostility to foreigners, the broadsheets distance themselves to appear neutral.

Rationalised xenophobia

In spite of all their attempts to present a balanced view (or in spite of their incoherence) the broadsheets use the same two arguments against the foreign presence (players and managers) in English football as the tabloids.[58] These arguments are spurious. They reveal attempts to justify baseless xenophobic prejudices through rational reconstructions. This phenomenon can therefore be called rationalised xenophobia and is thus unacknowledged by the journalists themselves. The repeated criticisms levelled at the lack of opportunities for young home-grown talent,[59] which is claimed to threaten the good health of the England team can be, at best, branded as a form of protectionism.[60] According to the Director of Development at the Football Association, Sir Trevor Brooking, these criticisms are also misplaced as young English players are lacking in technical quality compared to their foreign counterparts.[61] Furthermore, the English national football team cannot really be said to have performed any better or worse in tournaments following the *Bosman* ruling than in tournaments before. Newspapers have also reported that in the years 1998–2010, England had one of the most talented generations it has ever had. The idea that a club needs English players (a 'strong English backbone') to succeed at both or either national and European level is also put forward with startlingly predictable regularity every time Arsenal flounders.[62] It has been disproved by the team's subsequent ability to perform well (winning the league unbeaten in 2004 and reaching the final of the Champions League in 2006).

Casual xenophobia

The Englishness of the game is actually a source of countless clichés bearing witness to a rampant, if not omnipresent, casual xenophobia in all quarters of the press. The recurring assumption is that foreigners play in a way which is not compatible with the kind of football carried out in England. It is assumed foreign footballers may not be able to withstand the physicality (a euphemism for violence) of the English game. Foreigners are indeed regularly described in terms similar (though often slightly less belligerent) to 'a bunch of showboaters, who more often than not lack the guts for a proper scrap'.[63] Newspapers also ritually ask of a new foreign recruit: 'can he do it on a Tuesday night in Grimsby?'[64] The reference to a northern town, and the midweek date are anything but anodyne. It questions the 'foreign import's' ability to deal with the bad weather, the hostile crowds, the frequent games. Such statements or questions reflect only prejudice as, over time, many foreign footballers have doubtless proved their ability to adapt. There is enough proof in the fact that they have conspicuously and regularly trusted the end-of-year awards for best player.

When their abilities are not doubted, foreigners are routinely downplayed as 'mercenaries' (or collectively as a 'foreign legion').[65] It is implied, if not explicitly stated, that they have no interest in the English game, in their clubs and that their move to England was purely motivated by greed. Academic research on the matter has provided evidence that foreign players come to England for a variety of reasons, such as furthering their career or sampling a new football culture. Money is not the sole concern.[66] Some players such as Thierry Henry, Dennis Bergkamp or Kolo Touré have also stayed at Arsenal for a long time, and proved their attachment to their club.

Denigrated as mercenaries, foreign players are also accused of having brought vice and cheating in a hitherto virtuous game. Diving or play-acting is a 'foreign disease',[67] it is claimed. This is in direct contradiction to the renewed statements from UEFA that diving is only a problem in Britain.[68] Players such as Roy Keane have also emphasised that it is the illness of the time in British leagues as all players, English, British and foreign dive.[69] More important is the accusation that foreigners are fundamentally altering the game, destroying it: that they are 'losing the soul of English football' in the words of then West Ham manager, Alan Pardew.[70] This is common – as can be seen on the many occasions that foreigners have been accused of devaluing the FA Cup.[71] The assumption is that the foreigners' 'home nations lack cup tradition',[72] and therefore, they show no interest in the Cup in England. This seems to be in complete opposition to reality as, in the words of a former player, Tony Adams about foreign players:

> They're winners. If there is a game of tiddlywinks going on, certain players will always want to win. It's like me going to France and not wanting to win the French Cup. Are you mad? Of course I would want to win it.[73]

The stereotype is also ill-informed and based on the assumption that 'continental' players are all similar, regardless of the country they come from. In Italy, the Cup may be a trophy of much lesser value than the league, but in France, the Cup final is almost always the major game of the domestic season. For instance, the 2006 final of the Coupe de France, was then hailed on French television as the greatest game in French domestic football.

Parochiality and insularity

The lack of overt xenophobia, and the pretence that views are balanced, hides not only rationalised and casual xenophobia, but also the parochiality and the insularity of the English press. This is never clearer than when Arsène Wenger is presented as a great discoverer of hidden talent. He has certainly shown a good eye for young players such as Nicolas Anelka. But often footballers who are presented as his main 'discoveries'[74] were already proven talents, if not famous, before joining his team. Thierry Henry was already the leading goal scorer in a World Cup-winning side. Robert Pirès was elected best player at Euro 2000 by a panel of journalists just before signing with Arsenal. The *Evening Standard*'s headline 'Arsène who?' when his signing was announced on 16 August 1996 was similarly misguided. Mr Wenger had already won titles in both leagues in which he had coached (France and Japan). To any follower of international football, he was certainly not the unknown character that even broadsheets at the time claimed he was.[75] Although there might have been improvements in the second half of the 2000s, all these examples point to how ill-informed on world football the British press is.

This insularity perhaps explains why French players at Arsenal have frequently complained that the original meaning of what they said was lost when translated from the French to the English press. Thierry Henry, for example, wrote:[76]

> People have to know that what they put in the paper sometimes is a pile of rubbish … It's funny it always happens after I do an article in France. I have never spoken to that Sunday paper[77] since I've been in England. They love to say they have an exclusive, but I want people to know that sometimes they just make it up, quite often actually. They never put the original question in, so if you just have one line, you can do whatever you want with it out of context. Sometimes they misquote me too. If they want I can translate it for them. It's ridiculous.[78]

The ferocity of the English press

This also highlights the ferocity of the English press. Offered the management of the England team, World Cup winner coach Felipe Scolari, relented after some hesitation because of the media pressure that was already put on him.[79] This ferocity results chiefly from the tabloids' avidity in looking for 'scoops', which are later reprinted by the broadsheets. The dismissal of the previous manager of England, the Swede Sven-Göran Eriksson took place after he was tricked into talking to the same reporter of the *News of the World* disguised as a 'fake sheikh'.[80]

Overall, the whole of the English press (and not only the tabloids) take part in putting pressure on football players and managers. There is a difference in style between tabloids and broadsheets. Tabloids purposely rely more heavily (sometimes almost exclusively) on quotes, whereas the broadsheets prefer longer articles with more authorial input: in the words of journalists, more 'analysis' and 'narrative'.[81] However, the content of the newspapers (broadsheets and tabloids alike) is very similar when it comes to sport. The political orientation of the newspaper is not reflected in its sports coverage either. As Matt Scott from *The Guardian* puts it: 'There is no place for dogma in journalism and political dogmas don't translate in football'. Consequently, there is less difference between every newspaper on sport matters than on any other matter. The subjects dealt with have also become more and more similar over the ten years of this study. The only case where broadsheets differ fundamentally, in content and not only in tone, from tabloids is that they would usually not cover the personal life of players, managers and other actors of the game, unless they are deemed to have a clear impact on the results).

Yet, most conspicuously, broadsheets do not steer clear of other topics bereft of sporting relevance but which have scandalous appeal, and may even be potentially dangerous. A good example is the very high-profile verbal brawls with other managers that have successively engulfed Arsène Wenger. Stories have run in all newspapers, including all broadsheets considered, on Wenger's lack of answer to Mourinho's 2005 Christmas card, the claim that it had been treated as a bomb scare and subsequent episodes.[82] At *The Guardian*, Matt Scott explains that these stories are included 'for entertainment value'. John Brodkin even states that it is the journalists' duty to report on them, for each story constitutes a 'big talking point', and are also part of 'mind games' played before the matches. Such reports have been published on a regular basis in spite of a joint intervention from the Football Association and the police (or in the case of the Christmas card, the minister for sport)[83] calling both managers to make peace publicly, for fear that their verbal dispute might sour the rivalry between the clubs and rouse physical trouble between fans.[84] Unlike the Glaswegian case, where the broadsheets were trying to avoid stirring any trouble, in the case of Arsenal, both the tabloids and the broadsheets seem happy to take the risk.

What impact has all this had on the Arsenal supporters? The criticisms on the number of foreign players have certainly created some resentment towards the press. The supporters usually defend their club's decision to recruit abroad against attacks from the press. The disappointment created by eventually disproved rumours of transfer circulating from one newspaper to the other seems to have created some disaffection towards the press. Most supporters interviewed claim that they do not read the press and use alternative sources of information instead, such as the internet, radio, television, and for the older generation, fanzines. This resentment and disaffection are nevertheless fairly weak (especially if compared to PSG). Journalists have already registered that the press is nowadays only one source of information among others and act accordingly. Indeed, according to Matt Scott, the goal of a newspaper nowadays is 'to inform and stimulate the dialogue among fans happening on internet forums'.

It therefore appears that the English press, tabloids and broadsheets alike, are actually expressing a xenophobia which is not overt. No newspaper has a purely xenophobic agenda. Instead, the xenophobia expressed is rationalised (presented through arguments which have the semblance of rationality but eventually appear baseless) or casual (through a series of repeated false assumptions). The parochiality and insularity of the English press partly explains this state of facts. The ferocity with which the English press reports on matters related to sport only serves to give much more resonance to the xenophobia it expresses. This does not seem to have impacted on the supporters. As in the case of PSG, this puts the emphasis on the necessity to reassess the role of the press in the framework. The importance of the press in creating a common memory, and in shaping the opinion on matters such as the presence of foreign players cannot be doubted. But the supporters have proved their ability to reject the views expressed in the press – for example when they defend their club's policy on foreign recruitment. For the most dedicated of these supporters, alternative sources of information have also proved important. Their audience is still comparatively low though, so they certainly play a minor role in shaping the opinion of the whole society and they should only be studied as complements to the press study for a portion of the supporters.

Renovating emblems

Once a very conservative club, Arsenal has undertaken several changes since recruiting its first foreign manager in 1996. These have all affected the emblems and symbols, at the risk of altering or damaging it. From the examination of the major and most controversial changes, a redesigned crest and a move to a purpose-built larger stadium, it appears that the modernisation of Arsenal has indeed brought about controversy among the supporters, without significantly affecting their bond with the club in the long term.

A new crest, an old identity

As in the cases of Glasgow and Paris, the club crest or logo is considered by supporters as a major bearer of the club identity at Arsenal. Supporters have vehemently opposed new design of the club crest in 2002. Newspapers have extensively reported that the crest was booed when first presented before an Arsenal game at Highbury.[85] The audience proceeded on, chanting 'What a load of rubbish!', during the whole game.[86] Thereafter, a campaign against the crest was launched by two supporters' club (the Arsenal Football Supporters' Club – ASFC – and the Arsenal Independent Supporters' Association – AISA) together with two fanzines (*Highbury High* and *The Gooner*).[87] According to the Club secretary, Michael O'Brien,[88] no other subject has triggered as many emails to the club as the new design of the crest. Discontent was indeed running high as letters to the AISA newsletter testify: 'What are they trying to do; they want me to wear a crest on my shirt that's been designed by a 10-year old on his big brother's computer'.[89] Fans particularly resented not being consulted by the club in the elaboration of a design that did not fulfil their expectation:

> The history and traditions of Arsenal Football Club are important to us all. The Club needs to understand and reflect that, when planning major changes, such as to club colours and the crest.[90]

Moreover, it's the rupture with the past the new design of the crest created that was the main source of resentment: 'The new crest reminds me of the latest energy drink can, or a badly designed beer label. Not the image I held for my club – the club my grandfather, my father and my son have all supported'.[91] As in the case of PSG, the value of the crest as a realm of memory, i.e. its ability to provide a sense of continuity, has come to the fore.

But unlike the unsuccessful new design of PSG's emblem, which had got rid of the Eiffel Tower, the new Arsenal crest retained 'the cannon, the very epitome of Arsenal tradition and determination',[92] and the value of the crest as a realm of memory has not been completely undermined. Fans have therefore been able to project on the cannon at least some of the same meanings that they projected on the old crest. In parallel, the club has bolstered acceptance by emphasising the changes in the crest and how the new design, with the gun pointing to the 'west' was actually closer to an older design dating from 1922.[93] Some fans may still regret the old crest, notably its Latin motto, *Victoria Concordia Crescit*, or its 'black letter' writing. Yet, fans have come to accept the commercial considerations behind the change.[94] Supporters agree with the club's statement that it was too complex to achieve the goal set out by the club: conquer foreign markets: 'we're in a different marketplace today. We're playing in Europe every year. What does a Latin statement mean to a Japanese person?'.[95] They also understand that Arsenal's inability to copyright the previous crest or use it as a trademark[96] resulted in a hefty lack of earnings for the club. Anyone could sell merchandise with the Arsenal crest, without paying the club any fee. Consequently, the dislike for the crest subsided and campaigns against it ceased rapidly.

In this instance, it is surprising to see supporters' acceptance of the increasing commercialisation of the game, which they typically would fight. For example, fans also criticised the introduction of the new crest on the grounds that it meant the club betrayed the promise made in its charter that 'all replica strip designs have a minimum lifespan of two seasons'.[97] Fans also campaign for less expensive tickets ('Ticketing is a favourite topic' by AISA's own admittance).[98] However, fans now believe, often in a resigned manner, that widening the club's income is necessary and that, otherwise, the club would not remain able to compete at the highest level. As in the case of PSG, the management of the club has also been able to reconcile the supporters' longing for continuity and their target of bolstering their income. Like PSG, Arsenal has started to sell 'retro' shirts incorporating an older club logotype,[99] which did not include the gun, apparently at the fans' request.[100] This design was popular with the supporters because it featured heavily on the doors and walls of Arsenal's old stadium: Highbury.

A new local stadium

At the beginning of the 2006–7 season, Arsenal left Highbury and moved to a new, purpose-built, larger, stadium at Ashburton Grove. Though it may have raised a few eyebrows, this decision to change stadium registered surprisingly little opposition from the fans.[101] Coming after the debate about the crest, the increase of income (and therefore competitiveness on the field) that the new stadium would generate has been widely accepted as a legitimate reason to move grounds. Fans had also become accustomed to see Arsenal play at home in a stadium other than Highbury (Wembley for its Champion League's games between 1998 and 2000).[102] At some point, David Dein, the club's Vice-Chairman was indeed in favour of a move to a newly reconstructed Wembley.[103] Confronted with relocation outside North London, supporters showed a clear preference to a local move and welcomed the fact that the new stadium was built within walking distance of Highbury. Even supporters coming from far-away London boroughs or from abroad, seem to have been in favour of this 'local relocation': supporters are attached to a locale not because they reside there, but because of the values they have invested it with. For some supporters, it was quite clear that they could claim that they belonged to a part of London which increasing housing prices forced them to leave.

The creation of AISA testifies to the importance of locality for the supporters. It was largely motivated by some fans' desire for the club to stay in Islington.[104] AISA campaigned strongly against the opposition from some local councillors, representative of what AISA describes as a 'minority' of local residents.[105] Arsenal has certainly enjoyed a strong link with its neighbourhood. Although the club claims that it has 27 millions supporters worldwide and that most supporters no longer come from North London,[106] the immediate vicinity of Highbury's stadium is populated by supporters. It also bears the mark of Arsenal as it is full of shops (hairdressers, convenience stores, pubs, fish-and-chip shops) named after the team or its supporters ('Gooner car hire', 'Gunner's fish bar', 'Arsenal hairdresser'). On match day, Arsenal's imprint on the neighbourhood is even more visible. Many front gardens in the residential streets between the Tube stations (Arsenal, Finsbury Park) and the stadia are used to sell Arsenal merchandise, or food and drinks, to the spectators.[107]

The change was also smoothed out by the club's celebration of Highbury's past during the whole of the last season in the old stadium, in articles on the club website ('Highbury Highlights')[108] and in match programmes ('It happened at Highbury', 'Hidden Highbury').[109] All articles emphasised the club and the stadium history as a succession of changes: of 'first' and 'last'. Supporters were also regularly asked to share their memories of Highbury.[110] Most conspicuously, the home jersey was redesigned to use a darker shade of red, akin to the jersey worn during the first season in Highbury.[111] A formal ceremony of farewell to Highbury finally took place after the last home game in the league. It included a parade of 'Arsenal legends', presentations to 'distinguished Club members', a trophy parade, a crest parade, the final countdown of the Highbury clock and fireworks.[112]

During the first season in the new stadium, a correlative celebration of change was undertaken. 'Hidden Highbury' was replaced by 'Discovering Emirates', aimed at familiarising fans with the new stadium. Two new regular sections emphasising change appeared in the programme. One is a series of interviews with former club players who remember their 'First impressions' of Arsenal. The other focuses solely on 'Arsenal Firsts'.[113] Similarly, Arsenal insists on the inscription of the new stadium in the succession of places where the club has played. This double action of the club, celebrating memory and change, is particularly important. Arsenal's management has understood how important this is, and made extensive use of its ability to create new symbols by linking them to old ones.

A homely feeling

The new stadium seems to have been overwhelmingly accepted by supporters. It gives way to some mild criticisms: poor home results at the start of the first season; the quality of the food that can be bought. On the other hand, long-term fans are nostalgic about Highbury and dislike the lack of what they term a 'homely feeling' at the new stadium. In that respect, the name of the stadium, sold to a sponsor, Emirates Airlines for fifteen years, has proved to be hugely problematic for most supporters.[114] According to an AISA survey, 85 per cent opposed the idea of selling 'naming rights' for the new stadium before the transaction was completed.[115] At the end of the first season, the name Emirates stadium was as disliked as it was when the deal was announced. Many supporters still avoided using this name,[116] purporting to denounce the 'excessive' commercialisation of the game. It seems that changing the emblems themselves would justify the qualification of commercialisation as 'excessive'. At Arsenal, as in other football clubs, the name of the stadium is important to carry an attachment to locality or history. Hence some supporters prefer calling the stadium Ashburton Grove (or simply 'the Grove')[117] or occasionally 'New Highbury'.[118]

The problem with names is also illustrated within the stadium itself. Whereas different seat colours spelled out the name Arsenal at Highbury, the seats in the Emirates are uniformly red. The club has officially explained that since sponsor logos were forbidden during Champions League games, it would be disrespectful for the club to plaster its name around. Club secretary, Michael O'Brien has admitted that the real reason was more likely to be the wish to bid for lucrative events such as concerts or European Cup finals where displaying the name of the club could be seen as a disadvantage. Fans have nevertheless expressed to the club, and in interviews, their great disappointment at seeing the stadium bear so little mark of belonging to Arsenal. They are currently engaging in a strategy to colonise the stadium and invest it with symbols from Highbury, which they call 'Arsenalisation'.[119] During games, some have indeed been seen deploying banners claiming 'this is the Clock End' or 'this is the North Bank' in reference to the names of the two ends of Highbury. The supporters have also asked the club to reinstall 'Herbert Chapman's clock' from Highbury in the new stadium.[120] Promises were made by the club that a solution would be found.[121]

A continental modernity?

The stadium has been invested with Arsenal meaning through other practices, from the club and supporters. As a North London supporter in his fifties explained: 'since we now have a "continental" stadium, the club has tried to develop continental traditions'. The first of such traditions the supporter named is a mascot, 'Gunnersaurus', which had been seen for a few years at Highbury. Truly, it has more to do with the commercialisation of the game in England based on an American model than with practices from the European continent where they are actually largely unknown. He went on to refer to the practice of announcing the team in the sound system. Although some supporters claim that like Gunnersaurus, this is a new practice imposed by the club, Michael O'Brien said it originated from some fans who want the stadium to become livelier.

For years, Highbury had actually been known as 'the library', in reference to its traditionally largely silent crowds. Since 2003, before the move to the Emirates, a group of supporters named 'REDaction' (in reference to Arsenal's main colour) has undertaken to enliven the atmosphere of the stadium, by writing and singing chants dedicated to each Arsenal player.[122] They also meet regularly on game days at the weekend in The Rocket, a pub on Holloway Road where the songs are sung and learned by the supporters. Despite their strong emphasis on the British tradition of singing, REDaction is particularly interesting since it has occasionally organised the closest in England there has been to a *tifo*, the practice (originally from Italy) of welcoming the players on the pitch through a display of light and flags. REDaction also gained permission from the club to regroup in one section of the stadium (aptly called the REDsection), to use drums and a megaphone to initiate the singing. REDaction has therefore broken with the English tradition of individualised and spontaneous support for the team. It actually set out to accomplish what the Ultra group of supporters was founded for: bringing unconditional and *organised* support to its team. This 'European approach' was even mentioned twice by REDaction members.[123] REDaction is not an Ultra group though. The Ultra model is not only characterised by what the fans themselves brand an unconditional support for the team but also by vocal and sometimes powerful opposition to the club. REDaction still lacks the power to pressure the club (a power that Ultra groups use and arguably abuse). REDaction's possible convergence with AISA might provide them with this power: AISA is invited to the supporters' forums organised by Arsenal.

Fans who are unhappy with the club policies, and want to have their say in Arsenal's policy can also join another organisation: the Arsenal Supporters' Trust, born from AISA in 2002, when members of the latter saw a need for an independent organisation to deal with the club's governance issues.[124] The Trust therefore buys club shares and every Arsenal supporter can join and buy units of these shares for a price of £13. The stated goal is that they can therefore have their say in the running of the club without buying a whole share, the price of which (around £5,000) is prohibitive for most supporters. The real influence of the Trust is very limited, however. Representatives from its board get to meet the club managing director (Keith Edelman) two to three times a year. But the Trust owns only three shares out of the 54,000 that the club has issued. Even taking into account that the shares held privately by members of the Trust total 1 per cent of the club capital, it is unlikely that the Trust's voice can be decisive in any vote at the shareholders' general assembly. It is possible to wonder whether the role played by the Trust is not merely symbolic and aims at giving fans the impression that they are being heard. More crucially, supporters' trusts are uniquely British institutions, which can be found in more than a hundred clubs in Britain and which are supported by Supporters' Direct, a government-funded organisation. The changes that have recently affected Arsenal have therefore prompted two different kinds of response from the supporters: an internationalisation of the practices of support, based on a British version of continental practices; and the adoption of a purely British practise through the foundation of a supporters' trust.

The reactions from the supporters to the changes that have affected the emblems of the club (chiefly the logo and the stadium) illustrate the importance fans attach to them, mostly confirming the framework adopted for this study. The major upheaval that followed the redesign of the crest subsided rapidly. In contrast to the PSG case, the new design did indeed include a major element of the old crest, the cannon. The crest was thus able to retain the meaning that it had previously been invested with and to promote identification with the club. Furthermore, the club management emphasised that the new design marked a return to an older one. Change was linked with continuity and the crest therefore retained its value as a realm of memory. The club similarly emphasised change and continuity in the move to a new stadium and proved its ability to play on the processes through which the emblems are invested with meaning by the supporters. This has its limits, as the rejection of the corporate name of the new stadium shows. The increased commercialisation of the game is accepted by the supporters as a necessity to be able to compete with other clubs. It is rejected, though, when it changes the very nature of the emblems with which the supporters identify. Also, the club has partly failed to import traditions from abroad. The mascot or the practice of reading the names of the players out aloud before the game have not been widely adopted by fans. Supporters are not entirely hostile to imported traditions though. The development of a number of new and different supporters' associations, AISA and REDaction, shows that Arsenal supporters are willing partly to adopt foreign practises of support and adapt them to suit their needs. But these imported traditions are mixed with home-grown institutions, such as the Supporters' Trust, which promote an unquestionably British involvement of supporters with their club, through ownership of shares.

The question of the stadium has also brought to the fore the question of the locale. It has been shown in the two dimensions analysed by John Bale: space and place. The localisation of the new stadium (its 'place') within walking distance of the old one, in a neighbourhood which breathes Arsenal, certainly played a major part in its adoption by the supporters. The fans are now engaged in making the 'space' of the new stadium feel like home, just as PSG supporters were in the 1970s and 1980s.

'One of us'

In the years 1995–2006, Arsenal supporters' relations with their club were not affected by the change of emblems. How have the internationalised Arsenal teams been received by supporters? In the words of many of the club's supporters, 'fans do the voting with their feet'. If so, then the multinational Arsenal has received a clear vote of confidence. Audiences are on the increase. The new stadium has indeed been built to accommodate them; and, waiting lists for season or even game tickets are still growing. A few factors have facilitated the adoption by the public of the multinational Arsenal and its foreign players. Success comes first. Arsène Wenger indeed claimed a great number of domestic honours between 1996 and 2005, including League Cup doubles in 1998 and 2002, the Cup in 2003 and 2005 and remaining unbeaten in their victorious 2004 league campaign. The first few titles were also won with a side that included the ageing all-English Arsenal defence of the Graham era and the recruitment of foreigners was gradual: and fans never had the impression of a clear rupture with the club's established policy or identity.

Foreign style and English qualities

Style has doubtlessly contributed significantly to the public's espousal of the multinational Arsenal too. All supporters have spontaneously mentioned the style developed by Arsène Wenger as a source of enjoyment at the games and of pride in their club. This is certainly of great significance as Arsenal's current style is a total departure from the style for which Arsenal was famous and which earned it the tag of 'Boring Boring Arsenal' by rival fans, for its reliance on victories by the smallest margins ('1–0 to the Arsenal').[125] After scoring, the team would regroup in defence and not attack for the remainder of the match. In contrast, Arsène Wenger's teams are always prone to attack and playing a passing game.[126] As an old supporter (in her eighties) explained: 'we cannot watch English football any more, now we have seen Arsène Wenger's football'. Remarkably, the press and fans (in interviews and in the press) always brand the new Arsenal style as 'not English', or 'continental'. Even so, supporters never fail to express a preference for it. Style previously expressed the identity of the team, notably as a bastion of English traditions, thereby arguably prompting identification. It has now become an element of a spectacle offered to an audience. As *The Guardian*'s Matt Scott points out: 'Arsenal now see themselves as part of the entertainment industry, and believe they are competing with the opera and theatres'.[127] Because the change of style only happened in the last fifteen years, it is still difficult to assess whether this new style may herald a complete change in the nature of partisanship: will supporters come to follow a game because of the show on offer? Will they desert the team if it stops playing flamboyantly? For the supporters interviewed, style has proved to be only one determinant in their appreciation of Arsenal and, so far, proved compatible with traditional identification with the team.

The foreign players' ability to contribute to this attractive style of football is a major reason behind their general acceptance by fans. The award given every year by the Arsenal Supporters' Club to the best player is one of the signs of this acceptance: it has been regularly given to foreign players, starting with Bergkamp in 1997 and including Vieira (2001); Pirès (2002) and Henry (2000, 2003, 2004).[128] When asked, most supporters have also named at least one foreign player among their two favourite Arsenal players. Furthermore, on the occasion of a campaign organised by the English football authorities called 'football's anti-racism week' two supporters' association, AISA and REDaction joined together to publish a single-sided leaflet entitled 'Kick Racism out of Football; United Nations of Arsenal'. It shows eighteen Arsenal players and the flag of the eighteen different nations that they hail from and states that 'If ever a manager showed that colour and nationality means [*sic*] nothing, it is Arsene [*sic*] Wenger. We are proud to support the united nations of Arsenal'.[129] The support that Arsenal fans give their team's players, whether native or foreign, is unquestionable. They are prone to point out that criticisms against the omnipresence of foreigners in their club come chiefly from supporters of other teams. It therefore seems to constitute part of what Bromberger has described as: 'A rich rhetoric of glorification of their own people and denigration of others'.[130] Consequently, Arsenal fans are prone to glorify their own players, no matter their origin. In their words: 'As soon as they put the jersey on, you have got to love them'.

Identification to the players has appeared facilitated by three major factors. First, is the length of association with the club. A player such as Kolo Touré who, in 2006, was Arsenal's longest-serving defender,[131] became 'a firm favourite with the fans'.[132] Interviews with supporters further suggest he had even become an important symbol of the Arsenal team at the time. Second, some players are easier to identify with because of their prominence on the field. Either they have captained the team (Tony Adams, Patrick Vieira or Thierry Henry), or they have proved important in a number of situations. Thierry Henry owes his status as one of the club's 'idols' primarily to his being the most prolific striker in the history of Arsenal.[133] Third, it has also appeared, more crucially, that a foreign player can represent typically English values. Patrick Vieira, for example, has been commonly lauded for his total, physical (a common euphemism for 'often brutal') implication in the game, qualities which have been seen as typically English. The fans' sentiment has been corroborated by Arsène Wenger: 'We have the English character and resilience in the team, but you can get that as well with foreigners like Petit and Vieira'.[134] This finding is of major importance. English qualities can be associated with a foreign player in the same way that a foreign style can be associated with an English team, without detracting supporters from following the team.

A residual English identity

Nevertheless, the remaining English elements in Arsenal are being regularly emphasised by the club through its officials and its website. Topic headers such as 'Arsenal pair called up by England'[135] or 'Eight Gunners named in England squad'[136] have for example cropped up on the front page of the website. They are slightly misleading as these 'Eight Gunners' hail from the women's team and the Arsenal pair in question has been selected for the 'England Women's Under-15 Development Pool'. The website's selection of news is indeed rather prone to emphasising the English element in the women,[137] or occasionally in the youth teams.[138] In 2006, long before the club became foreign owned, and even before the possibility of foreign ownership surfaced, Arsène Wenger made a much publicised declaration on the necessity to keep the ownership of Arsenal English, as the only way to ensure that an English spirit would remain.[139] Both the *Evening Standard* and the *Daily Mirror* ironically entitled 'Beware us foreigners' on that occasion.[140] Confronted with the lack of English players of the first men's team (the only one that really embodies the club), Arsenal has promoted new symbols of Englishness. As in the case of PSG, where the management became a symbol of the club, this shows that when a symbol disappears, another one can take its place, at least partially. It is really unlikely that the young girls provide as much a support for identification as the professional players do. But as a supporter said: 'it shows Arsenal is still an English club'.

English and local players

The perceived need to associate with English elements has also been expressed by the club assistant secretary, Michael O'Brien with regard to players. According to him it stems from his perception that 'All Arsenal fans would rather win the title with an all-English team'. Interviews with supporters corroborate the impression gathered from supporters' written production on websites and mailing lists, that this is not quite so. Only three interviewees explained their preference for a team that would comprise at least a few English players, but mostly when Arsenal competes in Europe: they argued that Arsenal represents England in this competition. Yet this preference has proved wholly theoretical. None of these supporters could name a precise number of Englishmen in the team that would satisfy them. More significantly, they all explained that success was more important to them than the inclusion of English players. Arsenal has a history of success since the 1930s, which has certainly been very important in attracting fans. One of them has even commented in his published diaries that he could not understand why anyone could follow a team which never wins, such as Scunthorpe United.[141]

Michael O'Brien's assertion is also misleading as it defines a category, 'English player', which does not necessarily have great significance to the supporters. Undoubtedly, an English player such as Tony Adams has long embodied Arsenal for fans. Arguably, he still does represent the English era at Arsenal. Reasons abound. He was developed at Arsenal, captained the club for nearly fourteen years and, crucially, he never played professionally for another club. Yet supporters are quick to point out that he was not from North London. He was born in Romford (London Borough of Havering), which, as two fans have expressed 'is traditionally West Ham territory'. This emphasises a crucial point: in the London fans' attachment to Arsenal, local identity actually primes national identity. In domestic competitions, Arsenal represents London against other English teams. Against other London teams, Arsenal represents more specifically North London. A player from North London is therefore much more representative of these fans' identity than an English player from elsewhere (and even more so than a Brit: 'you have to remember Scots are seen as foreigners here', one Arsenal supporter pointed out). The case of Ashley Cole emphasises this essential element and how the local identity of the club links to the identification with a player. Developed at the club, and perceived as coming from the vicinity of the stadium, the player left to join the rival team Chelsea in the summer of 2006.[142] He later criticised Arsenal heavily in his autobiography.[143] The reaction from Arsenal supporters was so virulent that it prompted Arsène Wenger to make public declarations in order to discourage a planned display in a forthcoming game against Chelsea,[144] and to send an email to fans on the subject.[145] Supporters have explained the reasons behind this extreme dislike of Ashley Cole, explained most clearly by a 60-year-old woman from Islington:

> He betrayed us. He was from Islington. He was raised in one of the council estate flats near the stadium. He was meant to be *one of us*, Arsenal through and through.[146]

Unlike players from outside Arsenal's catchment area or who supported other clubs, the propinquity fans felt with Ashley Cole compounded the sense of betrayal. For supporters, he was another supporter who managed to fulfil their unspoken dream: play for Arsenal.

The most dedicated Arsenal supporters, those who attend the games most often, are clearly much more concerned with local than national identity. Yet, there are two categories of non-local English players that they are more likely to identify with. First are players developed at the club. Whereas foreign players are often seen as 'simply an opportunity to get talent cheaply', English players acquire some bona fide local identity during their training in the club's youth teams. Second are England players. This can be explained because in practical terms, Arsenal footballers selected for England are supported twice by the English supporters of Arsenal. Furthermore Arsenal players represent their club at country level, a clear source of pride for Arsenal fans. They also represent their country at club level and the national element in their identity thus becomes more important than the local one. That David Seaman was born in south Yorkshire became less important than the fact he represented England – another unspoken dream of Arsenal's English fans. It is important to emphasise here that, contrary to popular belief, very few of the English supporters of Arsenal do not support England. Arsenal supporters are less committed to England than they are to their club and will seldom follow the national team abroad or even in Wembley. Nevertheless, most do follow English games, if only on TV; most wish for England to win; most are happiest when an Arsenal player performs well for England.

National teams also play an important part in the identification of foreign supporters. A few Arsenal supporters have been prompt in mentioning the undoubted Irish component in the Arsenal team of the 1970s,[147] and to comment upon how it reflected on the Irish population found near Holloway Road. Contacts with supporters of Arsenal in Paris suggest that they are more likely to like Arsenal because of its large French contingent (which has, crucially, included World Cup winners).

The omnipresence of foreign players has clearly not deterred fans from supporting Arsenal. The foreign imports have even been far from rejected by supporters. The period of transition during which the team mixed Englishmen and foreigners certainly helped the supporters to get used to the presence of foreigners. The long association of some of the overseas players with the club, and the prestige and success they brought played its part too. Furthermore, Arsenal supporters have proved more prone to identify with a local, North London player, English or not, than an English player from elsewhere in England unless the player represented England or was developed at the club. It also appears that foreign players can bear English values, they can fit in with the English identity of the club, and thus provoke identification from English fans. They are also a source of identification for foreign supporters, an important factor at a time that football is increasingly concerned with internationalisation.

Conclusion

In their dealing with Arsenal Football Club and its foreign contingent, no newspaper has adopted an overt xenophobic agenda. All have presented arguments both in favour of and against the presence of foreign players in English football. Their view on the matter may appear balanced (or if Stephen Wagg is to be followed, 'incoherent'). A difference in the style explains why tabloids might be more commonly seen as xenophobic: they often seem to endorse comments made by players, managers or officials, some of which are undoubtedly xenophobic. Yet a rationalised and unacknowledged xenophobia is clear in the newspapers since the arguments used against the foreign presence prove largely unfounded. A rampant if casual xenophobia also appears in the stereotypes associated with the foreign players. This reflects the staggering parochialism and insularity of the English press and is made all the more apparent by the ferocity of the English written media.

The supporters have been largely unaffected by the press's xenophobia. On the contrary, they distance themselves with the criticisms made by the printed media of Arsenal's foreign recruitment. Fans have indeed for the most part accepted the internationalisation of their team. First, they have embraced, sometimes resignedly, the renovated emblems, even those perceived as foreign. Fans have accepted the commercial imperatives that prompted it, in view of the need for Arsenal to be able to compete with wealthier clubs in England and abroad. The new 'continental' stadium has been largely accepted, chiefly because of its location near the old one. There are limits to the acceptance of commercialisation. It is rejected if it affects the very nature of an emblem. Celebration of the past has also been used to soften the transitions to new emblems. An emphasis has been put on ruptures which happened in the history of the club so that the new emblems are simply seen as another stage in the evolution of Arsenal and not a departure from tradition. Even the symbols which have been identified as 'continental' by the supporters result more from the increasing commercialisation of football than from some internationalisation of the club. On the other hand, supporters have shown an interesting ability spontaneously to adapt foreign uses to their needs. The combination of two newly founded and increasingly close supporters' groups, AISA and REDaction may be seen as the beginning of a small scale replication of the Ultra model. The Arsenal Supporters' Trust, which has developed recently too, is clearly a British invention, though. Supporters have organised on a foreign model, but adapted it and added home-grown elements.

Second, fans have embraced the foreign players. The success enjoyed by the club explains the ease with which foreign footballers were adopted. The flamboyant style in which the team now plays, despite identified as 'foreign', has been another major reason for acceptance. Some of the players have also shown qualities that are traditionally considered English in football. More crucially, players are adopted by virtue of representing Arsenal. Showing unconditional support for the team is a self-defining characteristic of the 'true fan', so any player in the team is supported – and the longer the player stays at the club, the greater the increase in support. The club has nevertheless developed new symbols to emphasise its English identity: the women's team, the owners. This seems largely unnecessary as fans show a limited preference for English players. In domestic competitions, fans identify better with strictly local players (hailing from North London, as discussed above).

The Arsenal case shows clearly that the internationalisation of teams resulting from the *Bosman* ruling is less a challenge to fans' identification and to gathering support than the increased commercialisation of the game – even when it is as widely accepted as at Arsenal.

Notes

1 Nick Harris, *The foreign revolution: how overseas footballers changed the English game*. London: Aurum, 2006, p. 1 (hereafter Harris 2006). The fact has also been commented upon in many occasions during the week following the game, notably: Nick Harris, 'How Arsenal's imports have changed the game' and 'Overseas and over here', *The Independent*, 16 February 2006. Ken Dyer, 'England's top clubs lead Euro league for foreigners', *Evening Standard*, 17 February 2005. Jon Brodkin and Louise Taylor, 'Wenger in blast at critics of foreign policy', *The Guardian*,

19 February 2005. Mike Hammond, 'UEFA's new home-grown quota numbers don't add up', *The Times*, 20 February 2005.

2 This historical narrative of Arsenal is mostly derived from: Phil Soar and Martin Tyler, *The official illustrated history of Arsenal (1886–1999)*. London: Hamlyn, 1999 (hereafter Soar and Tyler 1999). Michael Wade, *The Arsenal story: an official history of Arsenal Football Club*. Edinburgh: Lomond Book, 1999 (hereafter Wade 1999). David Sims, *Arsenal: memories and marble halls*. London: Pavilion, 2000 (hereafter Sims 2000). Joe Rose, *Arsenal player by player: five decades of player profiles*. London: Hamlyn, 2004 (hereafter Rose 2004).

3 'A new home at Highbury', Soar and Tyler 1999: 34ff.

4 Keir Radnedge. *The complete encyclopedia of football: the bible of world soccer*. London: Carlton Books, 2004, p. 236 (hereafter Radnedge 2004).

5 Wade 1999: 21.

6 Soar and Tyler 1999: 34.

7 Wade 1999: 23.

8 Soar and Tyler 1999: 9.

9 Wade 1999.

10 Wade 1999: 39.

11 Soar and Tyler 1999: 34 and 49.

12 Sims 2000: 15; Soar and Tyler 1999: 18–19; Wade 1999: 38.

13 Harris 2006: 2 and 36.

14 Harris 2006: 358.

15 Rose 2004: 124.

16 Rose 2004: 124.

17 Radnedge 2004: 236.

18 Harris 2006: 192.

19 Wade 1999: 77.

20 Rose 2004: 124.

21 Dan Brennan, *The official Arsenal miscellany*. London: Hamlyn, 2004, p. 142 (hereafter Brennan 2004).

22 Soar and Tyler 1999: 163.

23 Soar and Tyler 1999: 201.

24 Soar and Tyler 1999: 50 and 54.

25 Harris 2006: 314.

26 Harris 2006: 4.

27 Harris 2006: 1.

28 Dave Kidd, 'March of foreign legion', *The Sun*, 21 August 2002.

29 Harris 2006: 1.

30 Harris 2006: 1.

31 Wade 1999: 14.

32 Soar and Tyler 1999: 171.

33 Harris 2006: 296.

34 Harris 2006: 225.

35 For a striking example, Soar and Tyler 1999: 170–171.

36 Christopher Davies, 'Global Gunners set for place in history', *Daily*

Telegraph, 15 September 2006. The team was: Jens Lehmann (Germany); Emmanuel Eboue (Ivory Coast); Johan Djourou (Switzerland); Justin Hoyte (England); William Gallas (France); Tomas Rosicky (Czech Republic); Gilberto (Brazil); Cesc Fabregas (Spain); Alexander Hleb (Belarus); Emmanuel Adebayor (Togo); Robin van Persie (Holland).

37 Salient examples include: David Lacey, 'Wenger's legion equipped to win in style', *The Guardian*, 17 May 2000. David Lacey, 'Until Wenger's team retain a title they cannot be called great', *The Guardian*, 27 March 2004. Ian Ridley, 'Wenger must be seething', *The Observer*, 16 March 2003. Brian Reade, 'Let's thank Wenger that a small corner of a London field will always be foreign', *The Mirror*, 1 April 2006. Oliver Holt, 'It's Real 0… the Real Arsenal 1', *The Mirror*, 22 February 2006. David Anderson, 'My success is all down to you, Wenger', *The Mirror*, 23 September 2006. John Sadler, 'Arsenal WILL be the best', *The Sun*, 24 February 2004. Henry Winter, 'Wenger puts style to the forefront', *Daily Telegraph*, 26 February 2003. Duncan Castles, 'Brazilian Beast desperate to show off his drive', *The Times*, 3 December 2006. Jon Culley, 'Warnock mind games outwit limp Arsenal', *The Independent*, 1 January 2007.

38 Gordon Tynan, 'Dein says "secret formula" produced exquisite vintage', *The Independent*, 28 October 2004.

39 For a good example, see: David Mellor, 'Why Wenger must tackle his bad guys', *Evening Standard*. 14 March 2003.

40 See for example, see Brian Glanville, 'Lost youth pay price', *The Times*, 25 July 1999.

41 Raoul Simons, 'Walcott deal can't hide Wenger's foreign fancy', *Evening Standard*, 24 January 2006.

42 'Petit: I've suffered for years', *The Sun*, 8 March 2000. Bill Pierce, 'Surgeon's knife looms large again for Adams', *The Independent*, 8 March 2000. Michael Herd, 'Please grow up Mr Anelka, French dissing is not our style', *Evening Standard*, 8 July 1999. Tommy Staniforth, 'McDermott's social call', *The Independent*, 5 July 1999.

43 A good late example is provided by Richard Williams, 'Foreign legion: beauty or blight?', *The Guardian*, 13 August 2003.

44 See Adrian Curtis, 'Keegan: My foreign fear', *Evening Standard*, 20 January 2000. David Mellor, 'Real stars don't need protection', *Evening Standard*, 4 February 2000.

45 Wagg 1991.

46 A small selection includes: Guy Hodgson, 'Growing pains for the league of nations: is football being stung – or saved – by the influx of foreign players?', *The Independent*, 23 November 1996. Alan Parry, 'Why January love: foreign imports', *The Guardian*, 12 July 1996. Joe Lovejoy, 'Increasing the interest rate', *The Times*, 11 August 1996. Rob Hughes, 'Fine tradition needs saving from the danger of continental drift', *The Times*, 5 March 1998. Clare Balding, 'Six of the best and worst for the season', *Evening Standard*, 11 May 2000. Henry Winter, 'Invasion force threatens to tilt the balance', *Daily Telegraph*, 6 August 1996.

47 Glenn Moore, 'The two sides to a foreign invasion', *The Independent*, 10 February 1996. Following a similar theme was, among others, Joe Melling, 'The foreign invaders', *Mail on Sunday*, 3 August 1997.
48 On at least twenty-eight Mondays between 11 September 2000 and 16 April 2001.
49 Joe Lovejoy, 'Passport to the stars', *The Times*, 20 February 2005. Martin Lipton, 'Europe or bust: goal feast at Highbury', *The Mirror*, 15 February 2005.
50 Bill Edgar, 'Neville has swipe at Arsenal as local talent row rages', *The Times*, 17 February 2005.
51 Toby Manhire, 'Critics fire salvo at all-foreign Arsenal', *The Guardian*, 17 February 2005.
52 Dave Kidd, 'You're a Brit out of order', *The Sun*, 10 March 2006.
53 Henry Winter, 'Wenger in racism row', *Daily Telegraph*, 11 March 2006. Charlie Wyett, 'Arsene: Pardew is racist', *The Sun*, 11 March 2006.
54 'Pardew: I'm not a racist', *The Sun*, 14 March 2006.
55 Aston Villa boss David O'Leary, players' union chief Gordon Taylor and Wigan chairman Dave Whelan according to John Cross. 'Wenger blasts Pards' "racism"', *The Mirror*, 11 March 2006.
56 Neil Moxley and Steve Curry, 'It's a disgrace', *Daily Mail*, 16 February 2005.
57 An article by Christopher Davies, on 16 February 2005.
58 See Michael Hart, 'McClaren faces fight to halt the foreign legion', *Evening Standard*, 12 April 2002 (where the author laments the presence of only one English coach in the FA Cup semi-finals).
59 A small selection of articles in which such critics appear over the years includes: Rob Hughes, 'Fine tradition needs saving from the danger of continental drift', *The Times*, 5 March 1998. Ben Webb, 'The foreign legion', *The Times*, 29 August 1998. David Mellor, 'Clever Alex has put one over the FA', *Evening Standard*, 2 July 1999. Charlie Wyett, 'Our kids just hit a brick wall', *The Sun*, 16 February 2005. Nick Harris, 'Hidden dangers of foreign policy', *The Independent*, 2 August 2006.
60 As Sue Mott does in 'Arsenal right to put Planet Football above England', *Daily Telegraph*, 14 March 2006.
61 Sir Trevor Brooking, 'Wenger would think of England… but our kids are second best', *Daily Mail*, 15 March 2006. Terry Land, 'Trevor: Wenger is spot on', *The Sun*, 15 March 2006.
62 See for example, criticisms made by former Arsenal coach, George Graham in John Cross, 'Arsenal's fall from power', *The Mirror*, 16 February 2006.
63 David Mellor, 'How to manage a decline from greatness', *Evening Standard*, 17 February 2006.
64 Quoted from: John Leigh and David Woodhouse, *The football lexicon*. Cambridge: Oleander, 2005. As it appeared in Tom Dart, 'Handbags at ten paces in row Z', *The Times*, 18 October 2004.
65 A very small selection of articles where the word appears, casually

includes: Henry Winter, 'England must learn foreign language', *Daily Telegraph*, 13 September 1996. Andy Totham, 'Cash and grab', *The Sun*, 14 August 2004. Jamie Jackson, 'Show me the money', *The Observer*, 8 January 2006.

66 Jonathan Magee and John Sugden, 'The world at their feet: professional football and international labor migration', *Journal of sport and social issues*, 26(4) (2002), 421–437. Joseph Maguire, 'Sport labor migration research revisited', *Journal of sport and social issues*, 28(4) (2004), 477–482.

67 In the words of Sir Alex Ferguson as quoted in Neil Custis, 'My Ron's no diver', *The Sun*, 16 September 2003.

68 As authors Kaveh Solhekol and Oliver Kay admit: 'Diving and play-acting were once seen as symptoms of a foreign disease, brought to Britain by overseas imports with no respect for the laws of the game', in 'Campaign gets on a roll as UEFA attacks "British" diving problem', *The Times*, 15 February 2006.

69 Simon Bird, 'The Premiership is full of cheats and divers, *Daily Mirror*, 10 November 2006.

70 Duncan Bech, 'Pardew rejects Wenger's charge of racism', *The Independent*, 14 March 2006.

71 Rob Hughes, 'Wenger revels in Double whammy', *The Times*, 5 May 2002. Glenn Moore, 'Do we care any more?', *The Independent*, 7 January 2006.

72 Matthew Syed, 'From romance to hollow farce', *The Times*, 10 January 2005.

73 David Mellor, 'Hoey takes the biscuit', *Evening Standard*, 1 March 2002.

74 See for example Simon Kuper, 'Revolutionaries face home truths', *The Times*, 18 November 2002.

75 Jasper Rees, 'Who is he?', *The Guardian*, 18 August 2003.

76 In the programme of the match against Sheffield Wednesday, 20 September 2006 and against Porto on 26 September 2006. Two of the articles that sparked Henry's latter reaction are: Martin Lipton, 'Thierry: my hero Dickov', *The Mirror*, 22 September 2006. Dominic Fifield, 'Davies thriving as Henry's unlikely hero', *The Guardian*, 30 September 2006.

77 Investigation suggests Henry is referring to Steve Morgan, 'Henry blast: January can't do it alone, lads', *Daily Star*, 17 September 2006.

78 In the programme of the match against Sheffield Wednesday, 20 September 2006.

79 One report is Clive Tyldesley, 'From very slim pickings, hail the Englishman at the coronation', *Daily Telegraph*, 5 May 2006.

80 Mazher Mahmood, 'Sven's dirty deals', *News of the World*, 15 January 2006. Rob Beasley, 'I was sacked from best job in the world', *News of the World*. 29 January 2006.

81 To quote the words used by all four journalists interviewed.

82 Among many articles, favourites include: Marina Hyde, 'The Christmas card is warfare by other means', *The Guardian*, 22 December 2005. Michael Hart, 'No Jose snub: Wenger says Xmas card has been treated

like CIA bomb', *Evening Standard*, 22 December 2005. Dave Kidd and Pat Sheehan, 'Jose: my regret. Peace on earth as Mourinho settles row with Wenger', *The Sun*, 23 December 2005. David Woods, 'Weng card trick', *Daily Star*, 23 December 2005. Matt Hughes, 'Wenger has final say in "ridiculous" card row', *The Times*, 23 December 2005. Henry Winter, 'A Christmas reminder: it's all about the silverware', *Daily Telegraph*, 24 December 2005. 'Get the message Arsène?', *The Mirror*, 21 December 2005. Sam Wallace and Jason Burt, 'Wenger rejects Mourinho card of friendship', *The Independent*, 20 December 2005.

83 Kieran Daley, 'Football: Caborn calls for truce in card row', *The Independent*, 21 December 2005.

84 Sam Wallace, 'Ferguson and Wenger agree truce', *The Independent*, 21 January 2005. Neil Custis, 'Say sorry boys, or you'll have to see the headmaster', *The Sun*, 20 January 2005. Daniel Taylor, 'FA calls for a truce in Wenger–Ferguson spat', *The Guardian*, 20 January 2005.

85 Anthony Clavane, 'Crestfallen Gunners go off the boil', *Mirror*, 3 February 2002. John Lisners, 'Crestfallen', *News of the World*, 3 February 2002.

86 Nick Callow, 'Tessem takes opportunity to steal the Gunners' thunder', *The Observer*, 3 February 2002. 'The fans don't like it... And even Arsene's stuck with the old one', *The Mirror*, 4 February 2002.

87 Interviews with supporters from AISA and Arsenal Football Supporters' Club. References were made to the 'Crestfallen', a document printed and published by Paul Matz, Tannington Terrace, Gillespie Road, London N5 1LE, and bearing the logos 'Arsenal Independent Supporters' Association' (AISA), 'Highbury High', 'the Gooner' and a logo which seems to be that of Arsenal football supporters' club.

88 In an interview with the author at the club's premises, on 9 November 2006.

89 Letter from T. Fitzsimmonds, *Arsenal supporter* (AISA's newsletter), *c.*2002, (4): 2.

90 'Crestfallen' (n. 87).

91 Letter from Richard Webber, *Arsenal supporter* (AISA's newsletter), *c.*2002, (4): 2.

92 John Ley, 'Adams still the man to lift Arsenal', *Daily Telegraph*, 4 February 2002.

93 Their press release detailing the argument can now be found on their website (at: www.arsenal.com/article.asp?thisNav=The+Club&article=344298&Title=Arsenal+Crest (last accessed 18 May 2007).

94 As expressed by Michael O'Brien, Arsenal's assistant club secretary (interviewed: 09/11/06).

95 Tom Dart, 'Design for life?', *The Times*, 9 March 2002.

96 Adam Fresco, 'Europe overruled in Arsenal dispute', *The Times*, 13 December 2002.

97 From the club charter, on their website (at: www.arsenal.com/article.asp?thisNav=News&article=344874&lid=Community&Title=Club+Charter; last accessed 12 February 2006). The problem was commented

upon in Andrew Norfolk, 'Arsenal gunned down over new badge', *The Times*, 23 February 2002.

98 A claim repeatedly made throughout all interviews and in all the various documents from the supporters' associations.

99 The shirts were on prominent display in the club's shop at Finsbury Park. Taking pictures of them was forbidden by shop assistants.

100 According to Michael O'Brien, Arsenal's assistant club secretary (interviewed: 09/11/06).

101 The only written evidence found was in a letter from Gary Quattromini, *Arsenal supporter* (AISA's newsletter), *c*.2002, (4): 2.

102 The move to Wembley for European games was first announced in 'Arsenal seek home help', *The Times*, 20 July 1998. A fan has abundantly commented on the 1998–1999 Wembley fixtures: Laurence Marks, *A fan for all seasons: the diary of an Arsenal supporter*. London: Warner, 1999 (hereafter Marks 1999).

103 The rumours 'rubbished' in Vivek Chaudhary and Jon Brodkin, 'Walker rubbishes rumour of Arsenal move to Wembley', *The Guardian*, 20 January 2001. Confirmed by Michael O'Brien, Arsenal club assistant club secretary (interviewed: 09/11/06).

104 Interview with Tony Bernhard-Grout, chair of AISA and member of REDaction.

105 'Ashburton Grove, almost there', *Arsenal supporter* (AISA's newsletter), *c*.2002, (4): 2.

106 Cited in Jim Holden, 'Battle for London now a deadly serious affair', *Daily Express*, 6 November 2005. According to Jill Smith, supporters' liaison officer at Arsenal, this figure was produced by the marketing department; she emphasised that a great number of supporters' club are located abroad and there are certainly many overseas supporters.

107 As experienced by the author before a game with Everton on 28 October 2006.

108 www.arsenal.com/article.asp?thisNav=The+Club&article=344869&Title=Highbury+Highlights; last accessed 13 January 2007.

109 Match programmes for the 2005–6 season, section 'It happened at Highbury'.

110 For example, fans contributed to an 'A–Z of Highbury' distributed at the last game and voted for their greatest memories of Highbury (at: www.arsenal.com/article.asp?thisNav=News&article=384724&lid=NewsHeadline&Title=Your+greatest+Highbury+moments+-+revealed!).

111 As explained by Michael O'Brien, Arsenal Club assistant club secretary (interviewed: 09/11/06).

112 Programme for the Arsenal–Wigan Athletic game, 4 May 2006.

113 Club programmes for the season 2006–2007, 'First impression' and 'Arsenal first'.

114 See among others, Adrian Warner, 'Arsenal's £100m sponsor jackpot', *Evening Standard*, 5 October 2004. Ashling O'Connor, 'Arsenal flex muscle with Emirates deal', *The Times*, 6 October 2004.

115 www.aisa.org/news/survey_results.html; last accessed 13 January 2007.
116 See for example, Brian Dawes, 'The "E" word', a column, 26 May 2006 on the supporters' website 'Arsenal World' (at: www.arsenal-world.co.uk/news/loadnews.asp?cid=TMNW&id=283908; last accessed 13 January 2006).
117 Attested in 262 emails to the REDaction mailing list between 10 March 2006 and 10 January 2006.
118 Attested in emails to the REDaction mailing list between 3 and 15 August 2006.
119 Email to the REDaction mailing list on 23 October 2006.
120 See for an early example, an email to the REDaction mailing list on 5 September 2005.
121 Programme for the Arsenal–Dinamo Zagreb match, 22 August 2006.
122 Presentation on the club website (at: www.arsenal.com/article.asp?thisNav=Fanzone&article=344239&Title=REDaction+Group; last accessed 13 January 2007).
123 Email to the REDaction mailing list, 4 September 2006 and 5 November 2006.
124 The information here comes from an interview with Richard Irving, Arsenal Supporters' Trust's Company Secretary, in March 2007.
125 References to the 'Boring Boring Arsenal' abound in writings on the club. For a selection, see Soar and Tyler 1999: 62; Wade 1999: 35, 48, 67; Simms 2000: 115.
126 Articles with a positive outlook on Arsenal's style include among others, Amy Lawrence, 'Wenger guns for Euro glory but vows to keep accent on style', *The Observer*, 21 August 2005.
127 Interview with Matt Scott from *The Guardian* (12/12/06).
128 Brennan 2004: 91, gives a list of all winners of the official Arsenal supporters' club player of the year between 1967 and 2004.
129 Both quotes from the leaflet, which states: 'Published by Paul Matz on behalf of the Arsenal Independent Supporters' Association and REDaction, designed by harderthansatan.com, printed by Hartington Fine Arts'.
130 Bromberger 1995: 292.
131 'Two ton Toure', Middlesbrough match programme, 9 September 2006.
132 www.arsenal.com/player.asp?thisNav=first+team&plid=60102&clid=4421&cpid=703; last accessed 24 January 2007.
133 Matt Hughes, 'Henry hits new heights with record-breaking return to action', *The Times*, 19 October 2005.
134 Mark Bradley, 'Wenger puts his faith in new boys', *The Independent*, 11 March 1999.
135 It appeared on 26 January 2006 (at: www.arsenal.com/article.asp?thisNav=ladies&article=361046&cpid=703&title=Arsenal+pair+called+up+by+England; last accessed 24 January 2).
136 It appeared on 16 October 2006 (at: www.arsenal.com/article.asp?thisNav=news&article=422225&cpid=703&title=Eight+Gunners+named+in+England+squad; last accessed 24 January 2007).

137 For the year 2006 only, see: 'Seven Ladies called up by England', 4 February 2006. 'Ladies: several stars earn international call-ups', 1 February 2006. 'Six Ladies called up by England', 28 February 2006. 'Five Ladies named in England squad', 16 March 2006. 'England international joins Arsenal Ladies', 19 July 2006. 'Ladies named for England training camp', 3 August 2006. 'Six Ladies play in England defeat', 26 October 2006. 'Kelly Smith fifth in FIFA World Player poll', 20 December 2006. All articles on Arsenal website (at: www.arsenal.com/newsarchive.asp?thisNav=Reserves+and+Youth&clid=4436&lid=Reserves%20News%20Archive; last accessed 24 January 2007).

138 'England call up three Arsenal youngsters' published on 23 January 2007 (at: www.arsenal.com/article.asp?thisNav=reserves%20and%20youth&article=443543&cpid=703&title=England+call+up+three+Arsenal+youngsters; last accessed 24 January 2007).

139 'Board are my reassurance policy', published on the website on 15 September 2006 (at: www.arsenal.com/article.asp?thisNav=the+match&article=416331&lid=fixture_298491&Title=Board+are+my+reassurance+policy+-+Wenger; last accessed 24 January 2007).

140 'Wenger: beware us foreigners', *Evening Standard*, 29 September 2006. Darren Lewis, 'Beware us foreigners', *The Mirror*, 29 September 2006.

141 Marks 1999: 222.

142 Sam Wallace, 'Cole on his way to Chelsea as Arsenal accept Gallas and £5m', *The Independent*, 1 September 2006.

143 Ashley Cole, *My defence*. London: Headline Book Publishing, 2006.

144 A full picture is provided in the following: Wayne Veysey, 'Gunners order fans to stop the Cole taunts; club act to prevent homophobic chants in showdown at Chelsea', *Evening Standard*, 8 December 2006. Matt Hughes, 'Wenger pours oil on troubled waters as Cole faces fans' fury', *The Times*, 9 December 2006. 'Don't flash your Ash cash', *The Sun*, 9 December 2006.

145 Neil Ashton, 'Don't bash Ash: Arsenal's email plea for fans to lay off Cole', *Daily Mail*, 9 December 2006.

146 Interviews with supporters (see p. 70). Author's emphasis.

147 On Arsenal's Irish heritage in the press see, Dave Hannigan, 'Seeds fall on stony ground', *The Times*, 23 April 2000. Patrick McGovern, 'The Irish brawn drain: English League clubs and Irish footballers, 1946–1995', *British Journal of Sociology*, 51(3) (2000), 401–418.

Conclusion*

This study has researched the processes through which supporters identify with their clubs in the post-*Bosman* era. It seeks to build on, modify and develop the hypotheses that the nationality and social identity of players as well as the composition of the team are the primary means through which supporters identify with their club. Other means of identification have been looked at too: the style of the team, and emblems such as the colours and the stadium. The study has also investigated whether the press plays a central role in the construction of the 'imagined communities' of supporters, as it has a major part in creating the collective memory of a club.

Three main sets of findings can be derived from the case studies. They show without any ambiguity that the influx of foreign players following the *Bosman* ruling has not fundamentally altered supporters' capacity to identify with their club. The role of the press in this process needs to be reassessed in the light of the reaction that the printed media have gathered from the supporters. The processes through which emblems and people have come to symbolise the

* Elements of this chapter have already been presented in: David Ranc, 'Vectors of identification and markers of identity', in Bettina Kratzmüller, Matthias Marschik, Rudolf Müllner, Hubert D. Szemethy and Elisabeth Trinkl (eds), *Contemporary European football, sport and the construction of identities*. Vienna: Verlag Turia & Kant, 2007; David Ranc, 'The impact of EU sports regulation on supporters', in Simon Gardiner, Richard Parrish and Rob Siekmann (eds), *Professional sport in the European Union: regulation, re-regulation and representation*. TMC Asser Press and Cambridge University Press, 2008; David Ranc, 'Les supporters de football et les réglementations européennes (Arsenal, PSG, Rangers and Celtic)', in Guillaume Robin (ed.), *Football, Europe et regulations*. Lille: Presses Universitaires du Septentrion, 2011; Paul Dietschy, David Ranc and Albrecht Sonntag, 'Parallel myths, popular maps', *Journal of educational media, memory and society*, 1(2) (2009), 125–144.

identity of the club and its supporters, thereby raising supporters' identification with the club, have also proved more complex than previously suggested in the literature.

The role played by the press

The hypotheses made following Benedict Anderson and Patrick Mignon on the role of the press in the construction of imagined communities and in raising support for clubs can only be partly confirmed. The succession of narratives in the press does seem to be important in constructing the public image of the club and of its members. This is particularly clear in times when the image has become out of kilter with the situation of the club and needs to be 'rebuilt'. The printed media have, for example, accompanied and emphasised the changes in Arsenal identity: from a thoroughly English club to the club most open to foreign influence. Yet, the xenophobic angle through which the question of the foreign presence at Arsenal and in English football has often been raised, may be less revealing of the club's characteristics than of questions which have a wider appeal in society, as has also been the case of sectarianism in Scotland, or, perhaps more arguably, the moral panic surrounding violence and security or the widespread anti-Parisian feelings in France. This confirms Boyle and Haynes' idea that the identities are echoed in the press and not created by them and that the press is not the sole factor raising identification.

The role played by the press in the construction of the identities of specific clubs may also be less important than first thought because it is not uniform. Some newspapers play a greater role because of the extensive coverage that they give to sport, football or even one team in particular, as is the case of the tabloids in Great Britain and, in Paris, *L'Équipe* or *Le Parisien*. Also, some parts of the press show a greater tendency to emphasise rivalries (an important element in the definition of the clubs' identities), while others, conversely, underplay these rivalries because they are potentially dangerous – and may therefore contribute less to both the identity of a team and partisan identification. In this instance, the press – and journalists – show their awareness of the role that their reporting may play in the creation of real events, and that they are influenced by the supporters too. What becomes clear is that the relationship between the press and the supporters is most certainly a two-way relationship.

Likewise, the role played by the press is more limited because fans tend not to read the press simply passively. They may disagree strongly with some articles, a particular newspaper or they may even reject the press as a whole, if they are unhappy with the portrayal of their club (or their own portrayal) therein. Supporters then resort to alternative sources to the press to read about their teams and, to paraphrase Mignon, learn about the games, events surrounding the team and most importantly to share their analyses. Fanzines have been the first alternative medium but the relatively recent development of the internet has multiplied the number of sources of information for the supporters: on-line releases from news agencies (such as AFP or Reuters) and supporters-run forums, websites or mailing lists. The press must therefore be envisaged as only one actor among others in the definition of both the public image of the team and the collective of supporters. Still, whereas the core of supporters will use a greater number of sources, the supporters who are less involved (and who are, *a fortiori*, the 'outsiders'), will resort only to the press. The image of a club, and the collective identity referred to by the supporters, may therefore depend on the level of involvement of the individual with the club or how far away they are from the club.

In the case of PSG, the relationship between the supporters and the press has even developed into a triangular relationship involving the club. Its officials have been seen to capitalise on the ill-feeling of supporters towards the press in order to gather their support (even if at times only momentarily). In this instance, the supporters' identities, individually as well as collectively, are constructed not only with sources other than the press, but also against it. A negative depiction of a club, its supporters or of the foreign character of some of its players leads less to a decreased ability to recruit supporters from the newspapers' readership than to antagonism with the press from the most dedicated of supporters. The role played by the press in creating a club's public identity and in raising supporters' identification is attested to but it appears less important and more complex than previously analysed.

Identification through foreign players

The suggestion that supporters' identification with a club might decrease with teams who have a large foreign contingent has proved unequivocally false in the three cases studied. That suggestion was based on the idea that supporters cannot (or would find it difficult to) identify with foreign players because clubs are representative of a national identity, and because the social identity of a player and the composition of the team are the main means of supporters' identification with their team. In contrast, the case studies have shown that clubs (at least in domestic competitions, though perhaps less so at European level) are representative of a local rather than a national identity. One of the reasons for PSG's success in recruiting its support has been the development of a local identity (strengthened even after *Bosman* by a policy of recruiting local players). Similarly Arsenal's identity is firmly located within North London, even for supporters from abroad or for supporters who have been forced to move out of the vicinity by the increase in property prices (emphasising that the locale is largely dreamed of). Even the identities of Celtic and Rangers are presented less in terms of a confrontation between Irish and Scots than between Catholic and Protestants.

The local identity of clubs underlined in the case studies also explains the need to widen our understanding of the means of identification suggested by Bromberger, Sonntag and Mignon. All three authors have emphasised the composition of the team as representing the way a community sees itself in terms of an ideal model. Bromberger has also insisted on how the social identity of a player provides a link with the social identity of supporters. It appears throughout this research that both insights must be revised to be more encompassing. A team may, indeed, include foreigners who are representative of local communities of immigrant descent (the Irish at Arsenal in the 1970s, North African players at PSG). In that case, the identification with a foreign player might be easier for supporters who share the same nationality. The importance of the locality also partly explains why supporters, especially at Arsenal, have tended to show a limited preference for native players. Arsenal supporters readily identify with a player hailing from North London, and to a lesser extent with an English player (as discussed above) developed at the club. They identify much less easily with an English player who comes from another locality (which may even be home to some rivals) and he may be perceived as no less of a stranger than someone from a foreign country, unless at the same time he plays for England. International games provide an opportunity for the player to represent both the club in the national team (therefore the contribution of the local to the national) and the English identity of some fans. Supporters have also shown that they are able to identify with foreign players, especially if they have contributed to the success of the club, or have long played for it.

More crucially, the insights from Bromberger *et al.* must be revised to include the fact that a foreign footballer can actually symbolise 'native' qualities: a French player like Patrick Vieira can be lauded by Arsenal supporters and officials for his 'English' qualities (his physicality and grit or determination). Likewise, a foreign style of play can be accepted – as is very clear at Arsenal where a style branded 'continental' is the pride and joy of supporters and praised by the press. The style of play associated with Celtic points to the need to develop the insights from Bromberger *et al.* who argued that style expressed the values of the community that the club represents. On the contrary, the description of Celtic style as foreign by those other than fans of the team, serves symbolically to exclude them from the Scottish community.

The cases of PSG and Arsenal have also revealed a hitherto unstudied aspect of style. The flamboyant styles of these teams indeed serve the same purpose: contrary to the insights of Bromberger and Sonntag, these styles do not express the identity of the club or its followers (which can enhance identification) any more but aim simply at producing an attractive show in order to attract an audience. There is thus a possibility that a 'showy' style transforms the followers of a club from supporters into spectators. It might, therefore, be regarded as running the risk of weakening the link between supporters and club. This fundamental change to a particularly important mean through which supporters identify with a team raises the question of how much the increasing commercialisation of the game is affecting support in ways previously undetermined (and underlines a possible area for future research). PSG's success in recruiting a faithful audience, which includes dedicated supporters, however, indicates that the matter is complex as the association between a club and its supporters is not yet threatened by the new role assigned to style. Indeed, the absence (or disappearance) of one means of identification (such as the composition of the team, or its style) is offset by the increased importance of other means or the creation of new means.

New symbols and processes of symbolisation

New emblems have been identified and added to the colours and logo already studied in the existing literature. Chief among these are names. They have provided a clear focus for identity in all three case studies: calling Celtic supporters the 'Bhoys' underlines the religious sympathies of the club; groups of supporters at PSG have similarly chosen names with local character. The three case studies have also shown quite clearly that people other than the players (individually or as part of the team) can play the part assigned solely to the players in the literature: to carry the club's identity and gather support. Other members of the club such as the manager and the president can carry the identity of the club. Crucially, supporters can play a similar role too. In Paris, it is even as important for some fans to be a member of a given Ultra group (say, the Lutèce Falco) as to support the club. The supporters' group indeed symbolises aspects of their identity that the club cannot symbolise (for example, their non-strictly-white identity in the Auteuil stand or conversely their white identity in Boulogne). More surprising perhaps, interviews suggest that this extends to phenomena of violence (relatively common at PSG until 1993). It seems that some men have liked to associate with the image of toughness that some PSG supporters (the so-called *'indépendants'*) have had.

More than the new means of garnering support and identification, it is the processes through which these are created that are particularly interesting, as they have not been studied in the previous literature, where the focus has been on existing means which have been dealt with in a static manner which fails, inevitably, to consider them from a dynamic perspective. A contribution that this research makes to the study of supporters' identification with their club is the distinction between markers of identity and vectors of identification. Markers of identity can be construed as means through which supporters demonstrate at least one facet of their identity. Vectors of identification are means through which the process of supporters' identification with their club takes place. Arsenal's colours and crest are clearly markers of identity. They are not vectors of identification, though. The difference between 'markers of identity' and 'vectors of identification' is therefore between static and dynamic. The same means can play either role or both roles in different contexts. The jersey takes on a very different value at Arsenal than at PSG. In Paris it has proved to be a vector of identification – even if occasionally in the negative: supporters went on strike and refused to support the club when the jersey they favoured was replaced. This finding sheds a remarkable light on factors other than those simply related to the composition of the team and the ability to identify with foreign players. Playing an all-Protestant team (Rangers) or an all-British team (Arsenal) was certainly a marker of identity, but its role as a vector of identification might have been more limited than first thought. Also, new emblems and symbols have been commonly introduced by club management often in order to make money out of them. Supporters, though, have the final say about them and decide to adopt or reject them. Of prime importance is the ability for the new emblem to retain some of the meaning of the one it replaces or complements. The new Arsenal stadium, for example, has been generally well accepted by supporters because of its proximity to the old one: it retains the sense of place that matters most for Arsenal supporters. As at PSG in the 1970s, supporters are still in the process of investing the stadium and making it 'their' space.

Significantly, an emblem which only results from business considerations (such as the name 'Emirates Stadium') is widely rejected even in a club such as Arsenal where commercialisation is generally accepted. Supporters also have to be able to invest the emblem with diverse meanings. A logo that simply says PSG is too unambiguous, whereas an Eiffel tower can take different meanings (modernity?, international standing and instant international recognition?) for various supporters and symbolise more identities. The emphasis on dynamic processes in periods of change can also explain why the main historiography paradigm that needs to be used here when studying the creation of a collective memory through new emblems is not the notion of 'invented traditions', but that of 'realms of memory'. The symbols which have been most successfully embraced by supporters are those which provide a sense of continuity (even through selection of some memories), as they link the present with the past.

Scope for further study

The Europeanisation and internationalisation of football teams have clearly not adversely affected the level of support that clubs receive. This is mostly because the factors prompting or maintaining support have proved their ability to adjust to a new context. However, some of these factors may have been fundamentally altered in this process of adjustment. Accordingly, there is a risk that in the long term these factors may cease to perform their role and may no longer raise (or even simply maintain) identification. This is the case of style in Paris and at Arsenal: the attractive style that these teams offer risks transforming supporters into spectators. The commercialisation of the game has also been shown to be rejected by Arsenal supporters when it changed an emblem of the club to the point that it could not prompt new identification: the name Emirates stadium is indeed widely reviled by supporters.

There is scope to renew research on commercialisation, through the investigation of whether commercialisation may pose a threat to the game because of the extent to which it affects emblems and therefore it discourages supporters' identification. Such a research would certainly benefit from theories on brand and icons developed by Douglas B. Holt in his revolutionary study of consumer culture.[1] In the case of football clubs, supporters do not show 'obeisance' to the 'cultural authority model' analysed by Holt. Supporters offer both a case of 'reflexive resistance' (they filter the marketing imposed on them by the club and through the press) and 'creative resistance' (supporters are producing cultural values, and contributing to the brand through opposition to the institution). Supporters seem to fall between the postmodern consumer culture and the consumer culture that has followed, called for want of a better term the 'post postmodern' consumer culture. This would allow for a better understanding of the behaviour of club managements: faced with the reflexive irony and distance of the post-fan or post-supporter, they have to capitalise on the cultural value of the brand and make it a real 'icon'.

This study of partisan identification hopes to have made a significant contribution, if only because the research has been conducted through three different 'national' contexts. At the time that competitions force clubs to internationalise, it has become perplexing to see that most research is still conducted on a purely national basis. Moreover, the research presented here hopes to have made a contribution that only an outsider, a foreigner, can make. As emphasised by Anthony King, in the UK, studies on sport, and most of all on football, are heavily determined by the values of the working class. Often, the writings of British academics on sport seem to be an attempt to maintain a tenuous link with a working class to which their family once belonged. The transnational analysis hopes to have contributed to showing the specificities of supporters' culture in the UK but also the increasing convergence with other football cultures in Europe and the banality of the structures of identification and identity ('working class' is here seen as one among possible identities expressed through similar means).

Finally, for a research that sits very firmly within the field of European studies, it is hoped that the main contribution is to show the importance of studying processes of Europeanisation, policy debates through cases studies, at the level of the everyday life of the European people. Convergence across the nations, phenomena of resistance (or adhesion) to Europe can be best understood at this level, rather than solely at the level of institutions and through statistical methods or formal modelling. Twenty-five years after the Adonino report, this research suggests that 'a People's Europe' cannot be built without a detailed study of this People's Europe.

Notes

1 Douglas B. Holt, 'Why do brands cause trouble? A dialectical theory of consumer culture and branding', *Journal of Consumer Research*, 29(1) (2002), 70–90.

Bibliography

Ad Hoc Committee, 'On a people's Europe', *Report to the European Council*, 1985 (at: www.ombudsman.europa.eu/historical/en/default.htm; last accessed 8 April 2007).

Anderson, Benedict, *Imagined communities: reflections on the origin and spread of nationalism*. London: Verso, 1991.

Ardoino, Jacques and Brohm, Jean-Marie (eds), *Anthropologie du sport: perspectives critiques/actes du colloque: Paris-Sorbonne, 19–20 avril 1991*. Paris: ANDSHA and Vigneux: Matrice and Montpellier: Quel corps?, 1991.

Armstrong, Gary and Giulianotti, Richard (eds), *Football cultures and identities*. Basingstoke: Macmillan, 1999.

Armstrong, Gary and Giulianotti, Richard, 'Afterword: constructing social identities: exploring the structured relations of football rivalries', in Armstrong and Giulianotti (eds), *Fear and loathing in world football*, pp. 267–279.

Armstrong, Gary and Giulianotti, Richard (eds), *Fear and loathing in world football*. Oxford: Berg, 2001.

Back, Les, Crabbe, Tim and Solomos, John, 'Racism in football: patterns of continuity and change', in Brown (ed.), *Fanatics! Power, identity and fandom in football*, pp. 71–87.

Bairner, Alan and Shirlow, Peter, 'The territorial politics of soccer in Northern Ireland', in Armstrong and Giulianotti (eds), *Football cultures and identities*, pp. 152–163.

Bale, John, 'Playing at home: British football and a sense of place', in John Williams and Stephen Wagg (eds), *British football and social change: getting into Europe*, pp. 130–144.

Bale, John, *Sport, space and the city*. London: Routledge, 1993.

Beck, Peter J., 'The relevance of the irrelevant: football as a missing dimension in the study of British relations with Germany', *International affairs*, 79(2) (2003), 389–411.

Blain, Neil, Boyle, Raymond and O'Donnell, Hugh, *Sport and national identity in the European media*. Leicester: Leicester University Press, 1993.

Boniface, Pascal (ed.), *Géopolitique du football*. Brussels: Complexe, 1998.

Boniface, Pascal (ed.), *L'Europe et le sport.* Paris: Presses Universitaires de France, 2001.
Bourdieu, Pierre, 'Comment peut-on être sportif?', in *Questions de sociologie,* pp. 137–195. Paris: Éditions de Minuit, 1984.
Bourdieu, Pierre, 'Programme pour une sociologie du sport', in *Choses dites,* pp. 203–216. Paris: Éditions de Minuit, 1987.
Bourdieu, Pierre, 'Les univers de possibles stylistiques', in *La Distinction: critique sociale du jugement,* pp. 230–248. Paris: Éditions de Minuit, 1992.
Bourdieu, Pierre, 'Les Jeux Olympiques: programme pour une analyse', *Actes de la recherche en sciences socials,* (1994), 102–103.
Boyle, Raymond, *Sports journalism: context and issues.* London: Sage, 2006.
Boyle, Raymond, '"We are Celtic supporters…": Questions of football and identity in modern Scotland', in Giulianotti and Williams (eds), *Game without frontiers: football, identity and modernity,* pp. 73–101.
Boyle, Raymond and Haynes, Richard, *Power play: sport, the media and popular culture.* Harlow: Pearson, 2000.
Boyle, Raymond and Haynes, Richard, *Football in the new media age.* London: Routledge, 2004.
Boyle, Raymond and Monteiro, Cláudia, '"A small country with a big ambition": representations of Portugal and England in Euro 2004 British and Portuguese newspaper coverage', *European journal of communication,* 20(2) (2005), 223–244.
Bradley, Joseph M., *Ethnic and religious identity in modern Scotland: culture, politics and football.* Aldershot: Avebury, 1995.
Bradley, Joseph M., 'The patriot game: football's famous "Tartan Army"', *International review for the sociology of sport,* 37(2) (2002), 177–197.
Brennan, Dan. *The official Arsenal miscellany.* London: Hamlyn, 2004.
Brohm, Jean-Marie, *Sport, a prison of measured time: essays.* London: Ink Links, 1978.
Brohm, Jean-Marie, *Le mythe olympique.* Paris: C. Bourgois, 1981.
Brohm, Jean-Marie, *Sociologie politique du sport.* Nancy: Presses Universitaires de Nancy, 1992.
Brohm, Jean-Marie, *Les meutes sportives: critique de la domination.* Paris: l'Harmattan, 1993.
Bromberger, Christian, *Le match de football: ethnologie d'une passion partisane à Marseille, Naples et Turin,* in collaboration with Alain Hayot and Jean-Marc Mariottini. Paris: Éditions de la Maison des sciences de l'homme, 1995.
Bromberger, Christian, *Football, la bagatelle la plus sérieuse du monde.* Paris: Bayard, 1998.
Brookes, Rod, *Representing sport.* London: Arnold, 2002.
Brown, Adam (ed.), *Fanatics! Power, identity and fandom in football.* London: Routledge, 1998.
Brown, Adam, 'Introduction', in Brown (ed.), *Fanatics! Power, identity and fandom in football,* pp. 1–7.
Brown, Callum G., *The social history of religion in Scotland since 1730.* London: Methuen, 1987.

Brubaker, Rogers, *Citizenship and nationhood in France and Germany.* Cambridge, MA: Harvard University Press, 1992.

Cagnacci, Astolfo, *Pays du foot: une passion et des styles.* Paris: Autrement, 1998.

Caiger, Andrew and Gardiner, Simon (eds), *Professional sport in the European Union: regulation and re-regulation.* The Hague: T.M.C. Asser, 2000.

Caillois, Roger, *Les jeux et les hommes: le masque et le vertige.* Paris: Gallimard, 1967.

Campbell, Tom and Woods, Pat, *Dreams and songs to sing: a new history of Celtic.* Edinburgh: Mainstream, 1996.

Carmeli, Yoram S. and Bar, Iris, 'Team selection and chosen people in Israel: the case of Hapoel Taibeh', in Armstrong and Giulianotti (eds), *Football cultures and identities*, pp. 164–175.

Carrington, Ben and McDonald, Ian (eds), *'Race', sport and British society.* London: Routledge, 2001.

Carrington, Ben, '"Football's coming home" but whose home? and do we want it? Nation, football and the politics of exclusion', in Adam Brown (ed.), *Fanatics! Power, identity and fandom in football*, pp. 101–122.

Clarke, Alan and Clarke, John, 'Highlights and action replays: ideology, sport and the media', in Hargreaves (ed.), *Sport, culture and ideology*, pp. 62–87.

Cole, Ashley, *My defence.* London: Headline Book Publishing, 2006.

Critcher, Chas, 'Putting on the style: aspects of recent English football', in Williams and Wagg (eds), *British football and social change: getting into Europe*, pp. 67–84.

Crolley, Liz, Hand, David and Jeutter, Ralf, 'National obsessions and identities in football match report', in Brown (ed.), *Fanatics! Power, identity and fandom in football*, pp. 173–185.

Da Matta, Roberto, 'Notes sur le *futebol* brésilien', *Le débat*, 19 (1982), 68–76.

David Rowe, *Sport, culture and the media: the unruly trinity.* Birmingham: Open University Press, 1999.

Defrance, Jacques, *L'excellence corporelle: la formation des activités sportives et physiques modernes, 1770–1914.* Rennes: Presses Universitaires de Rennes, 1987.

Devine, Fiona. 'Qualitative analysis', in Marsh and Stoker (eds), *Theory and methods in political science*, pp. 137–153.

Dietschy, Paul, 'Le Paris Saint-Germain dans le football français et européen', *Le bulletin des amis du vieux Saint-Germain*, 39 (2002), 273–291.

Dietschy, Paul, Ranc, David and Sonntag, Albrecht, 'Parallel myths, popular maps', *Journal of educational media, memory and society*, 1(2) (2009), 125–144.

Donavan, D. Todd, Janda, Swinder and Suh, Jaebeom, 'Environmental influences in corporate brand identification and outcomes', *Brand management*, 14(1/2) (2006), 125–136.

Drolet, Jean-Christian, 'Extra time: are the new FIFA transfer rules doomed?', unpublished paper.

Duke, Vic, 'Local tradition versus globalisation: resistance to the McDonald-isation and Disneyisation of professional football in England', *Football studies*, 5(1) (2002), 5–23.

Dumont, Louis, *German ideology: from France to Germany and back*. Chicago, IL: University of Chicago Press, 1994.

Dunning, Eric and Sheard, Kenneth, *Barbarians, gentlemen and players: a sociological study of the development of rugby football*. Oxford: Martin Robertson, 1979.

Dupriez, Bernard, *Gradus*. Paris: Union Générale d'Éditions, 1980.

Duret, Pascal and Mignon, Patrick, 'Faire vivre un club en Île-de-France: le cas du Paris Saint-Germain et de l'Olympique Noisy-le-Sec', *Les annales de la recherche urbaine*, 6(79) (1998), 119–125.

Ehrenberg, Alain, *Le culte de la performance*. Paris: Calmann-Lévy, 1991.

Elias, Norbert and Dunning, Eric, *Quest for excitement: sport and leisure in the civilizing process*. Oxford: Blackwell, 1986.

Elias, Norbert, *The civilizing process*. Oxford: Blackwell, 1994.

End, Christian M., Dietz-Uhler, Beth, Harrick, Elizabeth A. and Jacquemotte, Lindy, 'Identifying with winners: a re-examination of sport fans' tendency to bask in reflected glory (BIRG)', *Journal of applied social psychology*, 32(5) (2002), 1017–1030.

Faure, Jean-Michel and Suaud, Charles, 'Les enjeux du football', *Actes de la recherche en sciences socials*, 103 (1994), 3–6.

Fernandez, Luis and Grimault, Dominique, *Le Parc de mes passions*. Paris: Albin Michel, 1995.

Ferrier, Bob and McElroy, Robert, *Rangers, the complete record*. Derby: Breedon Books, 1996.

Finn, G. P. T., 'Racism, religion and social prejudice: Irish Catholic clubs, soccer and Scottish identity I: the roots of prejudice', *International journal of the history of sport*, 8(1) (1991).

Finn, G. P. T., 'Racism, religion and social prejudice: Irish Catholic clubs, soccer and Scottish identity II: social identity and conspiracy theories', *International journal of the history of sport*, 8(3) (1991).

Garland, Jon and Mike Rowe, 'War minus the shooting? Jingoism, the English press, and Euro 96', *Journal of sport and social issues*, 23(1) (1999), 80–95.

Gellner, Ernest, *Nations and nationalism*. Oxford: Blackwell, 1983.

Girardet, Raoul, *Mythes et mythologies politiques*. Paris: Seuil, 1986.

Giulianotti, Richard, 'Scoring away from home: a statistical study of Scotland football fans at international matches in Romania and Sweden', *International review for the sociology of sport*, 29(2) (1994), 172–200.

Giulianotti, Richard, 'Football and the politics of carnival: an ethnographic study of Scottish fans in Sweden', *International review for the sociology of sport*, 30(2) (1995), 191–223.

Giulianotti, Richard, *Football: a sociology of the global game*. Cambridge: Polity Press, 1999.

Giulianotti, Richard, 'Supporters, followers, fans and *flâneurs*: a taxonomy of spectator identities in football', *Journal of sport and social issues*, 26(1) (2002), 25–46.

Giulianotti, Richard, 'Sport spectators and the social consequences of commodification: critical perspectives from Scottish football', *Journal of sport and social issue*, 29(4) (2005), 386–410.

Giulianotti, Richard and Gerrard, Michael, 'Cruel Britannia? Glasgow Rangers, Scotland and "hot" football rivalries', in Armstrong and Giulianotti (eds), *Fear and loathing in world football*, pp. 23–42.

Giulianotti, Richard and Robertson, Roland, 'The globalization of football: a study in the glocalization of the "serious life"', *British journal of sociology*, 55(4) (2004), 545–568.

Giulianotti, Richard and Robertson, Roland, 'Glocalization, globalization and migration: the case of Scottish football supporters in North America', *International sociology*, 21(2) (2006), 171–198.

Giulianotti, Richard and Williams, John (eds), *Game without frontiers: football, identity and modernity*. Aldershot: Arena, 1994.

Goksøyr, Matti and Hognestad, Hans, 'No longer worlds apart? British influences and Norwegian football', in Armstrong and Giulianotti (eds), *Football cultures and identities*, pp. 201–210.

Gouguet, Jean-Jacques and Nys, Jean-François, *Sport et développement économique régional*. Paris: Dalloz, 1993.

Halliday, Stephen, *Rangers: the official illustrated history*. London: Arthur Barker, 1989.

Handley, James E., *The Celtic story*. London: Stanley Paul, 1960.

Hare, Geoff, *Football in France: a cultural history*. Oxford: Berg, 2003.

Hargreaves, Jennifer (ed.), *Sport, culture and ideology*. London: Routledge & Kegan Paul, 1982.

Hargreaves, John, *Sport, power and culture: a social and historical analysis of popular sports in Britain*. Cambridge: Basil Blackwell, 1986.

Harris, Nick, *The foreign revolution: how overseas footballer changed the English game*. London: Aurum, 2006.

Haynes, Richard, 'Every Man(?) a football artist: football writing and masculinity', in Redhead (ed)., *The passion and the fashion: football fandom in the new Europe*, pp. 55–77.

Haynes, Richard, *The football imagination: the rise of the fanzine culture*. Aldershot: Arena, 1995.

Henderson, Willie, *Forward with Rangers*. London: S. Paul, 1966.

Hobsbawm, Eric and Ranger, Terence, *The invention of tradition*. Cambridge: Cambridge University Press, 1983.

Holt, Richard, *Sport and society in modern France*. London: Macmillan, in association with St Antony's College, Oxford, 1981.

Holt, Richard, *Sport and the British: a modern history*. Oxford: Clarendon, 1989.

Hornby, Nick, *Fever pitch*. London: Penguin, 1998.

King, Anthony, *The end of the terraces: the transformation of English football in the 1990s*. London and New York: Leicester University Press, 1998.

King, Anthony, 'Football fandom and post-national identity in the new Europe', *British journal of sociology*, 51(3) (2000), 419–442.

King, Gary, Keohane, Robert O. and Verba, Sidney, *Designing social inquiry: scientific inference in qualitative research*. Princeton, NJ: Princeton University Press, 1994.

Kuper, Simon, *Football against the enemy*. London: Orion, 1994.

Law, Alex, 'Near and far: banal national identity and the press in Scotland', *Media, culture and society*, 23(3)(2001), 299–317.

Leigh, John and Woodhouse, David, *The football lexicon*. Cambridge: Oleander, 2005.

Loy, John W. and Booth, Thomas, 'Functionalism, sport and society', in Jay Coakley and Eric Dunning (eds), *Handbook of sports studies*, pp. 8–27. London: Sage, 2000.

Lüschen, Gunther, 'The interdependence of sport and culture', *International review of sports sociology*, 2 (1967), 127–142.

Lüschen, Gunther, Sage, George and Sfeir, Leila (eds), *Handbook of social science of sport*. Champaign, IL: Stipes, 1981.

Lüschen, Gunther, 'The system of sports: problems of methodology, conflict and social stratification', in Lüschen *et al.* (eds), *Handbook of social science of sport*, pp. 197–213.

Lüschen, Gunther, 'Towards a new structural analysis: the present state and the prospectives of the international sociology of sport', *International review for the sociology of sport*, 24 (1988), 269–285.

Lüschen, Gunther, 'On theory of sciences for the sociology of sport: new structuralism, action, intention and practical meaning', *International review for the sociology of sport*, 25 (1990), 69–83.

McArdle, David, 'They're playing R. song: football and the European Union after *Bosman*', *Football studies*, 3(2) (2000), 42–66.

McGovern, Patrick, 'The Irish brawn drain: English League clubs and Irish footballers, 1946–1995', *British journal of sociology*, 51(3) (2000), 401–418.

McNee, Gerard, *The story of Celtic: an official history, 1888–1978*. London: Paul, 1978.

Magee, Jonathan and Sugden, John, 'The world at their feet: professional football and international labor migration', *Journal of sport and social issues*, 26(4) (2002), 421–437.

Maguire, Joseph, Poulton, Emma and Possamai, Catherine, 'Weltkrieg III? Media coverage of England versus Germany in Euro 96', *Journal of sport and social issues*, 23(4) (1999), 439–454.

Maguire, Joseph and Poulton, Emma K., 'European identity politics in Euro 96', *International review for the sociology of sport*, 34(1) (1999), 17–29.

Maguire, Joseph, 'Sport labor migration research revisited', *Journal of sport and social issues*, 28(4) (2004), 477–482.

Marks, Laurence, *A fan for all seasons: the diary of an Arsenal supporter*. London: Warner, 1999.

Marsh, David and Stoker, Gerry (eds), *Theory and methods in political science*. Basingstoke: Macmillan, 1995.

Marx, Karl and Engels, Friedrich, *L'idéologie allemande*. Paris: Éditions Sociales, 1974.

Mason, Tony, *Association football and English society, 1863–1915*. Brighton: Harvester, 1980.

Mason, Tony, *Sport in Britain*. London: Faber, 1988.

Mason, Tony (ed.), *Sport in Britain: a social history*. Cambridge: Cambridge University Press, 1989.

Mason, Tony, *Passion of the people? Football in South America*. London: Verso, 1995.

Mignon, Patrick. *La passion du football*. Paris: Odile Jacob, 1998.

Moorhouse, Herbert F., 'Les foules de Glasgow', *Sociétés et representations*, 7 (1998), 193–200.

Moorhouse, Herbert F., 'On the periphery: Scotland, Scottish football and the new Europe', in Williams and Wagg (eds), *British football and social change: getting into Europe*, pp. 201–219.

Morgan, William J., *Leftist theories of sport: a critique and a reconstruction*. Urbana and Chicago, IL: University of Illinois Press, 1994.

Murray, Bill, *The Old Firm: sectarianism, sport and society in Scotland*. Edinburgh: John Donald, 1984.

Murray, Bill, *Glasgow's giants: 100 years of the Old Firm*. Edinburgh: Mainstream, 1988.

Murray, Bill. *The Old Firm in the new age*. Edinburgh: Mainstream, 1998.

National Heritage Committee, House of Commons, *Fourth report: press coverage of the Euro '96 football competition*. London: Stationery Office, 1996.

Niemann, Arne, Garcia, Borja, Grant, Wyn (eds), *The transformation of European football: the national games*, Manchester University Press, 2011

Nora, Pierre (ed.), *Les lieux de mémoir*, 3 vols. Paris: Gallimard, 1982–86.

Parrish, Richard and McArdle, David, 'Beyond *Bosman*: the European Union's influence upon professional athletes' freedom of movement', *Sport in society*, 3(7) 2004, 403–419.

Pérès, Jean-François and Riolo, Daniel, *OM–PSG, PSG–OM, les meilleurs ennemis: enquête sur une rivalité*, in collaboration with David Aiello. Paris: Mango Sport, 2003.

Pociello, Christian, *Le rugby ou la guerre des styles*. Paris: A. M. Métailié, 1983.

Radnedge, Keir, *The complete encyclopedia of football*. London: Carlton books, 2004.

Ranc, David, 'Le Paris Saint Germain dans la presse quotidienne française: une relation tripartite ambiguë', in Evelyne Combeau-Mari (ed.), *Sport et presse écrite en France au XXe siècle*. Paris: Le Publieur (Bibliothèque Universitaire Francophone), 2007.

Ranc, David, 'Vectors of identification and markers of identity', in Bettina Kratzmüller, Matthias Marschik, Rudolf Müllner, Hubert D. Szemethy and Elisabeth Trinkl (eds), *Contemporary European football, sport and the construction of identities*. Vienna: Verlag Turia & Kant, 2007.

Ranc, David, 'The impact of EU sports regulation on supporters', in Simon

Gardiner, Richard Parrish and Rob Siekmann (eds), *Professional sport in the European Union: regulation, re-regulation and representation*. TMC Asser Press and Cambridge University Press, 2008.

Ranc, David, 'Local politics, identity and football in Paris', *Modern and Contemporary France*, February, 2008.

Ranc, David, 'Les supporters de football et les réglementations européennes (Arsenal, PSG, Rangers and Celtic)', in Guillaume Robin (ed.), *Football, Europe et regulations*. Lille: Presses Universitaires du Septentrion, 2011.

Ravenel, Loïc, *La géographie du football en France*. Paris: Presses Universitaires de France, 1998.

Redhead, Steve (ed.), *The passion and the fashion: football fandom in the new Europe*. Aldershot: Avebury, 1993.

Rigauer, Bero, *Sport and work*. New York and Guildford: Columbia University Press, 1981.

Rose, Joe, *Arsenal player by player: five decades of player profiles*. London: Hamlyn, 2004.

Russell, David, 'Associating with football: social identity in England, 1863–1998', in Armstrong and Giulianotti (eds), *Football cultures and identities*, pp. 15–28.

Séguin, Philippe, Rapport à Monsieur le Secrétaire d'État auprès du Premier Ministre, chargé de la Jeunesse, des Sports et des loisirs, sur certaines difficultés actuelles du football français, établi par Monsieur Philippe Séguin, Auditeur à la Cour des Comptes, 12 février 1973.

Sims, David, *Arsenal: memories and marble halls*. London: Pavilion, 2000.

Sirinelli, Jean-François (ed.), *Dictionnaire historique de la vie politique française au XXe siècle*. Paris: Presses Universitaires de France, 1995.

Soar, Phil and Tyler, Martin, *The official illustrated history of Arsenal, 1886–1999*. London: Hamlyn, 1999.

Sonntag, Albrecht, 'Le football, image de la nation', in Boniface (ed.), *Géopolitique du football*, pp. 31–40.

Stevenson, Christopher and Nixon, John, 'A conceptual scheme of the social functions of sport', *Sportwissenschaft*, 2 (1972), 119–132.

Stevenson, Christopher, 'Sport as a contemporary social phenomenon: a functional explanation', *International Journal of Physical Education*, 11(1) (1974), 8–14.

Suaud, Charles, 'Espace des sports, espace social et effets d'âge: la diffusion du tennis, du squash et du golf dans l'agglomération nantaise', *Actes de la recherche en sciences socials*, 79 (1989), 2–20,

Sugden, John and Bairner, Alan, *Sport, sectarianism and society in a divided Ireland*. Leicester: Leicester University Press, 1993.

Sugden, John and Tomlinson, Alan (ed.), *Power games: a critical sociology of sport*. London: Routledge, 2002.

Szymanski, Stefan and Kuypers, Tim, *Winners and losers*. London: Penguin, 2000.

Vaugrand, Henri. *Sociologies du sport: théorie des champs et théorie critique*. Paris: L'Harmattan, 1999.

Wacquant, Loïc, 'Corps et âmes: notes ethnographiques d'un apprenti-boxeur', *Actes de la recherche en sciences socials*, 80 (1989), 33–67.

Wade, Michael, *Arsenal story: an official history of Arsenal Football Club*. Edinburgh: Lomond Books, 1999.

Wagg, Stephen, 'Playing the past: the media and the England football team', in Williams and Wagg (eds), *British football and social change: getting into Europe*, pp. 220–238,

Wagg, Stephen (ed.), *Giving the game away: football, politics and culture on five continents*. London: Leicester University Press, 1995.

Wagg, Stephen, 'Introduction and acknowledgements', in Wagg (ed.), *Giving the game away: football, politics and culture on five continents*, pp. xi–xii.

Wahl, Alfred (ed.), *Les archives du football: sport et société en France, 1880–1980*. Paris: Gallimard /Julliard, 1989.

Wahl, Alfred, 'Enjeux: le football, un nouveau territoire pour l'historien', *Vingtième siècle: revue d'histoire*, 26 (1990), 127–132.

Walsh, Stephen, *Voices of the Old Firm*. Edinburgh: Mainstream, 1995.

Walvin, James, *The people's game: the history of football revisited*. Edinburgh: Mainstream, 1994.

Weatherill, Stephen, 'Discrimination on grounds of nationality in sport', *Yearbook of European law 1989*, 10 (1990), 55–92.

Weatherill, Stephen, *Cases and materials on EC law*. London: Blackstone, 1996.

Whannel, Gary, *Fields in vision: television sports and cultural formation*. London: Routledge, 1992.

Williams, Gordon, *From scenes like these*. London: Allison & Busby, 1980.

Williams, John and Wagg, Stephen (eds), *British football and social change: getting into Europe*. Leicester: Leicester University Press, 1991.

Williams, John and Woodhouse, Jackie, 'Women and football in Britain', in Williams and Wagg (eds), *British football and social change: getting into Europe*, pp. 85–108.

Young, Kevin, '"The killing field": themes in mass media responses to the Heysel Stadium riot', *International review for the sociology of sport*, 21(2/3) (1986), 253–266.

Young, Percy M., *A history of British football*. London: Arrow, 1973.

Index